STRATEGIES FOR INCLUSION
A HANDBOOK FOR PHYSICAL EDUCATORS

STRATEGIES FOR INCLUSION
A HANDBOOK FOR PHYSICAL EDUCATORS

Lauren J. Lieberman, PhD
Cathy Houston-Wilson, PhD
State University of New York College
at Brockport

Human Kinetics

Library of Congress Cataloging-in-Publication Data

Lieberman, Lauren J., 1965-
    Strategies for inclusion : a handbook for physical educators / Lauren J. Lieberman,
Cathy Houston-Wilson.
        p. cm.
    Includes index.
    ISBN 0-7360-0324-X
    1. Physical education for handicapped children--United States. 2. Physical education
for children--United States. 3. Inclusive education--United States. I. Houston-Wilson,
Cathy, 1962- II. Title.

GV445 .L54 2002
371.9'04486--dc21

2001051560

ISBN-10: 0-7360-0324-X
ISBN-13: 978-0-7360-0324-7

Acquisitions Editor: Judy Patterson Wright, PhD; **Developmental Editor:** Jennifer L. Walker; **Assistant Editor:** Sandra Merz Bott; **Copyeditor:** Lisa Sheltra; **Proofreader:** Jim Burns; **Indexer:** Betty Frizzéll; **Permission Manager:** Dalene Reeder; **Graphic Designer:** Fred Starbird; **Graphic Artist:** Dawn Sills; **Cover Designer:** Keith Blomberg; **Photographer (cover):** Les Woodrum; **Photographer (interior):** Les Woodrum; **Art Manager:** Carl D. Johnson; **Printer:** Versa Press

Printed in the United States of America   10   9   8   7   6   5   4

Human Kinetics
Web site: www.HumanKinetics.com

United States: Human Kinetics
P.O. Box 5076
Champaign, IL 61825-5076
800-747-4457
e-mail: humank@hkusa.com

Canada: Human Kinetics
475 Devonshire Road Unit 100
Windsor, ON N8Y 2L5
800-465-7301 (in Canada only)
e-mail: orders@hkcanada.com

Europe: Human Kinetics
107 Bradford Road, Stanningley
Leeds LS28 6AT, United Kingdom
+44 (0) 113 255 5665
e-mail: hk@hkeurope.com

Australia: Human Kinetics
57A Price Avenue
Lower Mitcham, South Australia 5062
08 8277 1555
e-mail: liaw@hkaustralia.com

New Zealand: Human Kinetics
Division of Sports Distributors NZ Ltd.
P.O. Box 300 226 Albany
North Shore City
Auckland
0064 9 448 1207
e-mail: info@humankinetics.co.nz

This book is dedicated in loving memory to Lauren's grandfather, Lou Lieberman. His encouragement, support, dedication, and interest in adapted physical education were invaluable. He had consistently high standards and always pushed us to do our best work. He was instrumental in helping make our dreams reality.

Contents

Part I ■ Understanding Inclusion   **1**

*Grasp the current trends in inclusion and understand the importance
of making inclusion a priority in the physical education setting.*

Chapter 1 Defining Inclusion in Today's Classroom   **3**

*Gain valuable perspective on the history of the inclusion movement and its impact
on physical education programming. Influential legislation is explained and
pre-inclusion planning (IEP) is introduced.*

Chapter 2 Preparing for Inclusion   **13**

*Understand how accurate assessment in adapted physical education directly
affects inclusion planning. This chapter provides insight into both traditional assessment techniques and authentic assessment techniques and their strengths and
weaknesses.*

Chapter 3 Planning for Success   **33**

*Learn how effective Individualized Education Plans (IEPs) set the stage for successful
inclusion. Components of the IEP form, the IEP meeting process, and the IEP team
members and their roles are discussed and defined in detail.*

Chapter 4 Adapting the Curriculum to Fit Special Needs   **51**

*Discover new theoretical constructs that drive the adapted physical education field.
Concrete examples are provided to help bring these theories to life. Basic principles
of adapting games and activities as well as instructions on implementing the
adaptations suggested are also included in this chapter.*

Preface

Since 1975, the process of including children with disabilities in general physical education classes has become a reality for school districts across the country. Unfortunately, for far too many students with disabilities, the transition from traditionally segregated classrooms to supportive, inclusive environments has been clumsy at best.

Consequently, teachers of physical education have been forced to blindly navigate the maze of legislation and its accompanying mountains of paperwork, relying on the best intentions rather than the best information when it comes to integrating these students.

The purpose of this book is to educate and empower physical education teachers with the information and tools necessary for the successful classroom inclusion of children with disabilities.

We have worked diligently to create a solid resource filled with practical applications and easily implemented planning and assessment strategies for use by physical education teachers, coaches, and recreation directors. The book is divided into two parts. The first part provides background information, as well as a concrete roadmap to planning the successful integration of a child with disabilities into a traditional physical education setting. The second part of the book is filled with 38 teachable units, complete with assessment tools for curriculum planning.

This book can also be used by special education teachers, adapted physical education teachers, therapeutic recreation specialists, graduate and undergraduate students in the above majors, and parents. The book is organized to provide the reader with the most up-to-date and useful strategies to include children with disabilities. To reinforce the information and strategies, we have created several unique recurring chapter elements that go beyond the typical "chapter objectives" and "chapter summary." These "new" special elements were created to both guide and encourage readers throughout the book. For example, one recurring special feature is the chapter opening scenario. These brief case studies are designed to help the reader explore his or her thoughts and feelings regarding various aspects of inclusion and adapted physical education. Each scenario is followed by several questions that directly relate to the chapter's objectives. To tie the chapter information and case studies together, the questions are then reviewed and answered at the end of each chapter.

Additional unique chapter features are the "Teaching Tips" from the authors. These quick tips are designed to reinforce ideas and provide inspiration along the way. The following paragraphs provide more detailed information about each chapter of this book.

The first chapter, "Defining Inclusion in Today's Classroom," provides an overview of legislative mandates that directly affect physical education. Armed with knowledge of the legal requirements, teachers can advocate and receive support to successfully educate children with disabilities. A sample of a continuum of supports and placements is presented, so physical educators can see the various options available in the education of children with disabilities. It is not necessary for children with disabilities to stay in one environment at all times. A child may move from one placement option to another depending on the child's unique needs and the unit of instruction.

The second chapter in this book, "Preparing for Inclusion," deals specifically with assessment. Such topics as traditional forms of assessment and authentic assessment are discussed. The chapter highlights the purposes of assessment and the use of assessment data to drive instruction. Sample rubrics and additional examples of portfolio uses for children with disabilities are provided. In making placement decisions, teachers can take advantage of the sample Ability Description Form provided in this chapter.

Chapter 3, "Planning for Success," deals with Individualized Education Plans (IEPs). IEPs are a necessary component in the education of a child with disabilities; they help ensure that the child is making progress toward intended goals. The chapter provides physical educators with all the steps necessary to develop and implement a physical education IEP.

This chapter is followed by chapter 4, "Adapting the Curriculum to Fit Special Needs," which highlights adaptations. We outline four main theories that support the concept of adapting activities to include children with disabilities. Specific guidelines for adaptation are included. Four major variables—rules, equipment, environment, and instruction—can easily be adjusted to successfully include children with special needs.

Chapter 5, "Creating an Atmosphere for Achievement," deals with strategies for facilitating inclusion. This chapter gives the reader nine specific techniques for successfully including children with disabilities in general physical education. The use of these strategies will create a welcoming environment for all children, as members of the class are intricately involved in the inclusion process. The nine techniques discussed are overcoming blanket medical excuses, disability/ability awareness activities, training peer tutors, the use of support personnel to enhance instruction, the use of homework in physical education, the use of grandparents, the use of university practicum students, the use of community facilities, and the use of role models with disabilities.

Part II of this book introduces the reader to specific strategies for inclusion. Here, the reader learns how to use the curriculum provided in part I. Part II includes a step-by-step guideline for implementing an inclusive curriculum. It provides the reader with 14 elementary units, 11 sport units, 8 recreation units, and 5 fitness units, all with potential adaptations. The adaptations are divided into the categories of environment, equipment, instruction, and rules. In addition, each unit contains an assessment rubric with skills broken down both quantitatively and qualitatively.

Finally, the appendixes of this book provide extensive information that teachers can use to successfully include children with disabilities in general physical education. The authors hope that, with this book, teachers will be empowered to advocate for themselves as well as their students with disabilities, and will receive the necessary support to lead all children to healthy, active lifestyles.

It is also our hope that physical educators will use this book to empower all students with the knowledge that anything is possible and that hopes and goals can be achieved through understanding, cooperation, and creativity.

Acknowledgments

Colleagues who have helped:

Steve Hannigan-Downs
Shayke Hutzler
Deborah Shapiro
Frank Short
Joseph Winnick

SUNY Brockport Students who have helped tremendously in this project:

Amanda Chambers
Sal Estremo
Joe Howell
Chris Kasperzak
Wendy Kohler
Steve Leroux
Melissa Milewski
Carin Mulawka
Megan O'Connell
Mike Pecorella
Kyle Root
Annette Scorse
Amanda Tepfer
Sommer Tiller
Brian Wiskochil
Ryan Woodford
Chris Wright

The authors would like to acknowledge the children, teachers, parents, and families who have taught us what strategies are beneficial in promoting success. Without their honesty, commitment, and continuous information this book would not be a reality.

Acknowledgments from Lauren Lieberman
I would like to thank Janet Joseph, Stan and Linda Lieberman, Ann, Pat, Marc, Eric, and Katrina for all their love, support, and encouragement in the process. I could not have done it without you!

Acknowledgments from Cathy Houston-Wilson
I would like to thank Lauren Lieberman for giving me the opportunity to collaborate with her on this book. I would also like to thank my family, Kevin, Meaghan, and Shannon, for the constant support they give to me to pursue projects such as these. Finally, to all the children I have worked with and learned from, my experiences with all of you have been truly incredible.

■ UNIT FINDER

UNDERSTANDING INCLUSION

It has been documented that more than 93 percent of children with disabilities are included in public schools. This change from typically segregated placements to more inclusive environments has occurred as a result of Public Law 94-142, the *Education for All Handicapped Children Act,* now reauthorized as Public Law 105-17, the *Individuals With Disabilities Education Act Amendments.* The law requires that children with disabilities receive physical education and that, if necessary, physical education be adapted to meet their unique needs. The law also requires that children with disabilities be educated in the *least restrictive environment* (LRE) possible. This means an educational environment in which the child will be most successful. In physical education, the most successful environment could range from a totally inclusive class to a segregated class. The most important thing to remember, however, is that a child with a disability can receive adapted physical education in any environment, because adapted physical education is a *service,* not a *placement.*

Inclusion, the process of educating children with and without disabilities together at all times, has become a reality for most school districts across the country. And even if a district has not embraced the concept of "total inclusion," most children with disabilities are included in their general physical education classes.

Teachers of physical education are faced with the reality of providing an appropriate education for children with a variety of abilities. Many teachers lack the professional preparation to know how to successfully include children with disabilities (Block 2000). They may have good intentions, yet they often possess limited knowledge about how to adapt the curriculum. Most undergraduate professional preparation programs offer only one class in adapted physical education, which seldom qualifies an individual to adequately adapt the whole curriculum for children with a variety of disabilities. In addition, most schools do not offer in-service training to assist teachers in including all children successfully. As a result, teachers have very little knowledge of the variables that lead to success in the gymnasium.

The challenge faced by physical educators is compounded by the fact that children with disabilities are often behind in their levels of fitness (Lieberman and McHugh 2001; Shephard 1990; Winnick and Short 1985) and motor skills (Pender and Patterson 1982). The solution to these problems, as well as the purpose of the first part of this book, is to educate and empower teachers of physical education by introducing them to all the variables that can be adapted to ensure appropriate inclusion in physical education. It is only when teachers are willing to analyze their curriculum, instruction, rules, equipment, and environment that children with disabilities will have a chance at full participation in general physical education.

1 Defining Inclusion in Today's Classroom

Ian was a five-year-old boy with diplegic cerebral palsy. Diplegia is a condition in which the arms are slightly impaired and the legs are greatly impaired. Ian attended an inclusive preschool program at his local United Cerebral Palsy center last year and was ready to advance into kindergarten. He made great gains in his preschool, especially in the motor area. He could now walk slowly without a walker and even faster with a walker. Ian had been assigned a teacher's aide named Ms. Adams. Ms. Adams had worked with a child with cerebral palsy before and was looking forward to working with Ian. Preparing for kindergarten was a little scary for Ian, but once he met Ms. Adams he was more comfortable. Ian was attending an inclusive school. Ms. Adams and Ian's mother made sure the teachers in the school knew about Ian's disability, as well as his abilities, during an Individualized Education Planning (IEP) meeting. It was decided that Ian would be included in his general physical education class because his skills were adequate for the intended curriculum. The general physical education teacher, Mrs. Bishop, who attended the meeting, was honest and said that she did not have much experience teaching children with physical disabilities but was willing to do her best to accommodate Ian. Mrs. Bishop had taught elementary physical education for 13 years and had received support and recognition from parents and administrators for her creativity and encouraging spirit. Mrs. Bishop was assured that she would receive support from an adapted physical education consultant. The consultant showed Mrs. Bishop how to modify and adapt activities so that Ian could be successfully included in physical education. After a while, Mrs. Bishop began to think of her own strategies and also solicited advice from the students in the class. The children were very supportive and enthusiastic about helping Ian to succeed in physical education. Mrs. Adams modified some equipment, the pace of some games, and instructional grouping, and Ian was doing well. Mrs. Adams reflected on the experience and concluded that all good teaching is adapted.

Questions to Test Yourself

1. I am often invited to pre-planning meetings to discuss placement of students with special needs.

   Yes — No — Sometimes

2. If I cannot attend pre-planning meetings for students with special needs, my written or verbal input is always taken into consideration.

   Yes — No — Sometimes

3. My school employs adapted physical education specialists who aid in including students with special needs.

   Yes — No

4. My school provides in-service meetings so that I can learn more about students with disabilities and how to appropriately include these students in physical education.

   Yes — No

5. Through informative Web sites, contact with local universities, and consultations with an adapted physical education specialist, teachers can find ways to successfully include students with disabilities in a general physical education class.

   Yes — No

The purpose of this chapter is to help the reader

- understand legislative mandates that affect physical education for students with disabilities,
- understand placement options available to students with disabilities, and
- understand inclusion and its effect on physical education programming.

As illustrated in the opening scenario, schools are responsible for planning the intake of students with disabilities. The scenario also illustrated the need for and the value of including physical education teachers in preliminary discussions. For example, when Mrs. Adams described her limited ability and experience in working with students with physical disabilities, she was provided the assistance of an adapted physical education consultant. Unfortunately, scenarios like this may not be the norm for everyone. Sometimes physical educators are unaware until the first day of school that they will have children with special needs in their classes. Often these teachers are left out of the loop in planning for placements of students with disabilities. This lack of information and communication is frustrating for even the most competent and motivated teachers. However, as frustrating as the bureaucracy surrounding school policy and procedure on inclusion may be, the inclusion process has come a long way in the thirty years since the first fledgling legislation made its mark.

This chapter presents an overview of legislative mandates that have affected physical education for students with disabilities. These mandates have a direct effect on the placement options and the physical education program planning and implementation available to students with disabilities.

■ A Historical Perspective

Educating students with disabilities was not always required. In fact, before much attention was paid to the subject, several parent activist groups filed suit on behalf of their children with disabilities who were being denied an educa-

A student is left out of a basketball game.

tion. Two specific landmark lawsuits filed in 1972 (*Pennsylvania Association for Retarded Children v. Commonwealth of Pennsylvania* and *Mills v. Board of Education of the District of Columbia*) set the stage for the passage of several laws that ensured rights to schooling opportunities for all children with disabilities. Most notably, it was determined through these cases that excluding students with disabilities from public education violated the Constitutional law of due process. According to Sherrill (1998, p. 75), "due process, within the educational context, refers to fair treatment in the removal of students from regular education classes."

■ Legislative Mandates

As a result of these landmark lawsuits, two significant legislative mandates were passed. One was the *Rehabilitation Act of 1973* (Public Law 93-112) and the other was the *Education for All Handicapped Children Act of 1975* (Public Law 94-142). Part of the *Rehabilitation Act*, Section 504, stipulated that no person with a disability shall be discriminated against or be denied equal opportunity afforded to nondisabled individuals in any programs or activities that receive federal funding. This was especially significant, because all public schools receive some form of federal support. Thus, students with disabilities were guaranteed equal rights among their peers. This included not only educational opportunities, but also after-school and interscholastic programs.

The *Education for All Handicapped Children Act* stipulated that all children with identifiable disabilities (such as mental retardation, auditory or visual impairments, speech or language impairments, serious emotional disturbances,

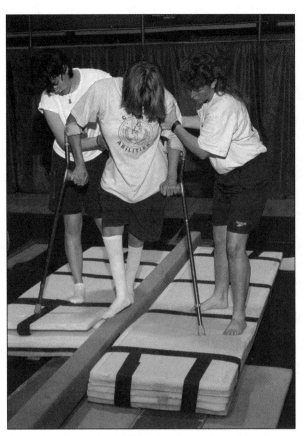

A student in an inclusive physical education class is assisted by a peer tutor and a teacher's aide.

orthopedic impairments, specific learning disabilities, or other health impairments) ages 5 to 21 be provided a free, appropriate public education with emphasis on special education services, which includes physical education. Specifically, the law defined physical education as the development of (a) physical and motor fitness, (b) fundamental motor skills and patterns, and (c) skills in aquatics, dance, individual and group games, and sports. In fact, physical education was the only curricular area specifically identified in the law. This distinction placed physical education as a *direct service*. Direct services are those services that must be provided to all students with disabilities. Related services, on the other hand, are only provided to students in order to allow them to benefit from special education services. Examples of related services include such things as occupational therapy, speech therapy, or physical therapy.

In addition to requiring physical education for all students with disabilities as a direct service, the *Education for All Handicapped Children Act* also stipulates that such education should be provided by qualified personnel. Although federal legislation does not define the term *qualified personnel*, most states define it in the regulations governing physical education in that state. For example, in New York state, *qualified personnel* is defined as anyone certified to teach physical education. Other states may allow classroom teachers to provide adapted physical education, while still others may require adapted physical education certification. Regardless of state definitions, whoever provides physical education to students with disabilities should be aware of appropriate adaptations and modifications to ensure successful physical education experiences.

Furthermore, this law requires students with disabilities to be provided with an Individualized Education Plan (IEP) that identifies specific educational needs and determines appropriate resources to address those needs. Typically, upon notification that a child with disabilities will be entering a district, an IEP team is assembled to determine an appropriate plan for the child. IEP team members usually include parents, the child (when appropriate), special education teachers, school psychologists, general education teachers, and any other representatives deemed necessary by the district or the parents. During IEP deliberations, placement decisions and modification and adaptation strategies are made, and goals and objectives are finalized. These goals are based on intended goals and objectives specific to each curricular area.

Finally, this law requires students with disabilities to receive their education in the *least restrictive environment* (LRE) and to be educated with their typically developing peers to the maximum extent possible. This means that students with disabilities should only be removed from the general education environment when the nature or severity of the disability will not allow the child to benefit from the program, even with the use of supplemental aids or supports (Rehabilitation Act of 1973, Sec. 794). Put simply, students with disabilities should be educated with their peers unless it would not be beneficial to the child. This model of providing services to students with disabilities in the typical environment rather than removing them from the regular class to receive services is known as *inclusion*. When a student with disabilities learns alongside his regularly developing peers this is called adapted education. Thus, adapted physical education is a service, not a placement. In fact, students with disabilities can and should receive their adapted physical education program in any appropriate environment as long as their goals and objectives are being met. Students with disabilities may be able to engage in physical education activities in an unrestricted manner, or they may need program adaptations. Thus, adapted physical education means physical activities modified or changed to meet the unique needs of students with disabilities.

According to Yell (1998), students with disabilities can only be pulled out of a general education class when

- the student needs additional related services (such as a 1:1 or higher teaching ratio with qualified professionals),
- the placement has a negative effect on other students (for example, the student's behavior or disability detracts from the ability of the nondisabled students in the class to learn),
- physical inability to perform is deemed significant enough to warrant alternative placements, or
- the student is not receiving educational benefits from the general classroom placement (the student cannot achieve class or IEP goals and objectives in the general education placement).

▓ Adapted physical education is a *service*, not a *placement*.

French, Henderson, Kinnison, and Sherrill (1998) also note that a student should be segregated from his or her typically developing peers for physical education if there is a probability of harm to the individual with a disability—if, for example, the child's disability may be exacerbated by involvement in general physical education.

The Lieberman and Houston-Wilson model given below shows the continuum of options, moving from a totally inclusive environment to a segregated environment, for including children with disabilities. Options are available on the continuum so a child can move freely from one environment to another based on unique needs.

A student who is out of his wheelchair stretches with his peers.

Lieberman and Houston-Wilson Model of Continuum of Supports and Placement

A. Inclusion Options

1. Full inclusion with no adaptations or support

2. Full inclusion with curriculum adaptations

   a. multilevel curriculum—presenting the same content but at different levels

   b. curriculum overlapping—presenting alternative curriculum goals within the same activity (Block & Horton, 1996)

3. Full inclusion with trained peer tutors

   a. traditional/unidirectional peer tutoring: peer tutor teaches the tutee the entire time, and the tutee remains the "student" in the dyad

   b. reciprocal/bidirectional peer tutoring: both students with special needs and their typically developing peers take turns tutoring each other based on the task at hand

   c. cross-aged peer tutoring: older students with or without special needs tutor younger students with special needs

   d. class-wide peer tutoring: teams are formed and given specific skill sheets to practice; tutoring occurs reciprocally; during competition, points are accumulated for appropriate skill performance by members of the team

    4. Full inclusion with teacher assistants

       a. full time: assistant accompanies child full time throughout the day

       b. flexible schedule: assistant accompanies child only when necessary

    5. Full inclusion with interpreter

       a. full time: interpreter accompanies child full time throughout the day

       b. flexible schedule: interpreter accompanies child only when necessary

B. Part-Time Segregated Placement Options

    1. Split placement without support

       a. student-directed: student directs unit modifications as needed

       b. teacher-directed: teacher directs unit modifications as needed

    2. Split placement with support

       a. flexible schedule: child attends both integrated and segregated classes, based on unit of instruction, with support

       b. fixed schedule: child attends both integrated and segregated classes with support

C. Community-Based Options

    1. Part time: child's time is divided between community- and school-based activities

    2. Full time: curriculum is implemented through community-based activities

D. Full-Time Segregated Placement Options Within a Regular School District

    1. Small group

       a. reverse integration: typically developing peers attend classes with peers with disabilities and assist as needed

       b. specialist-directed: specialist directs activity of group

    2. One-to-one

       a. reverse integration: typically developing peer attends class with peer with disability

       b. specialist-directed: specialist directs activity of student

E. Segregated Placement Options

    1. Day school for specific disabilities

    2. Residential school for specific disabilities

    3. Home schooling

    4. Hospital setting

Current Legislative Reauthorizations and Revisions

Subsequent to Public Law 94-142 were the *Amendments to the Education for All Handicapped Children Act,* Public Laws 98-199 (1983) and 99-457 (1986), which dealt specifically with services for infants, toddlers, and preschoolers. In 1990,

Public Law 101-476, the *Individuals With Disabilities Education Act* (IDEA), was passed. This law changed the terminology of legislation to describe individuals as having "disabilities" rather than "handicapping conditions," and also added two disability populations, individuals with autism and with traumatic brain injury. In 1997, IDEA was again reauthorized and is now known as Public Law 105-17, *IDEA Amendments of 1997*. This law has maintained all the regulations previously mentioned and includes preschoolers (ages three to five) in the same services afforded to those ages 5 to 21.

Roles and Responsibilities of Teachers of Adapted Physical Education

Although the tenet of the least restrictive environment remains the legislative mandate, inclusion has become common practice. More and more students are receiving their special education services in inclusive environments. Support services become the key to successful inclusion. Teachers of physical education for students with disabilities must be active participants in all intake and placement decisions about physical education. Necessary supports, such as personnel or equipment, need to be identified and agreed on during the IEP meeting for the child to be successful in physical education. More specific information about IEPs and IEP meetings is discussed in chapter 3.

> ## Teachers of adapted physical education should be involved in the decision-making process about placement in physical education.

Question Review and Summary

1. I am often invited to pre-planning meetings to discuss placement of students with special needs.

   As discussed, it is important that teachers of physical education for students with disabilities be active participants in deliberations about placement options and the supports needed to accommodate students with disabilities in physical education.

2. If I cannot attend pre-planning meetings for students with special needs, my written or verbal input is always taken into consideration.

   Because it is often difficult for teachers of physical education to attend all meetings, written or verbal input should be given to a designee so that physical education is addressed during the meeting.

3. My school employs adapted physical education specialists who aid in including students with special needs.

   Schools who do not have adapted physical education specialists on staff should provide physical education teachers with ongoing in-services and workshops to further their knowledge regarding adapted physical education.

4. My school provides in-service meetings so that I can learn more about students with disabilities and how to appropriately include these students in physical education.

   If your district has not provided in-service training on teaching students with disabilities, a designee should request such training.

5. Through informative Web sites, contact with local universities, and consultations with an adapted physical education specialist, teachers can find ways to successfully include students with disabilities in a general physical education class.

   Numerous resources are available to assist physical education teachers in successfully including and teaching students with disabilities. Appendix G provides a list of resources for implementing adapted physical education programs.

Through a brief historical overview of relevant legislation, this chapter has attempted to assist physical educators in understanding the legislative mandates currently affecting the education of students with disabilities. In addition, information was presented to help educators become aware of the many placement options made available to special needs students under the current legislation. Further discussion of inclusion and adapted physical education emphasized the vital role of physical education teachers in the planning and implementation of IEPs and in other aspects of adapted physical education programs.

There Is a Child Involved

By Michael Marsallo
A Total Commitment, 1998

Mainstream, self contain, integrate, include,
How's the wind blow what's the mood?
General education, special education, adapted or not,
Teachers everywhere are put on the spot. Lighter balls
Larger goals, shorter distances, too,
The menu's too large, no one's sure what to do.
These concerns each could be solved,
If we'd only remember,
"There Is A Child Involved"

Baseball, basketball, floor hockey too,
Do I have to adapt all of them for you?
Why can't you watch, maybe keep score,
Then the "regulars" will get to play more.
Gross motor, fine motor, wheelchairs and walkers,
And all those fancy augmentative talkers.
I went to college to learn how to teach,
But no one told me, there'd be so many to reach!
Relax, take a breath, for this too can be resolved,
If we'd only remember,
"There Is a Child Involved"

Frustrated kids who just want the chance
To score a goal, or join a dance.
They can't quite catch, or keep up the pace,

And seem to get lost in the midst of a race.
But you need not lower the ceiling
For those who stumble and fall,
Just adapt and level the field for one and all.
So, what's to be done, what's the goal to be?
Each decision we make,
should begin, and end, with a child.
You're ready to adapt, no challenge too great,
No problems that cannot be solved
So the Total Commitment you leave here with
Is to remember...
"There Is A Child Involved"

Olivia is a seventh grader who has arthrogryposis. Arthrogryposis is a condition that primarily affects range of motion. Individuals with arthrogryposis typically demonstrate extreme rotation at the shoulder joint, making their arms turn inward, and abnormal positioning of their knees and feet. Olivia, who just started middle school, has many friends. She uses an electric wheelchair to ambulate but also has good use of her left leg, which she uses as much as possible. Olivia loves swimming and swims independently all summer in her family's outdoor pool. She also swam independently during her swimming unit in elementary school. Unfortunately, her elementary school teacher, Mr. Long, never documented student skill ability, thus there were no records of students' abilities in swimming or any other unit of instruction. Olivia was excited about middle school physical education because she knew that swimming was offered once a week during the first quarter. She could not wait to show off her skills to Mrs. Bowman, her new physical education teacher.

When the first day of swim class arrived, Mrs. Bowman was very reluctant to allow Olivia to go into the pool. Judging Olivia's physical appearance, Mrs. Bowman had a hard time believing that Olivia could swim independently, despite the explanations of Olivia and her peers. Mrs. Bowman was just not going to take any risks and was fearful of possible liability. Mrs. Bowman only allowed Olivia to swim in the shallow water with a flotation device and a teacher's assistant to offer physical help. Olivia was crushed and very embarrassed. This was the one activity she could do independently and do well, and the opportunity was gone.

Olivia's mother contacted Mrs. Bowman at once. Mrs. Bowman agreed to a private evaluation to assess Olivia's swimming abilities. The whole situation was frustrating, embarrassing, and demeaning to Olivia. This entire scenario could have been avoided with the use of appropriate assessment practices.

Questions to Test Yourself

1. I would have acted in a similar fashion if I were Mrs. Bowman.

   Yes — No — Maybe

2. It is difficult to expect Mrs. Bowman to have assessed Olivia. Assessment is time consuming and not worth all the time and energy.

   Yes — No

3. The assessment tools for the regular class should be fine for assessing Olivia; after all, if she is to be included in the class, she should be expected to have the same goals and objectives.

   Yes — No — Not sure

4. Assessment is needed so that Individualized Education Plans can be written and progress toward meeting goals and objectives can be determined.

   Yes — No — Not sure

5. Assessment is needed for special needs students, but it's not my job. I think physical therapists or classroom teachers could do a better job. They could assess students with disabilities in the motor domain, develop goals and objectives, and report the findings to me.

   Yes — No — Not sure

The purpose of this chapter is to help the reader

- understand the use of assessment in adapted physical education,
- understand traditional assessment techniques, and
- understand authentic assessment techniques.

■ Effective Assessment in Adapted Physical Education

As noted in the previous scenario, assessment is needed to ensure students receive an appropriate educational experience. Lack of information about student abilities can compromise physical education programs, especially for students with special needs. Assessments need to accurately reflect what students can and cannot do in relation to the curriculum content. Poor, incomplete, or biased assessments yield weak and inaccurate information, which does little to shape the curriculum. On the other hand, effective assessments, those prepared and administered with a clear purpose and that relate to the curriculum content, will assist in the development of appropriate goals and objectives for all students and can really help to shape and grow student abilities (Henderson, French, and Kinnison 2001). Once information is obtained on what students (regardless of special needs) can and cannot do, program planning and specific activities can be identified and implemented. Failure to embed assessment into the physical education curriculum will produce programs that do not address the individual needs of learners and will have little benefit to the participants. Such programs can easily be targeted for elimination. Unless professionals can document learning, little value is placed on the subject matter.

What sets apart an effective assessment from an ineffective one is how accurately the assessment reflects the capabilities of the students being assessed. An effective assessment is objective, which means there will not be any guesswork

A teacher observes children to determine level of ambulation, abilities, comprehension, and behavior.

from the instructor as to the student's level of performance. Checklists that identify component parts of skills and that may also include a point system can be used as a form of objective assessment. The skills should be clearly identified, and the instructor should note which component parts of the skill the student has mastered. If points are attached, a score can be obtained, or the checklist could simply identify which component parts of the skill still need to be mastered. Once this information is obtained, specific activities can be developed to help achieve a high degree of mastery for any given skill observed.

Before a child with a disability can be assessed, it is extremely important to acquire information about the child. An Ability Description Chart, when completed, gives the instructor valuable information about the child. The instructor can ask the parents, previous teachers, therapists, or administrator for any information that is not known. With this information in hand, assessments will be much easier to implement. See the sample Ability Description Chart on page 16.

Effective assessments also produce data that are *valid, reliable*, and *functional*. Valid assessments are those that measure what one seeks to measure. For example, to assess students on throwing maturity, the assessment task must yield a throw. However, if the instructor adds the variable of accuracy to the throw (such as hitting a small target on the wall), the throwing assessment becomes invalid because a person can demonstrate a mature throw without having to hit a specific target. The addition of accuracy makes the test invalid if maturity is the variable being assessed. In addition to validity, assessments must also be reliable; that is, the test will give consistent results regardless of when or how often a particular task is assessed. For example, if a student scores a three on the standing broad jump for demonstrating three elements of the jump, he should be able to score the same two days later. Finally, assessments should be functional. Tasks that require students to place pegs in a pegboard are not functional to everyday living. Seldom, if ever, is a person asked to place pegs in a pegboard. Although fine motor coordination is a necessary skill, assessments that measure fine motor skills should relate to everyday life. An example of a functional fine motor skill

Ability Description Chart

Student:_____ School:_____

Birth date:_____ Grade:_____

Previous physical education teacher:_____

Phone number:_____

Previous adapted physical education teacher:_____

Phone number:_____

Form completed by:_____Title:_____

Please answer the following questions or descriptions as thoroughly as possible. This semester this student will be included in regular physical education class. Please answer all questions as positively as possible.

Disability:_____

Level of current function:_____

Ambulation method(s):

_____ Wheelchair and pushes independently   ___ Crutches   ___ Other

_____ Wheelchair and needs assistance   ___ Walker

Medical concerns:

___ Seizures   ___ Shunt   ___ Eye condition   ___ Ear condition

___ Diabetes   ___ Other:_____

Please elaborate:_____

Communication methods:_____

---

in physical education would be tying knots during a ropes unit. As evident, ensuring that tests are valid, reliable, and functional is the cornerstone of appropriate assessment.

Other features of an effective assessment include being easy to administer and easy to understand. Not only does the instructor need to understand how to implement the test and interpret the results, but the instructor must also be able to present the information in such a way that parents and administrators can understand the results as well. Various assessments can produce either limited or extensive statistical data. The key is being able to fully understand the assessment and to clearly articulate its findings, regardless of the extent of the data generated.

Utilizing appropriate assessments in physical education is also imperative in determining the need for adapted physical education for students with disabilities. Appropriate assessments can (a) determine the unique physical or motor needs of students with disabilities and appropriate placements based on those needs, (b) assist in the development of physical education goals and objectives,

> ### ◼ Assessment is the cornerstone of appropriate program planning, implementation, and evaluation.

and (c) monitor student progress. The following sections highlight these major outcomes.

Determining Unique Needs and Placement

Screening is the first step in determining if a child has a unique need and is entitled to special education services such as adapted physical education. Screening is the professional observation of student actions to determine if these actions differ considerably from typical behavior. Physical educators are often asked to screen youngsters to determine if any motor delays are evident and whether further testing is warranted. To conduct these screening tests, physical educators may develop checklists of skill performance and observe students as they perform various skills. Those who do not demonstrate developmentally or age-appropriate skill behaviors would be identified for further testing. This process of identifying students who may need further testing is known as a *referral*. Referrals are made to the *Committee on Special Education* (CSE) and can be made by any person who has a vested interest in the child, including parents, teachers, therapists, and physicians. Every district must have a CSE. Members of the CSE include the child's teacher; a school psychologist; and a district representative who is qualified to provide, administer, or supervise special education. The CSE will convene to determine if further testing is warranted. A variety of formal tests are available, and physical educators or adapted physical education specialists may conduct formal assessments to determine unique needs and eligibility for services.

Once students are deemed eligible, placement decisions are made about the appropriate environment in which the student will receive services. As noted in chapter 1 of this book, *IDEA-Amendments* (1997) requires that all students with special needs receive instruction in the least restrictive environment.

For example, let's revisit Olivia, the student introduced in the opening scenario. She was to receive general physical education with her peers two times a week and separate physical education once a week to further enhance her goals and objectives. Because Olivia has limited range of motion, her goals centered on increasing flexibility, muscular strength and control, and body coordination. In her general physical education classes, she participated in the same unit as her peers, incorporating her individual goals when possible. In her separate physical education class she worked predominantly on her individual goals. This program was least restrictive for Olivia, and she improved and excelled throughout the year. Not having assessment data for Olivia created an embarrassing and negative situation. On the other hand, assessing Olivia to determine her ability and placement needs will give her an advantage because she will be set up for success from the beginning.

Determining Program Goals and Objectives

A second outcome of assessment in adapted physical education is the development of program goals and objectives. Through assessment, physical educators can note individual strengths and weaknesses. Areas of weakness become *goals*, and specific activities employed to reach goals are *objectives* (Burton and Miller 1998) For example, Olivia's goal of developing muscular strength and control was incorporated into a gymnastics unit with her peers. A rubric was developed for the class, which included such tasks as the ability to perform front supports on the mat, crab walk, perform musical movements with ribbons, and do various rolls on the mat. These activities provided a way for Olivia to increase her muscular endurance and control in a typical physical education environment.

Knowing students' goals and objectives and enhancing them are tantamount to student learning. Olivia can work on her goals and objectives with her peers and improve her ability to do activities of daily living.

Monitoring Progress

The final outcome of assessment is that it provides physical educators with a way to monitor student progress. Through ongoing assessment, students and teachers can note individual progress. As one goal is achieved, others can be developed. This process is quite motivating for both student and teacher.

Monitoring progress can take many forms. One very easy and motivating way to monitor progress is to create an individual skill chart. Individual skill charts can be developed for students to keep in their portfolios. Olivia's upper-body strength was first evaluated using a *lat pull-down machine,* with straps tied around her wrists because of her difficulty with grasp. She could lift 20 pounds three to five times for three sets. During the gymnastics unit, she practiced wheelbarrow races on her elbows and started out with three steps. After four weeks on the gymnastics unit and working on this goal in her separate class, she could take 8 to 10 steps on her elbows and could do 10 to 12 repetitions on the lat pull-down machine.

Monitoring progress ensures that the student is working toward goals and objectives. It is extremely motivating for the student and teacher. Olivia continued to develop strength once she saw that she could improve.

This student challenges herself on the parallel bars during the gymnastics unit.

▓ Traditional Assessment Techniques

Assessment in general physical education has, since the 1950s, traditionally focused on the physical fitness domain. However, there has been a notable lack of testing instruments in the other areas of physical education. Testing in physical education was often viewed as time consuming, confusing, and unnecessary. With the recent advent of the National Association for Sport & Physical Education (NASPE) Content Standards (1995), a resurgence in the need for and value of assessment for all students in physical education has become apparent. NASPE (1995) has identified the following content standards for physical education:

1. Demonstrates competency in many movement forms and proficiency in a few movement forms
2. Applies movement concepts and principles to the learning and development of motor skills
3. Exhibits a physically active lifestyle
4. Achieves and maintains a health-enhancing level of physical fitness
5. Demonstrates responsible personal and social behavior in physical activity settings
6. Demonstrates understanding and respect for differences among people in physical activity settings
7. Understands that physical activity provides opportunities for enjoyment, challenge, self-expression, and social interaction

To maximize the impact of these new standards, teachers must utilize appropriate methods of assessment to ensure that students are meeting the standards. Physical educators realize that for programs to be held accountable, data need to be available to document student learning. These data can only be generated through assessment.

In the field of adapted physical education, assessment continues to be the cornerstone for effective programming. A variety of assessment instruments are available to assist professionals in determining whether unique needs exist, identify areas of strength and weakness, and document student progress and learning. When choosing an assessment tool for students with disabilities, professionals look for qualities such as purpose, technical adequacy (validity and reliability), ecological validity (testing in a natural environment), nondiscriminatory features, ease of administration, cost, and availability. Other factors that are considered are whether the test is norm- or criterion-referenced, curriculum-based, or has an instructional link (Zittel 1994). Some tests are designed primarily for screening, whereas others are used for placement and program decisions. Some tests are considered formal because they must be set up and administered utilizing a specific protocol. These tests may require additional time to administer and in some instances may require training before test administration. Other tests are considered informal because the teacher can gain the information necessary from observation or checklists with no strict protocol. Informal assessments can be conducted during class and can be administered by the instructor, a peer tutor, a teacher's aid, or support personnel. All tests yield data that can be used in the development of IEPs in physical education.

■ **Communication is essential to understanding students' unique needs, abilities, and achievements.**

To choose the most appropriate, efficient test for a particular situation, instructors may want to ask themselves some important questions. The following questions will assist the instructor in making the right decisions when it comes to choosing an assessment. After the questions is a list of commonly used assessment tests and their primary uses.

Assessing the Assessment

1. What is the purpose of the assessment? Screening? Placement? Programming? Documenting improvement? (Does the purpose meet my purpose?)
2. Is this test valid and reliable for the population I am testing?
3. Can I implement this test in my current setting?
4. Is the test qualitative or quantitative?
5. Does it give criterion-referenced results or normative results?
6. Can my district afford this test?
7. Does the test come with any curriculum suggestions or ideas?
8. Are the results understandable to parents and administrators?

A student with a disability is included in her general physical education dance class.

Commonly Used Tests in Adapted Physical Education

Developmental Tests

Name: *Denver Developmental Screening Test* (Frankenburg and Dodds 1991)

Ages: 0-6 years

Tests: Fine motor, gross motor, social and language skills

Name: *Peabody Developmental Motor Scales* (1974)

Ages: 0-7 years

Tests: Fine and gross motor

Features: Instructional link to motor activities

Motor Development Tests

Name: *Body Skills Inventory* (Werder and Bruininks 1988)

Ages: 2-12 years

Tests: Fine and gross motor

Features: Instructional link to motor activities

Name: *Smart Start: A Preschool Movement Curriculum* (Wessel and Zittel 1995)

Ages: 3-6 years

Tests: Locomotion, object control, orientation, and play skills

Features: Instructional link to a preschool motor curriculum

Name: *Test of Gross Motor Development* (TGMD) (Ulrich 2000)

Ages: 3-10 years

Tests: Locomotion and object control skills

Features: Criterion and normative standards

Name: *I CAN K-3* (Wessel and Zittel 1998)

Ages: 5-8 years

Tests: Locomotion, object control, orientation and play participation, and equipment

Features: Instructional link to an early elementary school motor curriculum

Fitness Tests

Name: *FITNESSGRAM* (Cooper Institute for Aerobic Research 1994)

Ages: 10-17 years and up

Tests: Health-related physical fitness components (aerobic capacity, muscular strength and endurance, flexibility, body composition)

Features: Criterion-referenced fitness standards, computer applications to generate fitness reports

Name: *Brockport Physical Fitness: A Health-Related Test for Youth With Physical and Mental Disabilities* (Winnick and Short 1999)

Ages: 10-17 years and up

Tests: Health-related physical fitness components (aerobic capacity, muscular strength and endurance, flexibility, body composition)

Features: Criterion-referenced fitness standards for youth with special needs, computer applications to generate fitness reports

Aquatics

Brockport Aquatics Checklist (see appendix D)

The checklist presented in table 2.1 summarizes the preceding information.

Table 2.1   Summary of Commonly Used Assessment Tools

Test	Age	Norm	Criterion	Screening/ placement	Program development	Curriculum
Denver	0-6	✓	✓	✓		
Peabody	0-7	✓	✓	✓		
Body Skills	2-12	✓	✓	✓	✓	
Smart Start	3-6	✓	✓	✓	✓	✓
TGMD	3-10	✓	✓	✓	✓	✓
I CAN	5-8	✓	✓	✓	✓	
FITNESSGRAM	10-17+	✓	✓	✓		
Brockport	10-17+	✓	✓	✓		
Aquatics	Any	✓	✓	✓	✓	

Problems With Traditional Assessment

Although the commonly used tests described here can be quite useful in screening students, making placement decisions, and developing program goals and objectives, they do have their limitations. For example, some students with severe disabilities may be unable to be tested in traditional ways. When a test is not conducted in the way in which it was intended, the results are invalid. In addition, some traditional tests are more developmental in nature and as such are targeted toward elementary students. Unfortunately, tests for middle and high school students are not readily available, and tests linking assessment to the middle and high school curriculum have been almost nonexistent. Because of these factors, a new and creative way to assess students, known as authentic assessment, was developed. A review of authentic assessment follows.

Guiding Principles to Authentic Assessment

1. Assessment should be embedded in the curriculum.

2. Data should be taken daily.

3. No ceiling should be placed on student learning.

4. All students should be expected to improve in their progress toward the objective.

New Assessment Options

Specifically, the tests of the past present four major problems for adapted physical education today (Block, Lieberman, and Conner-Kuntz 1998). First, standardized tests have been misused in determining IEP goals (Block 2000). Second, standardized tests offer little help in choosing instructional techniques (Wessel and Kelly 1986). Third, the accuracy of measuring a student's abilities by testing only once and with only one test is questionable (Davis and Burton 1991). Finally, some standardized tests are not related to the curriculum content of the physical education program. For example, although the *Bruininks-Oseretsky Test of Motor Proficiency* (Bruininks 1978) is considered a blue-ribbon standardized test to determine the need for special education services (such as adapted physical education), components of this test have little relation to typical physical education curriculum content. Tasks such as stringing beads (fine motor) or stopping a falling ruler (reaction time) do not correspond with physical education curricular content. These tasks are used, however, to develop an overall picture of the child's motor proficiency, and their value should not be minimized. Thus, although there is a purpose for standardized tests, other forms of assessment need to be examined that can provide more content-specific meaning. Authentic assessment fills this gap.

Authentic assessment is an ongoing feedback system that monitors and records student learning and outcomes under "authentic" conditions. Authentic assessment is conducted in real-life situations. Through authentic assessments, students demonstrate skills, knowledge, and competencies in age-appropriate, functional activities. It is a totally performance-based approach. This means that students are evaluated on skills that are directly related to outcomes of the program. The results provide unparalleled information on learning and achievement of students. Many in the teaching field today agree that this assessment technique should be infused into the teaching process (Wiggins 1997).

There are many benefits to using authentic assessment. These benefits include the following:

1. It can be used in the current curriculum.
2. It is created specifically for the goals and objectives of each unit.
3. It can be created to include every level of ability in the class.
4. Children are held accountable for their own learning.
5. Students know what is expected ahead of time.
6. It is motivating, challenging, and keeps children interested in learning.

Authentic Assessment

Authentic assessment is a clear, concise, measurable, and motivating way of assessing student learning, improvement, and achievement. Authentic assessment utilizes tasks based on those roles and responsibilities required in real-world settings. Because authentic assessment evaluates a student's abilities in real-world settings, the student must rely on higher-level thinking and concept application to complete the tasks. Also, the student is informed in advance and gets time to practice the skills required, because those skills are directly tied to the curriculum.

This advance knowledge gives the student ownership of the process. He or she can prepare mentally and physically for testing, thus performing at an accurate competency level. Finally, because of the interrelationship between teaching and assessment, students must demonstrate competence in a variety of skills and situations (Block, Lieberman, and Conner-Kuntz 1998; Melograno 1994; Smith 1997).

The following section describes rubrics, ecological task analysis, and portfolios, three examples of authentic assessment.

Rubrics

A rubric is a detailed guideline for making scoring decisions. The specific scoring criteria are used to evaluate student performance and progress (Smith 1997). Scoring is qualitative rather than quantitative.

Our culture already uses rubrics in a formal way, such as assigning levels of achievement in karate, gymnastics, or swimming. These rubrics have been successful because they are directly tied to instruction, students know what is expected in advance, and students can be made accountable for their own learning. Rubrics are created uniquely for each lesson and class; therefore, they can easily be individualized.

Rubrics used in previous years were better known as checklists, task analysis, or rating scales. The current rubric evaluation system combines all of these concepts to give students a comprehensive idea of how to perform, what to perform, and the number of trials to be performed. The instructor develops and

This student utilizes his choices and bats off a tee.

shares rubrics before the unit is taught so that students know what is expected of them.

There are many advantages to using rubrics. Because the rubrics must be measurable, clear, and observable, students can also learn to critically evaluate their peers' performance and achievement. Students are held accountable for learning and know exactly what is expected.

The rubric system can cover a wide range of abilities and can accommodate heterogeneous classes. A rubric can be developed to assess the *process*, or quality, of a movement skill; the *product*, or quantity, of a movement (how far, how fast, how many); and the *parameter*, or the conditions under which the movement skill was performed. An additional benefit of rubrics is that children can chart their own progress and note improvements based on their levels of achievement, so it is a great motivational tool as well. And because children must pass levels in a specific sequence and must possess prerequisite skills to move on, the hierarchy is excellent for ensuring safety.

The form *Rubric for Juggling*, on the next page, presents an example of a rubric for juggling that emphasizes both a qualitative and quantitative approach to scoring.

Rubrics are often created for a class of typically developing students. However, children with disabilities may need modifications within the rubric so that they can participate in the intended activity. The following list, based on the work of Block, Lieberman, and Conner-Kuntz (1998), presents adaptations that can be made to typical rubrics to ensure success.

1. *Rubric extensions.* There may be times when the rubric starts too high for a student with a disability or too low for a highly skilled student. The concept of rubric extensions allows the child to be an active part of the class. The levels of the rubric are extended higher and lower to accommodate more student abilities. For an example of a rubric extension, see the form *Scooter Board Relays* given on page 27.

2. *Rubric within a rubric.* Some children with disabilities may need to implement their IEP goals in the regular class setting. In some cases, this means they may be working on two rubrics at once. The concept of a rubric within a rubric means the child can be working on the overall class objective through the class rubric as well as on IEP goals and objectives through an individual rubric. An example would be Sam, a seventh grader with Down syndrome, working on endurance goals through a soccer unit. The child has low physical endurance and must keep his heart rate in its target zone for three sets of six minutes per class. The child can go into the game and be encouraged to actively participate in play for intervals of six minutes while moving continuously during the game. In this way, he is meeting his individual endurance goal through participation in the class unit.

3. *Rubric analysis.* In some cases, children with disabilities may need a skill to be further task-analyzed for them to put the parts of the skill together and to chart progress (Block, Lieberman, and Conner-Kuntz 1998). The idea of rubric analysis is that the skills are task-analyzed into very small parts to detect the child's progress and to teach the specific component parts of the skill. See the form *Rubric Analysis of Foul Shooting* for an example of a rubric analysis that breaks down foul shooting into its individual components.

Rubric for Juggling

Jester

- ☐ Student can throw and catch scarf with one hand.
- ☐ Student can throw and catch scarf with either hand.
- ☐ Student can throw and catch one scarf from one hand to the other.

Street Performer

- ☐ Student can throw 2 scarves in the air and catch one at a time.
- ☐ Student can throw 2 scarves in the air and catch both at the same time.
- ☐ Student can simultaneously throw one scarf from left hand to right and another from right hand to left.

Juggle Bug

- ☐ Student can cascade juggle 3 scarves, 1 time.
- ☐ Student can cascade juggle 3 scarves, 5 times.
- ☐ Student can cascade juggle 3 scarves more than 10 times.

Cool Clown

- ☐ Student can throw and catch a bean bag in both hands.
- ☐ Student can throw and catch 2 bean bags from one hand to the other.
- ☐ Student can simultaneously throw one bean bag from left hand to right and another from right hand to left.

Circus Clown

- ☐ Student can cascade juggle 3 bean bags, 1 time.
- ☐ Student can cascade juggle 3 bean bags, 5 times.
- ☐ Student can cascade juggle 3 bean bags more than 10 times.

Ringling Brothers' #1 Juggling Clown

- ☐ Student can cascade juggle more than 3 bean bags.
- ☐ Student can cascade juggle 2 to 3 clubs.
- ☐ Student can juggle while riding a unicycle.
- ☐ Student can perform various juggling tricks, such as behind the back, under the leg, twirls, or partner juggle.

Scooter Board Relays

Instructions: Place the abbreviated letter(s) next to the statement which best describes the child's performance.

TA = Total assistance   PA = Partial assistance   I = Independently

Slick rider

_____ Student lies on scooter while teacher, aide, or peer pulls across gym, 1 time.

Hammer hold

_____ Student sits or lies on scooter while teacher, aide, or peer pulls across the gym, 1 time, by holding on to a hula hoop or jump rope.

Speedster*

_____ Student sits on scooter and pushes self across gym, 1 time, with the legs, demonstrating control.

_____ Student lies on scooter and pulls self across gym, 1 time, with arms, demonstrating control.

Roadrunner*

_____ Student sits on scooter and pushes self across gym, 2 to 5 times, with the legs, demonstrating control.

_____ Student lies on scooter and pulls self across gym, 2 to 5 times, with arms, demonstrating control.

_____ Student lies on scooter while teacher, aide, or peer pulls across gym, 2 to 5 times.

_____ Student sits or lies on scooter while a teacher, aide, or peer pulls across gym, 2 to 5 times, by holding on to a hula hoop or jump rope.

Quicksilver*

_____ Student sits on scooter and pushes self across gym, 6 to 10 times, with the legs, demonstrating control.

_____ Student lies on scooter and pulls self across gym, 6 to 10 times, with arms, demonstrating control.

_____ Student lies on scooter while teacher, aide, or peer pulls across gym, 6 to 10 times.

_____ Student sits or lies on scooter while teacher, aide, or peer pulls across gym, 6 to 10 times, by holding on to a hula hoop or jump rope.

Blast-off

_____ Students ride scooters across gym, demonstrating control, and try to break their own speed records for 1, 2, and 3 times across.

* Original rubric element.

Rubric Analysis of Foul Shooting

Minnesota Lynx

1. Knees bent

Charlotte Sting

1. Knees bent
2. Eyes on basket

Cleveland Rocker

1. Knees bent
2. Eyes on basket
3. Body extends upward

New York Liberty

1. Knees bent
2. Eyes on basket
3. Body extends upward
4. Correct hand position on ball
    a. non-shooting hand supports ball held in shooting hand
    b. shooting hand is palm up, fingers facing shooter
    c. wrist flexed forward

Houston Comet

1. Knees bent
2. Eyes on basket
3. Body extends upward
4. Correct hand position on ball
    a. non-shooting hand supports ball held in shooting hand
    b. palm up, fingers facing shooter
    c. wrist flexed forward
5. Shooting arm extends up and forward
6. Follow through by fully extending arm toward basket and reaching with shooting hand

Taken in part from Block, M.E., Lieberman, L.J., and Conner-Kuntz, F. (1998).

4. *Individual rubric.* Children with special needs may require specific rubrics developed for their individual needs. Although the child may be able to participate in a specific unit of instruction (for example, dance), the child may be working specifically on balance while the rest of the class is working on mastering a variety of dance steps. The child with limited balance who is engaged in a dance unit is able to do such things as toe walking for distance, standing on one foot for a certain period, and challenging equilibrium without losing balance. This individual rubric would reflect these specific skills and the child's ability to perform them.

Ecological Task Analysis

Ecological task analysis (ETA) (Davis and Burton 1991) is another form of authentic assessment that has been used with students with disabilities. ETA provides students with choices within the environment to execute various skills. Thus, the teacher sets the parameters or objectives. Students then choose the type of equipment, the rules, and the pace of activity to execute the designated skill. Teachers observe and maintain data on these behaviors.

Data are then used by teachers to continually challenge students within their comfort level. The following presents an example of utilizing ETA for the skill of striking a ball.

Striking a Ball

1. Present the task goal, "striking or propelling" a ball.
2. Provide choices such as size, color, and weight of ball, size and weight of bat, and use of tee, pitch, or hanging ball.
3. Document student choices, such as a "red ball, off a tee, with tennis racket."
4. Manipulate the task variables to further challenge the student, such as hitting the ball with a smaller implement or decreasing the size of the ball.

The advantages of using this system are that the instructor learns what movement form and equipment are most comfortable to the student, the student starts out with success, and the teacher knows the student is being realistically challenged because the teacher has set the task goal. There are no right or wrong choices for equipment or execution of performance; however, the student is limited by the type of equipment made available by the teacher. This method is used to determine preferences and skill level and as a starting point to further challenge the child. To illustrate this point, consider the following example. Felicia is a middle school student with mild mental retardation. The class is participating in a volleyball unit. Felicia is being taught the underhand serve and is given a choice of balls, which include a beach ball, volleyball trainer, or regulation volleyball. She is also given a choice in terms of distance from the net in which to serve. Tape marks are clearly placed on the floor in one-foot increments from the net to the serving line. She chooses a beach ball and serves from a line two feet from the net. The teacher now knows that Felicia is a beginner based on these choices. The teacher can further refine Felicia's skills and slowly use smaller and harder balls until she feels comfortable with a regulation volleyball and an underhand serve from the service line.

Portfolios

Portfolios are a compilation of a student's best work. Portfolios can reflect how closely a student meets the necessary outcomes to be regarded as a "physically educated person" (Franck et al. 1992). Portfolios are also the most promising method to exhibit and record student performances. They give teachers a broad picture of student achievement because they reflect the outcomes of performance in each domain. This broad overview provides teachers with a genuine picture of student improvement. The visual presentation of student performance can be used as a motivational tool, a method of communication with the family, a means for grading, and for program promotion. Portfolios can also chart progress in all domains (psychomotor, cognitive, and affective) over the course of a unit, semester, year, or throughout school years (Melograno 1998). Table 2.2 provides ideas for the contents of a physical education portfolio.

Portfolios should be used to compile a profile of what the student has accomplished in all domains. This can either be done daily, or specific achievements can be included when they occur. Students can be evaluated on portfolio contents in various ways, depending on the age of the student or the content and purpose of the portfolio. If a portfolio is used as an evaluation or grading tool, the instructor can give an objective point or percentage value to contents in each domain for a composite score. For example, the portfolio can be divided into sections such as psychomotor, cognitive, affective, and physical fitness. Within each section, various components can be included with point values attached to each. Portfolio scores are then generated based on the portfolio content.

As we reiterated, children with disabilities may need assessments adapted to meet their unique needs. Table 2.3 presents strategies for adapting portfolios for individual needs based on the three domains of learning in physical education.

It should be noted that various forms of authentic assessment can be combined to present a total picture of students' abilities and accomplishments. For example, using the skill of juggling, teachers can utilize ETA to determine student comfort level by presenting students with choices such as scarves, soft balls, hard balls, bigger balls, or pins. Students can choose to juggle one, two, three, four, or more balls in cascade-style, behind-the-back, or up-and-down juggling. Once teachers are able to determine performance levels and students have opportunities to practice, skills can be assessed using a juggling rubric like the one developed in the form *Rubric for Juggling* given on page 26. Upon completion of the unit, the ETA data and the rubric can be placed in the students' portfolios. Teachers can also require reflection sheets, journals, and reports on circus arts. In total, comprehensive information about the skills of juggling are now available to the student, parents, and administrators.

Table 2.2   Contents of a Portfolio

Journals
Self-reflections or self-assessments
Rubrics, checklists, or rating scales
Peer evaluations
Fitness, cognitive, or affective tests
Articles, article critiques, or collages
Videos
Skill analysis
Game statistics
Special individual and group projects
Teacher comments
Interest surveys

Table 2.3 Adapting Portfolio Contents

Psychomotor Assessments
▨ extend or break down the checklist
▨ use peer tutor to assist with rating scales
▨ show video of skill several times to ensure understanding

Cognitive Assessments
▨ utilize picture descriptions
▨ utilize computers
▨ use peer tutors to teach and review cognitive concepts, rules, and strategies

Affective Assessments
▨ behavior expectations modified
▨ expectations clearly defined
▨ use of peer tutor to guide behavior
▨ alternative ways of evaluating the affective domain
▨ rating scale or checklist developed with student, if necessary

Question Review and Summary

1. I would have acted in a similar fashion if I were Mrs. Bowman.

   Mrs. Bowman's reaction was not that unusual. Physical educators are trained to think of safety first. Not knowing of Olivia's abilities at the outset required Mrs. Bowman to take a firm stance against allowing Olivia to swim in the deep end with her classmates. Obviously, if Mr. Long had maintained data on Olivia and participated in transition meetings from elementary school to middle school, this situation could have been avoided. Thus, communication between teachers, parents, and administrators is crucial to the successful inclusion of students with disabilities in physical education.

2. It is difficult to expect Mrs. Bowman to have assessed Olivia. Assessment is time consuming and not worth all the time and energy.

   Assessment is the cornerstone to effective program planning and implementation in physical education for all students, regardless of disability. All teachers are expected to conduct assessments on their students to determine present levels of performance and achievement of skills.

3. The assessment tools for the regular class should be fine for assessing Olivia; after all, if she is to be included in the class, she should be expected to have the same goals and objectives.

   Some students with disabilities may, in fact, be able to participate in general physical education class or specific units without any modifications; however, this may not always be the case. Students with disabilities are entitled to accommodations so that they can successfully attain the same or similar goals as their typically developing peers. Teachers should know that students with disabilities may need activities, assessments, and communication techniques modified to meet the unique needs of the child.

4. Assessment is needed so that Individualized Education Plans can be written and progress toward meeting goals and objectives can be determined.

   The answer to this question is yes. Assessment is needed to plan programs, set goals and objectives, and determine whether desired outcomes are achieved.

5. Assessment is needed for special needs students, but it's not my job. I think physical therapists or classroom teachers could do a better job. They could assess students with disabilities in the motor domain, develop goals and objectives, and report the findings to me.

   Teachers responsible for teaching curricular content are responsible for assessing students.

In this chapter, assessment has been described as the cornerstone of an effective physical education program, based on its importance to program planning (individual student needs and placements), implementation (goals and objectives), and evaluation (student learning and achievement). In light of this conclusion, information was provided about the availability of various traditional assessment instruments and their individual features and uses. In addition, some disadvantages of traditional assessment were enumerated. Authentic assessment, a more recent philosophy of evaluation, was discussed as a potential alternative to problematic traditional assessment, the benefits of which are evident in the example techniques described (rubrics, ecological task analysis, and portfolios).

3 Planning for Success

Mr. Thomas has been teaching at Susan B. Anthony Elementary School for the past 14 years. Mr. Thomas has had little contact with children with disabilities, because they were previously taught by an adapted physical education specialist. Recently, Mr. Thomas' principal informed him that the adapted physical education specialist had become the district's consultant, and Mr. Thomas would be directly teaching the special needs students in his building. Because the adapted physical education specialist acquired such a large caseload, Mr. Thomas would also be responsible for developing IEPs and serving as a member of the multidisciplinary team. As a member of this team, he would now be responsible for developing IEP goals and objectives in physical education for eight students with special needs.

Questions to Test Yourself

1. Mr. Thomas should not be expected to write IEPs for children with disabilities because he does not have the knowledge or experience to do so.

   Yes — No — Not sure

2. The goals and objectives of the general physical education class should be sufficient for the children with disabilities.

   Yes — No — Not sure

3. It is unrealistic to expect Mr. Thomas, a general physical educator, to serve as a member of the multidisciplinary team.

   Yes — No — Not sure

4. Mr. Thomas should contact the previous adapted physical education consultant for previous IEPs and ideas for goals and objectives.

   Yes — No — Not sure

5. With in-service training, professional development workshops, and consultations with an adapted physical education specialist, Mr. Thomas can write and implement IEPs.

   Yes — No — Not sure

The purpose of this chapter is to help the reader

- understand the need for IEPs for students with disabilities,
- know the components of the IEP,
- understand and be able to participate in the IEP process, and
- understand the roles of members of the IEP team.

▪ The Individualized Education Plan

This scenario may sound somewhat familiar to many general physical education teachers. If not, it could be something encountered in the near future. Because more and more students with disabilities are being included in general education, including physical education, teachers, whether they have extensive training or not, are being asked to teach all children under their care. According to LaMaster, Gall, Kinchin, and Siedentop (1998), adapted physical education specialists are taking on new roles, such as consultants, rather than serving as direct care providers. Thus, general physical educators are now being required to not only give input about physical education for students with disabilities but also to write IEPs and serve as members of the IEP multidisciplinary team (Dunn 1997).

The multidisciplinary team consists of a group of individuals who are responsible for teaching the student with a disability. These members meet at least three times a year to develop appropriate goals and objectives, discuss programs, and deal with any concerns that may arise. At a minimum, the team must consist of parents or guardians, a district representative, a school psychologist, a special education teacher, and the student (when appropriate). Other people, such as general education teachers, adapted or general physical education teachers, physical therapists, occupational therapists, and speech or other therapists, may also participate. Medical personnel, such as the school nurse, audiologist, vision specialist, orientation and mobility specialist, or other paraprofessional may also be present. A complete description of the members and their roles is included below.

Members of the IEP Team and Their Roles

Required Members of the Multidisciplinary Team

Parents or guardians: According to the *IDEA Amendments*, the parents' concerns as well as the information they provide about their child must be considered when developing the IEP.

Student with a disability: The child with the disability knows most about his or her level of ability, wants, needs, and preferences. Levels and types of participation may vary from student to student depending on age, disability, and ability to communicate.

District representative: A designee for the district must be identified and be present at all IEP meetings. This person is responsible for ensuring that all components of the IEP are addressed and that appropriate services are provided as indicated on the IEP.

School psychologist: The school psychologist is a vital member of the team and is responsible for testing, interpreting tests, and assisting in developing appropriate programs. In some cases the child will have ongoing meetings with the school psychologist, and in others the child will receive consultation from the psychologist. Either way, the psychologist is a good resource for test interpretation and psychological evaluation.

Special education teacher: The special education teacher is the primary advocate, planner, supporter, and organizer for children with disabilities. Other than the parents, the special education teacher will know the most about the student with disabilities. The special educator will know how to contact and communicate with other team members.

Recommended Members of the Multidisciplinary Team

Adapted physical education (APE) specialist: An adapted physical education specialist is a critical member of the team who should be qualified to provide information regarding the motor performance of the child with a disability. A qualified APE specialist should have a master's degree in adapted physical education or have passed the Adapted Physical Education National Standards Exam (APENS) (Kelly 1995).

General physical education (GPE) specialist: GPE specialists can provide critical information pertaining to physical education that no other team member can provide. They know and can describe the general physical education curriculum and can help to facilitate inclusion of children with disabilities into physical education classes. It is imperative that the GPE teacher be included on the IEP team if the child with a disability is in the GPE class setting.

General education teacher: When students with disabilities are included or are going to be included in general education classes, the general education teacher must be present at the IEP meeting to present the curriculum and secure the supports needed for successful inclusion.

Paraprofessionals: Paraprofessionals are also known as educational aides, instructional assistants, and teacher assistants. Paraprofessionals work under the supervision of the general education teacher or special education teacher to implement classroom goals and IEP goals and objectives. They may also be responsible for monitoring behavior and carrying out behavior plans if needed. Paraprofessionals are expected to attend physical education with the child or children they are assigned to supervise.

Therapists

Physical therapist: The physical therapist (PT) works in the area of gross motor development, daily living skills, and utilization of assistive devices such as wheelchairs, walkers, crutches, or braces. The PT can assist with contraindicated activities, positioning, reflex integration, and other issues. Not every child with a disability will have physical therapy, but if physical therapy is part of a child's program, the PT is a vital member of the team and can help with consultation in physical education. Physical therapy cannot replace physical education.

Occupational therapist: The occupational therapist (OT) focuses on activities of daily living, self-help skills, fine motor skills, sensory integration, and adapted equipment. The OT can be an important resource on the IEP team.

Speech/language therapist: The speech and language specialist primarily assesses communication and language skills, plans habilitation programs, provides services, prevents further disorders, and consults with other members of the team regarding the area of communication. The speech and language specialist can be a key player to assist the physical educator in implementing communication and language goals into their classes.

Medical Personnel

School nurse: The involvement of the school nurse will vary according to level and extent of disability. The nurse's responsibilities will often include dispensing medication, monitoring health in the case of asthma, cystic fibrosis, or AIDS, or medical procedures such as catheterization, cleaning a tracheotomy, or inserting the feeding tube. The nurse is a vital member of the IEP team and should be consulted regarding any health concerns about the child. In some cases the child may be so medically fragile that he or she will have a one-to-one nurse, and in that case, the one-to-one nurse should be the one involved in the IEP process. The nurse is also the bridge to the school physician and the child's physician can help support inclusion in the case of blanket medical excuses (see chapter 4).

Audiologist: An audiologist works with children who have a hearing loss or who are at risk for a hearing loss. The audiologist assesses level of function and recommends assistive devices such as hearing aids. The audiologist is a key member to assist physical educators with issues such as level of hearing and care of hearing aids.

Vision specialist: A vision specialist helps students with visual impairments by assessing vision. This specialist helps students use their vision effectively and works with assistive devices such as CCTVs, braillers, magnifiers, and computer technology. A vision teacher can help physical educators with guiding techniques for running and walking, auditory equipment, game adaptations, and rules for blind sports.

Orientation and mobility specialist: An orientation and mobility specialist (O and M) helps children with visual impairments travel in a variety of environments safely and efficiently. An O and M specialist can help children with visual impairments move independently to the gymnasium, as well as in the gymnasium, locker room, pool, or on the playground. The O and M specialist can also give the physical educator ideas on guidewires, activity setup, and adapting and modifying rules and activities.

This list was taken in part from Block, M.E. 2000. *A teacher's guide to including students with disabilities in general physical education.* 2nd ed. Baltimore, MD: Paul H. Brookes.

The thought of IEPs for physical education may make even the most experienced teacher cringe. The time required to participate in meetings and write the IEP is typically added on to an already busy day. However, the IEP can serve as

▪ Physical educators need to maintain constant communication with other professionals about students with disabilities.

a useful tool in securing the supports and services needed to provide quality programs for students with disabilities, and as such they can become the physical educator's best ally. Although the IEP can be an invaluable tool in securing appropriate support and services, LaMaster and colleagues (1998) have determined that general physical educators are often left out of the entire IEP process and are therefore not gaining the intended benefits of the IEP. For example, the same study found that general physical educators were often

1. unaware of the existence of an IEP for a particular child;
2. aware that the child has an IEP, but had no input in developing the IEP for physical education;
3. aware of an IEP, but not encouraged to review previous goals and objectives on past IEPs; or
4. familiar with the IEP, but the IEP does not address physical education.

Although this list is by no means exhaustive, it highlights key problem areas in IEP development and implementation for physical educators. The purpose of this chapter is to inform physical educators about the IEP process and the need for their involvement in the process. This involvement will help to secure the necessary services and supports for both the student and the teacher of physical education.

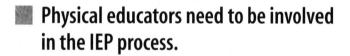

Physical educators need to be involved in the IEP process.

Overview of the IEP

In order to become effectively involved in the IEP process, teachers need to understand the purposes of the IEP and the legalities associated with it. All students who are identified as having disabilities must receive an IEP.

The IEP is a legal written document that is developed to ensure quality educational programming for each child with a disability. IEPs describe current level of performance, identify goals and objectives for the future, and list educational services to be provided to meet these goals (Short 2000). Because no two students with disabilities are exactly alike (nor, for that matter, are typically developing students), each student is first assessed. Then, unique needs are determined based on the assessment data. Individualized goals and objectives are then generated for various academic and social areas of development, including physical education, to ensure that the student receives an appropriate education. Once a service or support is identified on the IEP, school districts are held accountable for providing such services or supports. Periodic reviews and *due process* (the right to appeal decisions when disagreements occur) help to ensure that an appropriate educational program is being provided to the student.

Components of the IEP

Physical education IEPs typically address present level of performance, annual goals, short-term objectives, procedures for evaluation and parental reports, and support services and supplementary aids. District personnel are responsible for ensuring that each component of the IEP is fully addressed. The IEP contains the following components:

1. Present level of performance
2. Annual goals and short-term objectives
3. Support services and supplementary aids
4. Statement of participation in regular settings
5. Assessment modifications
6. Schedule of services
7. Transition services
8. Procedures for evaluation and parental reports

Because physical education is a direct service, federal law mandates that it be identified on every IEP. The extent to which physical education is addressed, however, will vary depending on the needs of the student. A sample IEP cover sheet, given in the form *Individual Education Plan Melrose School District*, identifies physical education within the context of the IEP. Some students with disabilities can participate in unrestricted general physical education without any modifications.

Students who fall under this category would have "general" physical education checked off on their IEPs, and physical education goals and objectives would not be developed for the IEP. Students who have unique needs and who require modifications or specially designed physical education would have "adapted" physical education checked off on their IEP. Goals and objectives related to physical education would then need to be developed. It is important to note here that an adapted designation on the IEP does not mean that the student receives separate physical education. Remember, adapted physical education is *a service*, not a placement. The environment in which adapted physical education is provided will vary depending on the needs of the student.

A child is assessed during an aquatics unit.

Individual Education Plan for Melrose School District

Meeting date:_____ Triennial review date:_____

Name:_____ DOB:_____

Parent's name:_____ Grade:_____

Address:_____

Phone (w):_____ (w):_____

Phone (h):_____(cell):_____

E-mail:_____ /_____

School year:_____ Anticipated year of graduation:_____

County residence:_____

Other information:_____

The Individualized Education Team

The Individual Education Program (IEP) Team makes the decisions about the student's program and placement. The student's parent(s), the student's regular teacher, and a representative from the local education agency are required members of the team. A regular education teacher may also be included if the student participates, or may participate, in regular education.

IEP Team Signatures

Name		Signature
_____	Parent	_____
_____	Parent	_____
_____	Student	_____
_____	Regular Ed. Teacher	_____
_____	Special Ed. Teacher	_____
_____	Local Ed. Agency	_____
_____	Physical Education	_____
_____	Medical Personnel	_____
_____	Related Service	_____
_____	Related Service	_____
_____	_____	_____

Summary of Performance in Current Educational Program

Strengths:_____

Needs:_____

The student's disability affects involvement and progress in general education in the following ways:

(continued)

(continued)

Physical Education Programming

___ General physical education   ___ Part-Time GPE   ____ Full-Time Separate PE

Full description of placement programming: _____

Present Level of Performance #1

Annual goal: _____

Short-term objective: _____

Present Level of Performance #2

Annual goal: _____

Short-term objective: _____

Present Level of Performance #3

Annual goal: _____

Short-term objective: _____

Present Level of Performance #4

Annual goal: _____

Short-term objective: _____

Criteria for evaluation: _____

Schedule for evaluation: _____

Nature and type of support services: _____

The IEP Process

The IEP can be a time-consuming yet rewarding process. To simplify the process it has been broken down into the following steps: assessment, present level of performance, goals, objectives, procedures for evaluation, support services, and the IEP meeting.

Assessment

In order for students with disabilities to be eligible for adapted physical education, a thorough assessment must be conducted. Questions may arise as to who should be responsible for assessing students for adapted physical education. Some districts may employ adapted physical education specialists, or contract out to specialists who are responsible for assessing students, determining unique needs, and serving as members of the multidisciplinary team. These individuals may or may not be responsible for program implementation. If they are not responsible for program implementation, they should meet with the general physical education teacher, present the results, and collaborate on goals and objectives. Most schools, however, will have the general physical education specialist conduct the assessment and fulfill the roles identified above. These teachers will also be responsible for implementing the adapted physical education program if such a program is indicated.

Various formal assessments exist, such as the Test of Gross Motor Development (Ulrich 2000), which allow professionals to determine unique motor needs. In lieu of formal assessment, authentic assessments may also be used to determine if unique needs exist. (See chapter 2 for more details on assessment.) Regardless of the type of assessment chosen, assessment data serve as the avenue for developing relevant IEP goals and objectives in physical education.

Goals and Objectives

Writing IEP goals and objectives for physical education can easily be done by following a simple procedure known as the three *P*s (Houston-Wilson and Lieberman 1999). This procedure has the teacher analyze the *process* of the movement, the *product*, or outcome, of the performance, and the *parameters* under which the performance is exhibited. The following provides a description as well as an example of each term.

Process

Process information relates to the form or quality of a movement. Skills can be analyzed into component parts through task analysis or through the use of ready-made checklists. Fronske (1997) provides a variety of task-analyzed sport skills that teachers can utilize to determine which parts of a particular skill are lacking. Skills that are deficient serve as the basis for the goal, and the component parts that are lacking serve as the objectives. Using the underhand volleyball serve as an example, assume that Joey, a middle school student with cerebral palsy, is

This student serves a modified ball at half-court.

able to perform only two of the five components of the skill (step toward net with opposite foot of serving arm, and palm up making fist with serving hand). A goal for Joey would be to perform the underhand volleyball serve correctly in three out of five trials, because the serve is the deficient skill. Objectives would be to (1) shift weight forward, (2) contact ball in front of body, and (3) follow through. These objectives reflect the inadequate component parts of the skill.

Underhand Volleyball Serve

1. Step toward net with opposite foot of serving arm.
2. Put palm up and make fist with serving hand.
3. Shift weight forward.
4. Contact ball in front of body.
5. Follow through.

Product

The *product* of the skill relates to the quantitative value produced by the student's performance. Skills will be quantified differently depending on the desired outcome, age of the student, and goals of the class. Again using the underhand volleyball serve as an example, the product could be quantified by: (1) the number of components the student was able to master, (2) the number of times the student served the ball, or (3) the number of times the ball went over the net.

Parameter

Parameter refers to the conditions under which the skill was performed. Examples of parameters that could be examined include (1) type of equipment used, (2) distance at which the skill is executed, (3) environmental arrangement (indoors, outdoors, group, or 1:1 setting), and (4) levels of assistance (independent, verbal cue, demonstration, physical assistance). For the underhand volleyball serve, the equipment parameters could include a regulation volleyball, a volleyball trainer, or a beach ball. The distance parameter may describe the distance served from the net. The environmental parameter in which the serve takes place could be indoors or outdoors, during a game or drill situation, or in small or large groups. Lastly, the level of assistance required will depend on the individual student's functional level. Students may require verbal cues, demonstrations, or physical assistance. Assistance may come from a peer, teacher's aid, or the teacher directly (Houston-Wilson and Lieberman 1999). It should be noted that a child's parameter on a skill may change with developmental or motoric gains or increases in dependence. This should be continually monitored, as should the process and product of the skill.

The three P system is an effective way to develop IEPs based on assessment data. Typically, a physical education IEP would include a minimum of three goals and corresponding objectives. Students in elementary school would receive goals and objectives related, but not limited, to the following:

1. Locomotor skills
2. Object control skills
3. Perceptual motor skills

4. Lead-up games and sport-related skills

5. Physical fitness

6. Aquatics

7. Rhythms and dance

Secondary students may receive IEP goals and objectives related to the following:

1. Sport skills

2. Physical fitness

3. Aquatics

4. Lifetime activities

5. Rhythms and dance

6. Community-based activities

Areas targeted would be those in which the student shows the greatest deficit. Even though these areas are targeted, in no way should this be interpreted to mean that these are the only areas worked on throughout the year. Students with disabilities should receive a comprehensive program just as any other student in the district would receive.

Other IEP Components

The following section identifies the components of a physical education IEP and incorporates the process of the three *P*s in addressing each component.

The first component of the physical education IEP is *present level of performance* (PLP). A present level of performance statement must be written in objective, observable, and measurable terms, and the statement must be written positively to reflect what the individual is able to accomplish.

Example

"Rachel can serve a volleyball trainer underhand by having her palm up, making a fist with her serving hand, and contacting the ball in front of her body, four feet from the net, with demonstration, in three out of five attempts."

You can see the process involves Rachel completing two of the five components of the underhand volleyball serve. The product consists of Rachel being able to execute the skill in three out of five attempts, and the parameters under which the skill is executed are from a distance of four feet with assistance at the demonstration level.

The second component of the physical education IEP is *annual goals*. Annual goals are broad, generic statements that reflect units of instruction in physical education. The *Individuals With Disabilities Education Act–Amendments* now requires annual goals to be measurable.

Example

"Rachel will serve a volleyball underhand in three out of five attempts."
"Rachel will swim the crawl stroke one length of the pool."
"Rachel will complete 10 laps during the PACER test."

The third component of the physical education IEP is *short-term objectives* (STO). Short-term objectives are realistic yet challenging increments of improvement that students strive to achieve. STO statements are based on annual goals and serve as a direct link between the PLP statement and desired outcomes. Increments for improvement should be attainable within six months to one year of the development of the IEP.

Example

"Rachel will be able to serve a volleyball trainer underhand, stepping with her opposite foot, with her weight shifted forward, and utilizing appropriate follow-through, six feet from the net, with verbal cue, in three out of five attempts."

The process has been expanded so that Rachel would be expected to perform all components of the underhand volleyball serve. The parameter was also expanded to six feet, and the level of support was decreased from a demonstration to a verbal cue. Because of increases in the task demands, the criteria for execution (product) remained the same (three out of five attempts).

The fourth component of the IEP is *procedures for evaluation.* Procedures for evaluation describe how the teacher knows if the student is making progress toward or has met the stated objectives. It also allows the teacher to determine if goals and objectives are no longer appropriate. In that case, the goals and objectives must be rewritten. Most schools require teachers to examine and update IEP goals and objectives quarterly. Examples of evaluation methods include teacher-made tests, rubrics, authentic assessments, standardized tests, criterion-referenced tests, teacher observations of specific skills, and checklists. The form *Checklist for Volleyball Skills* provides a sample checklist sheet for evaluating a child's progress on the skills needed for playing volleyball.

It should be noted here that many school districts are utilizing a "goal bank" system in which goals, objectives, and evaluation procedures are listed by number. Teachers choose the appropriate goals, objectives, and criteria for evaluation by number and identify these numbers on a standard grid sheet. (See the form *Sample IEP Goal Bank Grid Sheet* for an example.) Computers are then used to print the actual goals, objectives, and evaluation criteria for each subject area. This procedure is considered somewhat controversial. If needed goals are not identified in the goal bank, then IEPs should be written by hand. (See the form *Sample IEP Using a Goal Bank* on p. 46.) The table below provides an example of a goal chosen from a goal bank.

Sample Goal Drawn From a Goal Bank

Annual Goal: Goal Code: 7.8 Objective Codes: 7.8.1 7.8.2 7.8.3 7.8.4	
Short-term objectives written in measurable terms (minimum of three objectives):	
7.8	Demonstrate an improvement in early development gross motor skills.
7.8.1	Demonstrate the ability to reach with one hand to grab a toy held at eye level while propped on elbows.
7.8.2	Demonstrate the ability to push up on extended arms to observe a dangling toy while lying on stomach
7.8.3	When lying on back, demonstrate the ability to reach with one or two hands to grab an object held overhead
7.8.4	Demonstrate the ability to roll from back to stomach with increasing independence

If this goal was appropriate for a child, then goal 7.8 would be identified on the grid sheet. Specific objectives for meeting goal 7.8 would be identified based on the appropriate number, and the criteria for determining whether or not the child met the identified objective would also receive the appropriate number. The following scenario offers some ideas to facilitate improvement on specific IEP goals in common physical education units.

Jeffery is a 12-year-old boy with athetoid cerebral palsy in Mr. Thomas's sixth-grade class. Mr Thomas' goals for the class are taken directly from the National Association for Sport and Physical Education sixth-grade benchmarks (NASPE 1995). Jeffery uses a walker and can also use crutches. He has four major goals on his IEP for physical education. Mr. Thomas is trying to embed them into as many units as possible so Jeffery will improve toward his short-term objectives as soon as possible. Jeffery's goals from the school's goal bank are as follows:

Jeffery's Goals

7.7.10	Demonstrate improved overall muscle strength in lower extremities to perform ambulation activities.
7.7.13	Demonstrate improved stability in weight bearing positions.
7.9.29	Demonstrate the ability to stand unsupported without losing balance, for increased periods for duration.
7.10.71	Demonstrate the ability to run up and kick a medium size, stationary ball without losing balance.
7.12.18	Demonstrate the ability to assume standing using crutches with increasing independence.

The table below is just an example to demonstrate how the instructor could embed Jeffery's IEP goals into the general physical education curriculum.

Unit	General class goals*	IEP goal(s)	How unit will be implemented
Soccer	Cardiovascular endurance Eye-foot coordination	7.7.10	Jeffery will play offense for 5 minute periods at a time.
		7.9.29	Jeffery will stand stationary while waiting for ball to come to offensive area.
		7.10.71	Jeffery will have a no defense rule giving him time to practice kicking in the game.
Gymnastics	Body awareness Upper body strength	7.7.13	Jeffery will perform tripods, wheelbarrow races, three point stances.
	Balance	7.9.29	Jeffery will perform mat routines with reaching, changing levels, and movement across the mat without crutches.
Softball	Striking Physical activity Teamwork/respect	7.7.13	Jeffery will stand in the field and at bat with support from the walker only when needed.
		7.12.18	Jeffery will sit to wait his turn and stand independently when it is his turn to bat or be in the field.

*According to NASPE sixth-grade benchmarks.

Checklist for Volleyball Skills

Name: _____ Date: _____

Evaluator: _____

Situation: ☐ 1:1 ☐ small group ☐ small-sided game situation ☐ game

	Bump	Set	Spike	Serve
Motor appropriate				
Motor inappropriate				
Used at the correct time				
Ball over net				
Placement appropriate				
Total				

Comments:

_____

_____

_____

_____

Sample IEP Goal Bank Grid Sheet

Name:_____ Subject: _____

Measurable Annual Goals and Short-Term Objectives

Annual goal: Goal code: _____ Objective codes: _____ _____ _____ _____

Short-term objectives written in measurable terms (minimum of three objectives)

   STO   Evaluation procedures   Criteria   Progress update

1. _____

2. _____

3. _____

Annual goal: Goal code: _____ Objective codes: _____ _____ _____ _____

Short-term objectives written in measurable terms (minimum of three objectives)

   STO   Evaluation procedures   Criteria   Progress update

1. _____

2. _____

3. _____

Sample IEP Using a Goal Bank

Name:_____   Subject Area:_____

Measurable Annual Goals and Short-Term Objectives

Annual goal: Goal code:_____   Objective codes:_____ _____ _____ _____

Short-term objectives written in measurable terms (minimum of three objectives)

   STO   Evaluation procedures   Criteria   Progress update

1. _____

2. _____

3. _____

4. _____

Annual goal: Goal code:_____   Objective codes:_____ _____ _____ _____

Short-term objectives written in measurable terms (minimum of three objectives)

   STO   Evaluation procedures   Criteria   Progress update

1. _____

2. _____

3. _____

4. _____

Criteria for evaluation:

1. _____ teacher-made tests

2. _____ rubrics

3. _____ authentic assessment

4. _____ standardized tests

5. _____ criterion-referenced tests

6. _____ teacher observations of specific skills

7. _____ checklists

     The final component of the physical education IEP is the *support services and supplementary aids.* For teachers of adapted physical education, this is an extremely important component of the IEP, because it provides an avenue to secure needed supports so that students can be successfully included in physical education class. The nature and type of support may vary depending on the unique needs of the student. Two typical types of support requested include personnel support and equipment support. Personnel support ensures that there are enough "hands" in the gymnasium to provide a safe and successful program. Equipment support ensures that there is specialized or adaptive equipment available to allow the student to experience a high degree of participation and success. It is important to review your curriculum to determine any types of specialized equipment that may be needed in order for the child to be appropriately included and successful in your physical education program. Once these areas of support are agreed on, the district is responsible for supplying the requested resources.

Examples of Personnel Support

Personnel support may include adapted physical education consultants, teacher's aides, interpreters for deaf students, or trained peer tutors.

Examples of Equipment Support

Samples of specialized equipment could include beep balls, adjustable basketball baskets, or bowling ramps and switches. This equipment can be used by students with severe disabilities who may lack the ability to utilize large muscle groups. Most of this equipment can be purchased through physical activity catalogs.

The preceding information provides an overview of the components of a physical education IEP. Attention should be drawn to the fact that each PLP statement is numbered consecutively, and each corresponding component parallels the initial PLP statement. Thus, one would not identify a PLP area in volleyball and then develop a short-term objective statement related to soccer.

■ The IEP Meeting

IEP meetings for students with disabilities are always held at the beginning, middle, and end of the school year. The exact dates and times are available from the Office of Special Education in each school district. Teachers of students with disabilities should be informed of the meeting dates and times for students under their care. If this information is not readily transmitted, teachers are encouraged to contact the appropriate personnel and secure the information. According to Sherrill (1998, p. 89), "most adapted physical activity authorities believe that a physical educator should be present at the IEP meeting to provide input concerning performance and needs in the psychomotor domain." If general physical educators are unable to attend the IEP meeting, written recommendations should be provided to the classroom teacher or other individual, such as a parent, who can speak on behalf of physical education.

Some school districts require that the IEP team members only bring present level of performance information and recommendations to the meeting. After the meeting, in which the child's performance and goals are discussed, the team is given 10 days to complete the full IEP for the parents to read. During the meeting, the team, especially the parents, will give valuable information and insight about the child's performance. All of this information is taken into consideration when writing the IEP. Only after the team has met and agreed on the child's performance do the members write the IEP. The teacher who wrote the IEP, administrators, and parents sign the written document to signify agreement. In other instances, teachers are requested to bring a draft of the IEP to the meeting and then make necessary adjustments based on the meeting results. A similar procedure follows in which all parties sign the IEP to signify agreement.

> ### What to Bring to the IEP Meeting
>
> List of child's strengths and weaknesses
>
> Description of child's learning style
>
> Assessment results for the child's PLP
>
> Suggestions for goals and short-term objectives
>
> Suggestions about extent of inclusion in general physical education
>
> Suggestions for supports needed in physical education
>
> Suggested evaluation schedule
>
> Paper and pen to make notes
>
> A positive, open mind

Role of the Physical Educator

Becoming involved in the IEP process is by far the most important role of any physical educator who teaches students with disabilities. Because it is not always possible to attend meetings, having a strong ally (such as a parent or special education teacher) available to represent your recommendations will aid in the inclusion of students with disabilities in your classes. Unless you or someone else is available to request support personnel or equipment, chances are you will not receive them. Physical educators must also become familiar with appropriate assessment tools, whether they be traditional or authentic, so assessment data can be shared and utilized to determine appropriate programming and placement.

Involving the parents will assist in the development of the IEP goals and objectives because they have a unique perspective. In addition, the parents should know the child's physical education strengths and weaknesses because parents are to be informed about the educational progress of their children at least as often as the parents of children without disabilities (Auxter, Pyfer, and Huettig 2001).

Question Review and Summary

1. Mr. Thomas should not be expected to write IEPs for children with disabilities because he does not have the knowledge or experience to do so.

   By following described protocol, teachers such as Mr. Thomas can successfully write IEPs for their subject area, and they are required to do so.

2. The goals and objectives of the general physical education class should be sufficient for the children with disabilities.

   Goals and objectives for students with disabilities must be individualized to meet the unique needs of the student.

3. It is unrealistic to expect Mr. Thomas, a general physical educator, to serve as a member of the multidisciplinary team.

   Although initially it may seem overwhelming to serve as a member of the multidisciplinary team, Mr. Thomas should welcome the opportunity. By actively participating in the development of the IEP, Mr. Thomas can be sure that he receives the necessary personnel support and that his students receive the appropriate equipment support.

4. Mr. Thomas should contact the previous adapted physical education consultant for previous IEPs and ideas for goals and objectives.

   Yes. It is important that teachers maintain constant communication about students with disabilities to learn as much as possible about the student.

5. With in-service training, professional development workshops, and consultations with an adapted physical education specialist, Mr. Thomas can write and implement IEPs.

   Yes. Mr. Thomas and any other professional can learn how to write IEPs and teach students with disabilities.

After reading this chapter, educators should have a clearer understanding of the IEP itself—both what it consists of and how it functions in providing an appropriate physical education for children with disabilities. Each specific component of the IEP has been described and explained. In addition, this chapter detailed the development process that yields an effective IEP, beginning with assessment of the student and progressing to development of goals and objectives and determination of necessary services and supports. Finally, an overview was given of the IEP meeting and its participants. This overview should assist physical educators in understanding their vital role as a member of the multidisciplinary IEP team.

4 Adapting the Curriculum to Fit Special Needs

*E*ric is a sixth grader who has mild spina bifida. He uses a wheelchair to get around, but he can also walk with a walker. Eric has many friends and loves being active. Eric's physical education teacher, Mr. Anderson, allowed Eric to be included in activities such as swimming or track, but when there was a unit that involved games or sports he always had Eric keep score or watch on the sideline. Eric had been involved in most of his elementary school physical education classes, but most activities were developmental and were not competitive situations. Eric wanted to be involved with the other kids and was not used to sitting out. He complained to his parents, and they called a meeting with the principal and the teacher. Mr. Anderson said that Eric could not safely or successfully compete in sport and games units in his class. Eric's parents, friends, and his special education teacher came up with a variety of ways Eric could participate.

Mr. Anderson was skeptical, but he tried some of their suggestions. For the skill development portion of the volleyball unit, Eric was involved by using a trainer volleyball (an air light volleyball). Modifications included allowing Eric to catch the ball, making sure Eric touched the ball before his team could score, and allowing the ball to bounce once before catching. A few of the adaptations were expanded to include the whole class, such as the catch and bounce, and the points often went on for two or three minutes! Another game Eric had new access to was hockey. The teacher did not adapt the rules for Eric but provided a Nerf soccer ball instead of a puck, and the other kids in the class were given the same movement pattern as Eric was given. All the students had to play on carpet squares. They all moved like Eric, so the pace of the game was more conducive to his successful participation. The kids liked the new games so much that they started playing them at recess, and some of the kids in Eric's neighborhood included Eric in games he had never been included in before.

Questions to Test Yourself

1. There are many ways to include Eric in just about any activity.

   Yes — No — Not sure

2. Eric should only be allowed to participate in selected games and sports because he may be a danger to himself or others.

   Yes — No — Not sure

3. If a game is modified too much, the other kids will get frustrated, act out, or complain.

   Yes — No — Not sure

4. All sports should be taught and played by the traditional rules so that students know the real rules and strategies.

   Yes — No — Not sure

5. Children with and without disabilities should be involved in any game and all necessary modifications to that game.

   Yes — No — Not sure

The purpose of this chapter is to help the reader

- understand the theoretical constructs driving the necessity to adapt activities;
- understand basic principles of adapting games and activities; and
- understand and be able to implement adaptations related to equipment, rules, the environment, and instruction.

The previous scenario demonstrates that, with a little creativity, games and activities can be adapted and can still be fun and effective in helping all children meet their physical education goals. The adjustments made were ideal for Eric. As can be seen in this situation, it was not difficult to come up with a few variables that would ensure appropriate inclusion of everyone. Many teachers may not know what to do for a child like Eric, but this chapter will provide the instructor with many options for making the general physical education classroom work for all children who are included.

Theoretical Constructs

The following theories support the need to adapt activities. Without these theoretical constructs, the necessity of adapting activities to include all individuals may not be realized. Teachers need to embrace the idea of being empowered with choices to implement full and active inclusion.

Theoretical Constructs

Adaptation theory: The concept that many activities will only be accessible to children with disabilities if adapted.

Normalization theory: The idea that children with disabilities should be afforded the same opportunities in life as their same-aged peers.

Self-determination theory: The belief that individuals with disabilities should be provided with choices, creating autonomy over their own lives.

Empowerment theory: The theory that, should individuals with disabilities take advantage of the choices given whenever possible, empowerment will become intrinsic.

This student gains empowerment through a variety of activities, including rock climbing.

A quick glance at these theories gives the reader an overall understanding of the power inherent in each one. It is imperative to note that individuals cannot be empowered unless some variables are adapted. Volleyball would not have been a realistic choice for Eric without some adaptations. Since adaptations drive the theories, it makes perfect sense to assume that if students are to reach the empowerment stage, games, skills, sports, and activities must be adapted! The following paragraph describes the first of these theories, adaptation theory.

Adaptation Theory

"Adaptation theory is the art and science of managing variables so as to achieve desired outcomes" (Sherrill 1997, p. 60). Adaptation theory, or the process of adapting, was first introduced by Kiphard (1983). He further described this theory as individual and environmental interactions that maintain homeostasis. Individuals adapt to and alter the environment each time they respond to it, which makes their relationship reciprocal (Sherrill 1998). Sherrill (1998) further describes the process of adaptation as continuous, dynamic, and bidirectional (or reciprocal). She describes seven variables that can be promoted to ensure success.

Adaptation Theory Variables (Sherrill 1998)

Temporal environmental variables

Physical environmental variables

Object or equipment variables

Psychosocial environmental variables

Learner variables

Instructional or informational variables

Task variables

Each of these seven variables can be adapted individually or together. The adaptation of one area may facilitate the adaptation of another, and so on. Adaptations can be made within a lesson, skill acquisition, activity, game, scrimmage, practice, sport, or entire program.

Playing basketball in a group on an outdoor court is normal for these teens.

For example, in the opening scenario, Mr. Anderson included Eric in a volleyball game. He knew it was not developmentally appropriate to immediately begin with a game at this age, so he spent two weeks working on volleyball skill development. Eric used the volleyball trainer, a peer tutor (see chapter 5), and task analysis of all the volleyball skills. In this case, Mr. Anderson modified the temporal, equipment, learner, and task variables. The task and temporal variables could not have been modified without the equipment modification.

Normalization Theory

The second theory, normalization theory, refers to making available to persons with disabilities educational conditions as close as possible to the norms of children without disabilities (Sherrill 1998). Basically, what is "normal" for people without disabilities should be available to people with disabilities. The concept driving this important theory is that children with disabilities should be afforded the same opportunities as their same-aged peers. They are not isolated from the norm; rather, they are embraced. This theory was first introduced to the United States by Nirje (1969) and has been recognized as a major contribution to the integration of individuals with mental retardation into the community. The normalization theory is important to adaptation because it includes children with disabilities in culturally acceptable games and activities with their peers. We adapt so that children will have the same social and educational opportunities in physical education and society.

According to Auxter, Pyfer, and Heuttig (1997), the following attitudes must be present for normalization to become a reality.

Attitudes That Must Precede Normalization

Individuals with disabilities

- must be perceived as humans,
- must be perceived as having a legal and constitutional identity,
- must be viewed as individuals who can acquire skills throughout their lifetimes,
- must be provided an opportunity by society to take full advantage of their culture,
- must be provided services by competent, trained personnel in education and habilitation,
- must be cared for and provided opportunities by human services that are valued and well understood by society, and
- must be provided opportunities to play valued roles and lead valued lives in our culture.

Auxter, Pyfer, and Huettig 1997, p. 23.

Self-Determination Theory

The third theory, self-determination, is the right to possess control, power, and decision-making ability over your life (Wehmeyer, Agran, and Hughes 1998). When individuals with disabilities are included side by side with their peers in normal activities, they are viewed as valued in society (Wolfensberger 1972). The concept of being valued can be promoted through adapting activities so that all can participate and achieve. In addition to being viewed as valuable and worthwhile, being valued in society provides opportunities for choice in participation, affiliation, and adaptations. This concept is frequently referred to as self-determination and is particularly significant when considered from a global perspective. Specifically, the question teachers must ask themselves to define this perspective in terms of a child with disabilities is this: "Does this child have the same choices and options as her same-aged peers?" In many cases, he or she does not (Wehmeyer, Agran, and Hughes 1998).

All people should get to make their own choices, whether they have a disability or not. Opportunity is one of the essential characteristics that must be present for an individual to be self-determined (Wehmeyer, Agran, and Hughes 1998). Therefore, it is essential for teachers to ensure that all children be given equal opportunities.

Empowerment Theory

The fourth theory, empowerment theory, emphasizes a common set of beliefs that individuals are their own change agents and that such agency only emerges when there is a shared responsibility for planning and decision making (Powers et al. 1996).

Teachers of individuals with disabilities and other social minorities must study this theory to enable students to take charge of their lives. Individuals with disabilities must be empowered to change what needs to be changed so that they can live normal, active, healthy, and fulfilled lives. Like adaptation, normalization, and self-determination, empowerment theory advances the vision that chil-

Swimming with physical assistance increases this student's success rate.

dren have the right to live in the mainstream of society, to be included in everyday activities, to have choices, control, power, and dreams. Teachers can help them realize this potential every day by showing students how to make the most of opportunities to learn; they must teach students how to take advantage of community resources and consistently encourage empathy in every child they teach. Empowerment theory has especially strong implications for the child's life beyond school. A strong educational background and adapted experiences should lead these children to be strong, independent self-advocates.

These four theories serve as the basis for understanding the nature of disability and the need by those with disabilities to feel a sense of belonging. As educators, we must ensure safe, successful, enjoyable educational experiences for all students under our care. Realizing the importance of these theories helps educators in framing their ideas about inclusion and may serve as an avenue for changing attitudes from fear to acceptance.

▇ Types of Adaptations

For many children with disabilities, making the most of their lives may mean manipulating some of the surrounding variables so that they can be successful and attain control.

For example, if the equipment, rules, environment, and instruction were not modified, Eric would not have as many sports, games, and activities available to him. Eric, the youngster with spina bifida, now added hockey and volleyball to his repertoire of sports and games. Eric now knows how to play the same games as his peers do, which is "normal." Therefore, Eric has the same options available to him as his peers and can be a self-determined young man as he grows up. His self-determination will empower him to make decisions, advocate for himself, and have a better quality of life.

In many cases, parents are the strongest advocates and should be consulted for functional ideas when creating modifications. In addition, modifications that are successful should be shared with parents so that they can implement the modifications in the child's leisure time.

The following section will give instructors ideas for the adaptation of variables that will allow a child to participate in a game, activity, or sport with their peers. These principles have been modified from Block (2000) and Lieberman (1999).

Basic Principles for Adapting Activities

1. Include the child with the disability in adaptation decisions when possible. Some children will not mind having the activity modified to ensure success. In middle school and senior high school, however, many children with disabilities would prefer to "fit in" rather than be successful. Any adaptation that makes them look different or be perceived as different is unwelcome. Any well-meaning teacher must first consider the child's attitude toward the activity, peers, and oneself.

2. Give the child as many choices as possible. The more types of equipment offered, teaching styles used, rule modifications available, and environmental

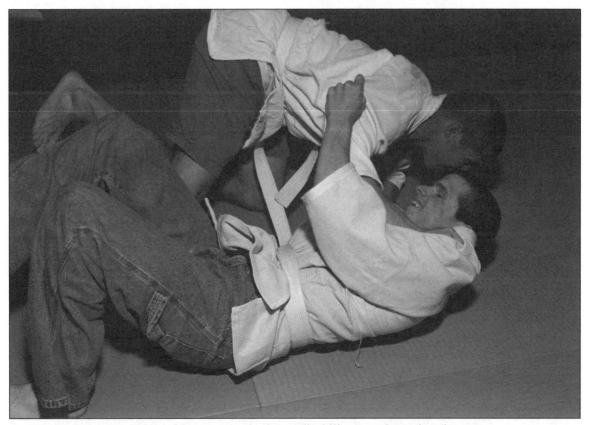

A peer demonstrates judo so his partner who has a disability can also enjoy the sport.

options there are, the more options the child has to be successful in the activity. The teacher may want to discuss all the options with the child before the unit and allow her to try out a few so that she can make the best decisions. This way the child can start out the unit with success, and the teacher can further adapt if needed.

3. Partial participation or physical assistance is acceptable and preferred over sitting out the activity. The use of physical cues, hand-over-hand, or total physical assistance is appropriate to ensure participation in the activity. The amount of assistance should be decreased to "normal" cues when possible.

4. Children with disabilities should be offered the same variety of sports, games, and recreational activities as their peers are offered. This will ensure that students learn lifetime activities and a variety of skills.

5. Community-based activities should be taught in the community whenever possible.

Adaptations should be ongoing and continually evaluated. Adaptations should not be a one-time occurrence. This consistency will ensure that when the child increases independence, becomes frustrated, or becomes embarrassed the instructor can modify any adaptation to meet the need of the child.

■ Adapting Activities

The following section on adaptations is broken down into four areas: equipment, rules, instruction, and environment. These four areas cover different attributes of the teaching and learning environment. Some variables could fit into more than one area. An attempt has been made to put each variable into the most appropriate adaptation area for the reader.

Equipment Modifications

Equipment modification is any modification that would make the participant more successful than when using the pre-existing equipment. Individuals with disabilities may need equipment adapted for a number of reasons, including limited mobility, limited grip strength, lack of vision or hearing, decreased cognitive function, or inability to attend for a long period. Examples of equipment modifications include the use of longer rackets, beeper balls, guide wires, Velcro mitts, or softer balls. It is important to remember that equipment used should be age-appropriate. The following scenario about Tamiqua presents examples of equipment modifications used to help her successfully participate in a tennis unit.

Equipment Example

Tamiqua is a ninth-grade girl with a spinal cord injury. This condition has resulted in impairment of all four of her limbs. She has some use of her arms, as she is able to move them up, down, and to the front, but she has limited grip strength. She uses a wheelchair to ambulate and can move her chair independently. Before the tennis unit, the teacher, Ms. Meehan, brainstormed with Tamiqua, the physical therapist, and Tamiqua's mother to identify necessary modifications. They decided to try using a badminton racket, indoor Nerf tennis balls, and an ace bandage to attach the racket to her hand. At first, Tamiqua could not get the timing right and became frustrated, so they switched to a balloon to help with the timing. By the second week of the unit, they switched back to the Nerf tennis ball and utilized the two-bounce rule. Tamiqua could rally at least five times in a row! Tamiqua has been practicing on the weekends with her brothers and is now learning how to serve the ball.

Tamiqua gains skills in tennis with a few minor equipment adaptations.

As can be seen in this scenario, a few minor equipment modifications and rule changes can greatly improve the opportunities available for children with disabilities. In addition, the modifications led her down a path to beginning tennis, and there is no ceiling on how much she can improve on her tennis, upper-arm strength, mobility, and speed.

Rule Modifications

A rule modification can be anything that deviates from the original or culturally accepted rules of the game. People with disabilities may need to have the rules adapted so that they can be successfully included. Examples include slowing down the pace of a game, allowing more chances, taking away rules, allowing for no defender, limiting or adding responsibility, utilizing one-part commands, and making sure all players are involved before a team can score (Lieberman 1999). Remember, children are not miniature adults. It is not beneficial to just "water down" adult sports and expect them to be appropriate for children, particularly those with disabilities (Housner 2000). In addition, the instructor may want to change a task completely for a specific person rather than just modifying the rules. For example, a student may throw a ball in a game instead of striking the ball (Rink 1998).

The following scenario about Jane presents rule modifications used to help her successfully participate in a softball unit.

Rule Modification Example

Jane is a fifth grader with mild paraplegic cerebral palsy. She can run, but she is slower than her peers and has a scissors gait. The class had done a disability awareness unit and learned what Jane could and could not do. Before each unit, the physical education teacher, Mr. Short, allowed all the children in the class (including Jane) to brainstorm appropriate adaptations for Jane. The softball unit was no exception. Jane batted, ran, and fielded on her own. The only modifications were that Jane used some physical assistance to bat, and she would score a point for every base she touched. Instead of one point for her runs, for example, she received four points. If she ran to second base before being called out, she received two points. This was a simple rule modification, and it accounted for her mild disability. The kids were very accepting, and they fought over which team Jane would be on! Jane considers herself a good softball player and will be joining a league for the summer!

Modifications to rules in many cases are natural when keeping normalization theory in mind. The two rule modifications increased accessibility to softball for Jane. For many children, inclusion in a game with traditional rules would be

Jane is successfully included in the softball unit with some minor rule adaptations.

impossible. Keeping the normalization theory in mind, physical educators must consider alternative rules to ensure inclusion of all children in general physical education.

Environmental Modifications

Environmental modifications may be necessary to successfully include a child with a disability. Often these modifications are not noticed until they become a problem. It is never too late to modify the environment to increase a person's success. To know what needs to be modified, the instructor may ask the parent, previous teachers, or the child. Environmental modifications include decreasing distractions, increasing visual cues, limiting noise, changing lighting, and increasing accessibility of the playing area.

The following scenario about Chuckie presents environmental modifications used to help him successfully participate in a swimming unit.

Environmental Modification Example

Chuckie is a third grader who was new to his elementary school. He has autism and limited communication skills, and his teacher's aid was out on maternity leave. The special educators in his new school read his IEP and found no goal related to physical education, although general physical education was checked off on the front page. They had no idea what Chuckie could do or what he needed in terms of instruction. The teacher, Mr. Wilkinson, wanted very much for Chuckie to be included in his general physical education class. The class was working on a three-week swimming unit at the middle school. Chuckie's mother had signed the permission form for swimming and checked off intermediate level. Mr. Wilkinson was happy about that and allowed the new teacher's aide, Ms. Bowman, to go into the pool with Chuckie. There were 33 students in the class, and Mr. Wilkinson was busy with the other kids. Chuckie's immediate reaction to the pool was very negative. He screamed, kicked, and continuously tried to swim to the deep end. He had no communication skills, so the teachers were very puzzled about what was wrong. His mother had said that he could swim well. After 30 minutes of struggling to keep Chuckie in the shallow end with the other kids, Mr. Wilkinson and Ms. Bowman gave up and let him swim in the deep end. This was the answer to the problem. Chuckie's autism made him hypersensitive to noise and distractions, and he could not tolerate swimming in the shallow end with the other kids. So, with a simple modification in environments (using the deep end of the pool), Chuckie swam and improved greatly in the three-week unit. He even started using a trained peer tutor in the deep end; this tutor became his friend throughout the school day.

Environmental modifications can greatly increase the amount of involvement in physical education for children with disabilities. As can be seen with Chuckie, swimming in the designated area was not possible or conducive to learning. Changing the environment is not always this simple; in many cases the instructor must gain added permission or personnel (such as a lifeguard for Chuckie, if necessary). Other examples of environmental manipulations include acquiring additional keys to lights, closing folding doors, covering windows that create glare, or minimizing decorations that distract. In any case, the increased involvement of children with disabilities is the reward for all the extra work of changing the environment.

Instructional Modification

Teachers have many variables they can change, adapt, and modify when teaching a lesson. The equipment, rules, and environment are just a few. Teachers can also modify the way they instruct a class, a small group, or an individual. The following is a list of teaching cues presented in a hierarchy from least invasive to most invasive. Sometimes these techniques need to be paired, such as verbal cueing and modeling, whereas at other times a simple cue can elicit the desired behavior.

1. *Verbal cues* (explaining in simple terms what you want the child to do)
   - should be clear, specific, and concise with no jargon or slang;
   - should be done in the mode of communication that the child understands;
   - should be repeated in a different way if the child does not understand the first time; and
   - should be used with demonstration to ensure understanding if the child has usable vision.

2. *Demonstration or modeling* (showing with actions what you want the child to do)
   - should be done in the child's field of vision,
   - should be done by someone as close as possible to the child's size and ability, and
   - should be done whole-part-whole when possible (that is, you should demonstrate the whole skill, then the task-analyzed parts, then the whole skill again).

3. *Physical assistance or guidance* (assisting the child physically through the desired skill or movement)
   - should be documented in terms of where you physically assisted, how much assistance you gave, and for how long;
   - should be preceded by telling the child you are going to touch him or her; and
   - should be decreased to "normal" touch cues when possible.

4. *Brailling* (allowing the learner to feel a peer or the instructor execute a skill or movement that was difficult to learn with the three previous approaches) (Lieberman and Cowart 1996)
   - should be preceded by telling the child where and when to feel you or a peer executing a skill;
   - should be documented as to when and where the child touched you or a peer, and why;
   - should be repeated as many times as necessary to ensure understanding; and
   - should be combined with the other teaching methods to increase understanding.

The following list enumerates a variety of teaching styles that can be combined with the various teaching cues previously mentioned. These teaching styles range from a more direct instructional approach, which is predominantly teacher-

Brailling helps this student learn the skills needed for performing on the uneven bars.

controlled, to a more indirect, predominantly student-controlled instructional approach (Rink 1998). The teaching style will depend on the lesson focus and content, the cognitive component, the learner, and the lesson objective (Rink 1998).

1. *Command style.* The teacher is in total control of all decisions.

2. *Task style.* The teacher develops a series of task cards (which may be brailled or in pictures) that progressively lead to the achievement of an instructional objective.

3. *Guided discovery style.* Through the use of questions or short statements, the teacher guides the students in a progressive series of steps resulting in a discovery of movement solutions that meet the criteria stated by the teacher.

4. *Problem-solving style.* Like guided discovery, the problem-solving style emphasizes the development of multiple solutions to a given problem posed by the teacher (Winnick 2000).

Good teachers teach to the learning style of the students. For most students one instructional style will be more beneficial than another. It is up to the instructor to discover the instructional style(s), as previously presented, that is most conducive for learning.

Adaptation Checklist

1. ___ Is the adaptation safe?

2. ___ Does the modification maintain the concept of the game?

3. ___ Was the child included in the adaptation and does he or she embrace the concept?

4. ___ Is the game still age-appropriate?

5. ___ Is the child still included successfully?

6. ___ Is the adaptation holding the child back and not affording a challenge?

7. ___ Does the adaptation still allow the child with the disability to work on either class goals or IEP goals?

8. ___ Does the adaptation alienate the child from the rest of the class?

9. ___ Could the adaptation be minimized or eliminated?

10. ___ Other?

Providing a sighted guide while running gives true ownership.

Question Review and Summary

1. There are many ways to include Eric in just about any activity.

   As demonstrated in this chapter, there are numerous ways to include students with disabilities in a variety of activities.

2. Eric should only be allowed to participate in selected games and sports because he may be a danger to himself or others.

   In instances where adaptations would not be feasible and there is a danger of injury to the student or other classmates, alternative programs must be provided.

3. If a game is modified too much, the other kids will get frustrated, act out, or complain.

   Although this is possible, disability simulation and discussing modifications with classmates and allowing them to assist in rule changes leads to more understanding and a willingness to play the game as indicated. Providing options to classes by having various game formats going simultaneously allows students to choose the type of play that is most suited to his or her ability level and interest.

4. All sports should be taught and played by the traditional rules so that students know the real rules and strategies.

   This is not true. Physical education is for all children, and games and sports do not need to be played in traditional formats. There are numerous other opportunities available to students to play competitive or recreational sports following traditional rules. Physical education does not need to conform to these standards.

5. Children with and without disabilities should be involved in any game and all necessary modifications to that game.

Including students in the decision-making process aids in the development and implementation of appropriate games and activities.

This chapter presents an overview of theoretical constructs related to adapting activities. In many cases the instructor may not even be able to think about including a child because of unnecessary blanket medical excuses. Modifications and adaptations are crucial to ensure safe and appropriate inclusion for any child in this placement. This discussion was followed by specific guidelines on adapting activities to meet the unique needs of children with disabilities. Examples of four common ways to adapt activities were presented. These common adaptations include equipment modifications, rule modifications, environmental modifications, and instructional modifications.

Creating an Atmosphere for Achievement

Amanda is a fourth grader who is visually impaired because of retinopathy of prematurity. She has just begun to attend Katie Stanton Elementary School. Prior to this, she went to the State School for the Blind. This school was out of the district and required Amanda to ride on the bus two hours each way. Her parents decided that she should attend her home district, and the district supported this decision. Amanda has limited vision and needs a cane to walk independently. Her physical education teacher, Mr. Aiello, had created a wonderful adapted curriculum for her and welcomed her into his physical education class. Mr. Aiello noticed that when he told the class to get a partner, Amanda was always left with no partner. She felt very isolated and told her parents she did not want to go to school anymore. This was her first year with her new peers, and by October she had withdrawn herself and stopped talking to her peers altogether. Her parents spoke with Amanda's teachers, and Mr. Aiello had a good idea. He would create a disability awareness unit to increase her classmates' understanding of visual impairments. In fact, Mr. Aiello created disability awareness activities for each new unit he taught so that the children would have a better understanding of individual differences. The children's understanding and empathy for Amanda increased, and her classmates began to play with her at recess, sit with her at lunch, and ask to be her partner in physical education. Amanda soon had partners and was even invited to her first sleepover during the winter break!

Questions to Test Yourself

1. Amanda should have spoken to her peers so that they would better understand her.

   Yes — No — Not sure

2. Amanda's parents should have gone to the school and educated the teachers and her peers about her skills, abilities, and potential modification needs.

   Yes — No — Not sure

3. Amanda should have been in a separate physical education class if her peers did not accept her.

   Yes — No — Not sure

4. Mr. Aiello should be commended for his efforts toward the disability awareness program, because most teachers have no time to do "extra" work.

   Yes — No — Not sure

5. The peers should be more sensitive toward others. They should know better
   than to ignore a child just because she is different.

   Yes — No — Not sure

The purpose of this chapter is to help the reader

- understand how to work with support personnel and the physician to overcome blanket medical excuses,
- understand and be able to develop disability awareness programs,
- understand and be able to plan and implement peer tutor training programs,
- understand and be able to use support personnel,
- understand and be able to use community resources, and
- understand the importance of role models with disabilities in sport and physical education.

◼ Understanding the Disability

People with disabilities have gone through different eras of oppression, separa-
tion, and discrimination over the years. The era of acceptance is a possibility, yet
many misconceptions, myths, and prejudices surrounding individuals with disabilities still linger. Many nondisabled people still believe that people with disabilities are second-class citizens, are all retarded, are unemployed, have no physical relationships, and do not contribute to society, just to name a few.

In physical education, students with disabilities have been routinely excused
from class due solely to their disability. Medical personnel without a clear understanding of physical education content have provided medical excuses re-
stricting participation in physical education. The first step to ensuring appropriate inclusion is to ensure that children participate fully in class.

Overcoming Blanket Medical Excuses*

Many children with and without disabilities cannot be fairly included in general
physical education due to blanket medical excuses from the physician. In many
of these cases the child's physical or medical problems can be safely accommo-
dated in general or adapted physical education. However, the child's physician
does not believe or has not been made aware that the child can safely participate
in any form of physical education. Physicians simply may not understand the
current nature of physical education (it is not all dodgeball and regulation games),
and they may not realize the support and modifications that can be provided to
enable the child to participate safely and successfully in physical education.

Unfortunately, due to the initial physician's recommendations, the child's parents and physical education teacher will often fear involvement in general physical

education classes. Parents will fear the worst due to the recommendation from the well-meaning physician and concur with exclusion from physical education. They believe they are doing what is best for their child and are often not aware of any alternatives such as adaptations, partial participation, or small group work. Physical education teachers should never defy a physician's orders. Even though they may disagree with a physician's orders, they must adhere to the order for "no physical education" until such time as the physician can be persuaded to alter the order. It is never acceptable to ignore a doctor's order.

*This section is taken in part from Lieberman and Cruz 2001.

Possible Solution

While physicians often take on a god-like quality when it comes to making medical decisions, parents and educators must realize that most physicians simply do not know what modern-day physical education entails. As noted earlier, physicians may picture physical education as 11 v. 11 soccer games or 5 v. 5 basketball games, or mass dodgeball games. Most physical education programs are much more developmentally appropriate and individualized. In addition, physicians may not realize the numerous types of modifications that can be made to make physical education safe, such as lighter, softer equipment, smaller groups, modified rules, and the availability of teacher assistants and even nurses.

Physical educators, parents, and even children themselves need to take a more proactive approach in order to educate physicians who want to excuse students with disabilities from physical education. The key is to explain to the physician that the child with disabilities should and can be involved in an ongoing quality physical education program that is safe, beneficial, and that meets the child's unique needs. The key to providing this program rests upon open lines of communication between the general and/or adapted physical education teacher and the child's special education teacher, parents, nurses, and physician. When a physical educator is faced with a blanket medical excuse there are three major steps to safely including the child:

1. Become familiar with the disability to determine possible modifications.
2. Communicate these modifications to the physician to procure permission for participation.
3. Implement the modified program and reevaluate.

1. **Become familiar with the disability.** There are many different types of disabilities that involve many complications and contraindications (see appendix A). It is not possible for anyone to know all of the important characteristics of each one. In order for the instructor to learn about a child's specific needs, it is important to confer with other members of the child's IEP team (e.g., parents, special education teacher, the physical therapist, the school nurse, or the student) as well as resources on the Internet or in books. With this information, it is possible to explain to the child's parents and physician the types of things that can be worked on (e.g., fitness, improved gait, development of leisure skills), the type of program (general or adapted), and the types of modifications that will be made to ensure safety (see table 5.1 for sample modifications).

Table 5.1   Common Contraindicating Conditions Leading to Exclusion and Appropriate Modifications

Contraindications	Action to avoid	Modification
Atlantoaxial instability	Forward rolls (jerking of the neck), diving, heading a soccer ball, neck rolls	Log rolls, jumping in the pool, catching the soccer ball or using a Nerf ball, forward head stretches
Asthma	Extrinsic factors (pollen, dust, grass), skipping a warm-up, skipping necessary medication	Avoid extrinsic factors, use warm-up at all times, utilize prescribed medication, take breaks when necessary
Cystic fibrosis	No mucus excretion plan, sustained activity with no breaks, no medication	Utilize mucus excretion plan, take breaks in physical activity when necessary, utilize prescribed medication
Juvenile rheumatoid arthritis	Flexion strength exercises, twisting, bending during periods of pain, inactivity	Walking and low-impact activities, mild range of motion activities, mild strengthening activities, exercise in water when possible
Osteogenisis imperfecta	Pounding and jumping, contact sports, undue stress on joints	Walking and low-impact activities, noncontact positions in games (peer tutor), light balls and rackets
Seizures	Heights without support, swimming under water without support	Use spotting or harness when rock climbing, climbing ropes, or high beam, use a one-to-one qualified observer in the pool.
Shunt	Head jerking activities such as tumbling, heading a soccer ball, or diving	Activities that do not jerk head such as log roll, catching ball with hands, and jumping in the pool
Visual impairment (severe)	Running alone, using a hard ball with no auditory devices	Use peer tutor when running and in games, and use ball with bells or beeper
Other	Look at contraindicated activity for that disability	Create alternative safe activity with the same objective as the class or IEP

Lieberman and Cruz 2001.

Another source of information is the list of children with allergies, health problems, medications, and contraindications that is created at most schools. A confidential list is often provided to the teaching staff at the beginning of the school year. Unfortunately, this list often provides just a name and a health condition. However, the physical educator, nurse, and physician can be proactive and add a third column which would be a potential modification list for physical education staff. This column would state any necessary modification to ensure appropriate physical education (see table 5.2).

2. **Communicate directly with the physician.** Most physical educators and physicians are busy people, and it is often difficult to contact the physician and even more difficult to get a timely response. However, it is important that the physician be apprised of the physical educator's familiarity with the child's condition and the suggested modifications. Table 5.3 gives an example of a one-page form that can be presented to the child's physician by the child's parents. Approval of the suggested modifications is tantamount to the inclusion of the

Table 5.2   List of Students With Medical Issues and Modifications

Student name*	Medical issue	Modification
Marcus Anderson	Atlantoaxial instability	Log rolls, jumping in the pool, catching the soccer ball or using a Nerf ball, forward head stretches
Jennifer Chandler	Asthma (pollen, dust, grass, mold)	Avoid extrinsic factors, use warm-up at all times, utilize prescribed medication, take breaks when necessary
Gary Clinton	Attention deficit disorder	Utilize prescribed medication (Ritalin)
Sarah Evans	Severe asthma (stress, pollen, animals)	Avoid extrinsic factors, stress relaxation, use warm-up at all times, utilize prescribed medication, take breaks when necessary
Valerie Kingsly	Retinal detachment	Noncontact positions in games (peer tutor), softer balls (Nerf or beach balls), activities that do not jerk head such as log roll, catching ball with hands, and jumping in the pool
Eric Musso	Shunt	Activities that do not jerk head such as log roll, catching ball with hands, and jumping in the pool
Susan Oreint	Allergies (nuts, peanut butter)	Avoid allergen
Jonathan Rutherford	Profoundly deaf	Use signs, utilize interpreter, use visual cues, face him when speaking
Michelle Timms	Seizures (grand mal)	Avoid heights, avoid being under water for lengths of time, utilize peer tutor

*All names are fictitious.

Lieberman and Cruz 2001.

child into physical education. The following are some suggestions to get this approval form filled out and signed by the physician.

- *Physical educator empowers the parents to act as advocates.* Because parents are seen as consumers, it will often behoove the physical educator to empower the parent to bring the form and discuss proposed adaptations with the physician. The physical education teacher must meet with the parent and educate the parent about all the options for each physical education unit discussed. The parent can then contact or meet with the physician to discuss all the options. After this initial contact by the parent it may be easier for the physical educator to communicate with the physician directly (e.g., via e-mail, fax, phone, or in person).

- *Physical educator meets with the school nurse.* The school nurse is often more accessible and very willing to meet and discuss possible modifications for physical education. The parent can be part of this meeting, and, when all three parties agree, the permission of the physician and implementation can be expedited. After the initial meeting with the school nurse, the contact with the physician for consent can be made by the nurse. The advantage of contact through the nurse is that often he/she will already have a positive professional working relationship with the physician.

Form Letter to Physician

To:_____ Phone:_____

From:_____ Phone:_____

Dear _____,

At this time _____ is excluded from physical education because of _____. Full exclusion from physical education has detrimental lifelong effects on children. Sitting out of physical education decreases physical activity levels, decreases skill levels, decreases time spent socializing with peers, decreases self-esteem, limits number of choices for future activity, and decreases overall quality of life. We understand that the condition of _____ is not an optimal status for full participation, but we are hoping you would agree that the student can participate with some modifications.

Please consider the following adaptations to facilitate inclusion of _____ into physical education.

Unit:_____ Equipment:_____

Dates of unit:_____ Time of day:_____

Fitness warm-up:_____

Lead-up activities:_____

Focus of lesson:_____

_____

Closure activity:_____

Proposed modifications to unit include _____

Equipment	Rules	Environment	Instruction
_____	_____	_____	_____
_____	_____	_____	_____
_____	_____	_____	_____

Other:

Please indicate appropriate adaptations to create a safe environment for _____.

If you have any questions please contact me at_____

or fax this letter to _____ with your modifications and signature.

Thank you very much for your continued involvement with _____.

_____   _____
Physician signature   Physical educator signature

_____   _____
Parent/guardian signature   Child signature
Lieberman and Cruz 2001.

■ *Physical educator sets up a meeting with the physician.* To facilitate communication and after obtaining permission from the child's parents, the physical educator can set up a direct meeting with the physician in person, by e-mail, or by phone contact. This way the physical education teacher can directly explain the various units in the curriculum as well as the various adaptations planned to ensure safe participation. The physical educator is likely to gain some good insight into the child's disability and medical condition, and in turn the physical educator will be able to educate the physician about physical education and possible modifications and adaptations. Although time costly at first, if the educator were to make the time to meet with individual physicians, then a lot of time would be saved explaining and correcting later. After this initial contact, it may be easier to send faxes or e-mails back and forth.

3. **Implement the program.** Once approval has been obtained, the instructor can feel comfortable implementing the program. It is imperative that only the activities approved by the physician are implemented. Also, professional courtesy would dictate that the physical education teacher share early results of the child's success in physical education with the physician. This can be in the form of a simple note or e-mail. If there is a teacher's assistant or nurse who works specifically with the child with the disability, the instructor must provide appropriate and continuous training in the modifications to this individual to make sure he/she is implementing the program as prescribed. Finally, the physical educator should conduct ongoing assessment of the program to ascertain the comfort level and success of the child, that contraindications are avoided, and that the child is meeting the intended objectives of the unit or individualized education plan. This ongoing assessment can then be shared with the child's physician and parents in the form of a quarterly progress report.

Physical educators should be prepared to deal with well-intentioned physicians who give blanket medical excuses to children with disabilities. Too often children with even relatively mild disabilities are being unnecessarily excluded from physical education, because physicians perceive that physical education is not safe. This practice can have detrimental lifelong effects on children with disabilities who have limited motor, fitness, and leisure skills and who already are prone to sedentary lifestyles. The three-step approach provided should give the instructor a way to combat unnecessary exclusion in physical education (Lieberman and Cruz 2001).

■ Methods to Facilitate Inclusion

Disability Awareness

One way to overcome misconceptions and misunderstandings is through the use of "disability/ability awareness" activities (Wilson and Lieberman 2000). Disability awareness programs have been proven to improve attitudes of children without disabilities toward children with disabilities (Loovis and Loovis 1997). Disability/ability awareness should be one of the first activities presented to a class that includes a child with a disability because, unfortunately, simply placing students with disabilities into environments with students without disabilities does not guarantee social acceptance (Blinde and McCallister 1998; Tripp, French, and Sherrill 1995). Table 5.4 provides basic principles for implementing a disability awareness program. If followed, these principles can prove to be helpful in achieving understanding and success for everyone involved.

In addition to the principles outlined in table 5.4, children need to gain an awareness of disabilities. There are three levels of awareness that people go through in their understanding of disabilities (Wilson and Lieberman 2000). Level I is centered on exposure, level II is centered on experience, and level III is centered on ownership. These levels of awareness are described in the following section.

Table 5.4 Basic Principles of Disability/Ability Awareness Programs

1. Discuss the proposed program with all children with disabilities in the class to ensure comfort and understanding of activities.
2. Parents of all children should also be informed of any sensitivity activities planned throughout the year.
3. Always use "person first terminology" when discussing individuals with disabilities (in other words, put the name of the person before the disability).
4. Do not promote pity. Individuals with disabilities do not want pity, they want people to understand who they are and what they can do as people. Promote the idea of ability over disability. Show the children what people with disabilities can do.
5. Disability/ability awareness activities should not be a one-week or one-month unit. Awareness activities should be ongoing throughout the school year and throughout the children's schooling. This will show children that disabilities do not go away, but that they are lifelong and need to be considered in every unit and in every place they go.
6. The goal of all these activities is to bring all children to level III, the level of ownership.

Taken from Wilson, S. and Lieberman, L. 2000. Disability awareness in physical education. *Strategies* 13(6):12, 29-33

Three Levels of Awareness

These three levels of awareness when presented in a sensitive, deliberate, and matter-of-fact way can foster understanding and acceptance. The goal of the program is to have all students achieve the level of ownership.

Level I: Exposure

At this level of awareness, children are exposed to individuals with disabilities through various methods. A good starting method is to simply describe the disability itself. Appendix A provides definitions of disabilities described in "kid terms," which can be used to enhance level I. This is a great resource for giving children an understanding of disabilities without leaving them feeling overwhelmed or scared. The descriptions define disabilities and emphasize what is similar about the child with the disability rather than just focusing on the differences between the children. Other ways of enhancing level I awareness are described in the following section.

Level I Disability Awareness Methods

Invite speakers who have disabilities.

Read and distribute newspaper articles, books, and literature about people with disabilities.

Watch videos about people with disabilities.

Visit Web sites about people with disabilities.

The experiences at this level help children without disabilities realize that they share characteristics with those who have a disability. They help children examine situations from a different perspective and see the bigger picture. They also help children to understand their own feelings related to disabilities and learn how to handle interactions, solve problems, overcome challenges, and be sensitive to the needs of others. By being exposed to people with disabilities and vicariously experiencing their struggles, children without disabilities can come to a better understanding and acceptance of others (Andrews 1998).

Level II: Experience

At this level, students in the class have opportunities to actually experience a disability for a short time. Level II activities might include children ambulating in a wheelchair or with a walker, participating in activities with a visual impairment, trying to follow instructions with limited hearing, or playing a game using a scissors gait. The attitude the teacher has toward these activities is the key.

Playing goal ball during a disability awareness unit increases peers' understanding of visual impairments

Cross-age peer tutoring while swimming benefits both the student and the tutor.

The teacher must introduce the activities so that a positive, comfortable environment is created. The atmosphere is considered positive when the teacher introduces the material in a nonthreatening, nonpitying, matter-of-fact, informative way. If the teacher answers all questions in a positive way, with no negative emotion or regrets, the atmosphere will remain positive. This type of atmosphere will allow all participants to ask questions, express concerns, and become sensitive to the obstacles that individuals with disabilities may face daily. Appendix B contains specific experiential activities teachers can implement with their classes.

Level III: Ownership

At this final level of awareness, children with and without disabilities become advocates for individuals with disabilities. They take it upon themselves to ensure that people with disabilities are being treated fairly and equally by society and that they have financial stability, accessibility, independence, and recognition. It isn't unusual to find students taking on teaching roles at this level of awareness. They may choose to make peers or community groups aware through fundraisers or through advocacy for such things as sighted guides and wheelchair categories at running events or interpreters during concerts. They may even be found picketing a building that is inaccessible for those with disabilities. Ultimately, the goal for both students with and without disabilities is to reach this level of awareness.

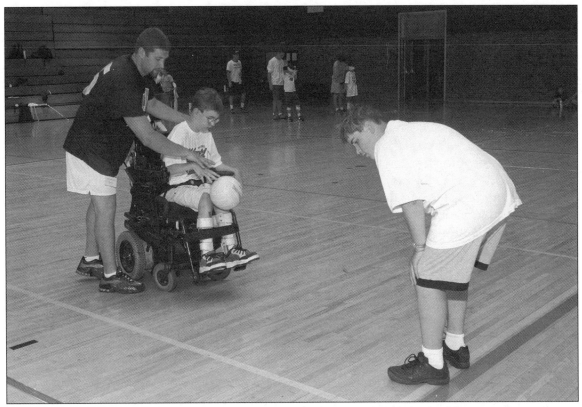

This student bounce passes a ball to a peer with the assistance of a teacher's aide.

Peer Tutoring

In addition to the use of disability/ability awareness activities, the use of peer tutoring programs can help to facilitate inclusion. The concept of peer tutoring in physical education is not new. Project PEOPLE was started in 1980 (Long, Irmer, Burkett, Glasenapp, and Odenkirk 1980) and included a training protocol and specific guidelines for implementation. There are several key reasons to implement a peer tutoring program in physical education. Table 5.5 presents the rationale behind the use of peer tutoring programs. The most important reason, of course, is that it allows for individualized instruction. Peer tutoring gives students with disabilities time in class to work on developmental skills vital to their involvement in physical activity in the future. Peer tutoring provides a situation in which the child with a disability receives instruction, increased practice, increased reinforcement, and continuous feedback on progress by the tutor on a one-to-one basis (Delquadri, Greenwood, Whorton, Carta, and Hall 1986). Peer tutoring is an appropriate, effective way to set up meaningful practice with the opportunity for high rates of motor-appropriate practice. The simple implementation of a trained peer tutor can improve the level of skill for the student with a disability. When students are inconsistent or do not perform skills correctly, not only do they fail to appropriately learn the skills but they also may actually learn them incorrectly. Besides its high success rate, peer tutoring is appealing because it is an inexpensive way to help students with disabilities succeed in the general physical education class (Barfield, Hannigan-Downs, and Lieberman 1998; Houston-Wilson, Lieberman, Horton, and Kasser 1997).

Peer Tutoring Choices

There are several types of peer tutoring options for teachers. Keep in mind that peer interactions and peer tutoring are two different things. If there is no formal training of the peers, the term *peer interactions* is used. If there is some type of peer tutor training, the term *peer tutoring* is used. Table 5.6 summarizes the peer tutor options.

1. *Unidirectional peer tutoring.* Unidirectional peer tutoring means that the trained peer tutor teaches the entire time, and the child with a disability remains the student in the pair. This method is effective when working with children with more severe disabilities such as severe autism, mental retardation, visual impairment, or cerebral palsy. The benefits of this option are that the tutor and student always know their roles, and the peer tutor carries the responsibility throughout the entire program.

Table 5.5   Justifications for Using a Peer Tutor Program

1. Children with disabilities need smaller ratios for learning than children without disabilities.
2. One-to-one instruction increases academic learning time (DePaepe 1985; Webster 1987).
3. Tutors learn skills better than if they had not taught them (Briggs 1975).
4. Peer tutoring increases leadership experience among the tutors (Rink 1998).
5. Peer tutoring stimulates socialization among peers.
6. Cooperative learning experiences promote more interpersonal attraction between students with and without disabilities, higher self-esteem, and greater empathy on the part of all the children (Johnson and Johnson 1983).
7. Participation together as partners and equals will encourage positive relationships (Sinibaldi 2001).

Table 5.6   Types of Peer Tutoring

Type of peer tutoring	Definition	Effective when used with
Same-age peer tutoring	Children tutor peers in the same class	Individuals with disabilities in the same class (3rd grade and older)
Cross-age peer tutoring	Older children tutor children in younger class	Children 2nd grade and younger, children with more severe disabilities
Unidirectional peer tutoring	The typically developing peer tutors the child with the disability	Children 2nd grade and younger, children with more severe disabilities
Bidirectional, or reciprocal, peer tutoring	The tutor and student take turns teaching each other	Any disability and any age can use this method, promotes leadership
Class-wide peer tutoring	Entire class, in pairs, utilizes reciprocal peer tutoring	Most disabilities; benefits the children because all are in pairs and all have opportunity for leadership

2. *Bidirectional, or reciprocal, peer tutoring.* A child with and a child without a disability form a dyad (pair). Both children take turns at being the tutor while the other serves as the student. The instructor can have these children switch roles for each skill, class, week, or unit. This method is most effective with children with mild disabilities. The main benefit of this approach is that each child has an opportunity to be the teacher and experience leadership opportunities.

3. *Class-wide peer tutoring.* Class-wide peer tutoring involves breaking the entire class into dyads. Each child participates in reciprocal peer tutoring by providing prompts, error correction, and help to their partner (Greenwood, Carta, and Hall 1988). Class-wide peer tutoring is unique because all children are given task cards to keep them focused on the objectives of the lesson. The tutor takes the task cards and fills in the skills that are mastered by the student. This method is most effective with children with mild disabilities. The main benefit of this approach is that the entire class is involved in the tutoring activity, so no children are singled out because of disability.

4. *Cross-age peer tutoring.* Cross-age peer tutoring occurs when an older child is chosen to tutor a younger child. This method works best when the peer tutor is interested in working with children with disabilities. A cross-aged peer tutor is more effective than a same-aged peer tutor when the student is very young (below first or second grade) or the disability is more involved (such as severe cerebral palsy, mental retardation, or autism) (Houston-Wilson, Lieberman, et al. 1997; Lieberman, Newcomer, McCubbin, and Dalrymple 1997). The cross-aged peer tutor can be chosen according to willingness, physical skills, and availability. The main benefit of this approach is that the tutor gains valuable teaching experience while the student experiences effective individualized instruction and feedback.

These students enjoy playing racquetball at a community center.

The parameters for this child during a bicycling unit include verbal assistance and a tandem bike.

Peer Tutor Training Program

Experts believe that training tutors is essential to the success of the program (Houston-Wilson, Dunn, van der Mars, and McCubbin 1997; Lieberman, Dunn, van der Mars, and McCubbin 2000). The peer tutor training program can take one hour or more, depending on the age of the tutor, the child's disability, and the units of instruction. For example, if a hearing child is in a reciprocal peer tutoring program with a deaf child, he or she will need to go through the basic training program with additional time spent learning important signs. If a student is in a unidirectional peer tutor program and is tutoring a student with autism during a dance unit, then the tutor will first need to understand the dance steps before attempting to teach them to the student with autism. In this case, the tutor would require more time in training.

Setting up peer tutor training programs is not difficult. The following are simple steps that aid in the development and implementation of a peer tutor program.

Step 1: Develop an Application Procedure

One rule of thumb when setting up peer tutoring programs is that tutors should *want* to participate. Some programs use tutoring as punishment. This is not conducive to fostering positive relationships. In addition, we believe the desire to tutor should be intrinsic. Therefore, there should be very little extrinsic reward for tutoring. Buttons, stickers, or certificates at the end of the program are fine, but higher grades or monetary rewards would be inappropriate. Some programs throw an ice cream or pizza party at the end of the year, and that is acceptable. Parties such as these allow students to celebrate the year's accomplishments. To ensure intrinsic motivation and strong desire, many schools choose to have tutors apply for positions just as they would apply for a job. The form on page 82 is an example of a peer tutor application.

Qualities of a Good Peer Tutor

Desire and interest in tutoring

Same-sex or opposite-sex (preference of student being tutored)

Average skill performance

Well behaved and reliable

Has younger siblings with or without disabilities

Enthusiastic

Patient

Previous experience working with kids with disabilities

Lieberman, Houston-Wilson, and Aiello 2001.

Step 2: Obtain Permission

In many cases, if the formal program is an additional part of the physical education program and there is out-of-class-training involved, the permission of parents, tutor, student (if appropriate), and administrators is imperative. A sample Parental Permission Slip appears on page 83. In a case where the entire class is part of the tutoring program, such as with class-wide peer tutoring, there may be no need for permissions.

Step 3: Develop Disability Awareness Activities

Understanding the disability is essential to effective training programs for peer tutors. Describing a disability in children's language can be difficult. Simple descriptions of many disabilities can be found in appendix A. Instructors are also encouraged to review the information about disability awareness levels, which is described earlier in this chapter.

Step 4: Develop Communication Techniques

The next step in the training program is training the tutor in the student's mode of communication. It is important for the peer tutor to understand the student's full expressive and receptive means of communicating. For example, if the child is nonverbal, how will the peer tutor know if the student needs to go to use the rest room, if the skill is too hard, or if the skill is too simple? In addition, if the student has a behavior problem, it is important for the peer tutor to know what words, activities, or expressions will send the child into a negative behavior pattern and what to do if such behaviors begin to show themselves. Sample modes of communication include sign language, communication boards, gestures, or augmentative talkers. Tutors need to become familiar with these communication devices so that they can use them effectively in their teaching.

Application to Be a Trained Peer Tutor

Name: _____ Grade: _____

Teacher's name(s): _____

Periods free to tutor:

1st choice _____

2nd choice _____

3rd choice _____

Availability for Training (minimum of 2 hours)

May be four 30-minute time periods, or six 20-minute time periods (one day if it is Superintendent Day)

_____ Recess: time _____

_____ Before school: time _____

_____ After school: time _____

_____ During lunch: time _____

_____ Superintendent Day (choice): time _____

_____ Study halls: time _____

_____ Portion of physical education class: time _____

_____ Other time: _____ (be specific)

Previous experience:

_____

_____

_____

_____

Please briefly describe why you want to be a peer tutor.

_____

_____

_____

_____

_____

_____

Please get a parental permission slip from the physical education office and have your parent or guardian fill it out before the training dates. Please check Mr. Wilson's door in three weeks for tutor placements and training schedules. Thank you for your interest in our peer tutoring program.

Parental Permission Slip

Dear Parents/Guardians,

The physical education department would like to start a peer tutoring program in physical education. We are writing to ask your permission to allow your child to participate in this program. Your child has expressed a desire to serve as a peer tutor, and we believe that he (she) will be effective. Tutors will be trained during free time and will be matched with a student who is experiencing difficulty in physical education. Your child will continue to participate in physical education activities but will also help teach and monitor skills. Your child may decide to terminate this experience with no form of penalty. If you agree to allow your child to participate in the peer tutoring program, please sign the permission slip below and return to the physical education staff. Also please have your child fill out the peer tutoring application enclosed. If you have any questions, please feel free to contact us at (000) 000-0000. Thank you.

Sincerely,

The Physical Education Staff

I give my child permission to participate in the peer tutoring program.

_____   _____

Signature of parent/guardian   Date

Step 5: Teach Instructional Techniques

Training peers to teach students with disabilities effectively requires a good understanding of a teaching process known as the *system of least prompts* (Dunn, Morehouse, and Fredericks 1986). Basically, the goal is to allow individuals to perform skills as independently as possible. Thus, the least prompt would be a verbal cue, followed by a model or demonstration, followed by physical assistance. These skills are taught to the tutor through the use of scenarios. For example, if the tutor provides a verbal cue requesting the student to throw a ball, and the skill is executed incorrectly, the tutor should then model the skill appropriately to facilitate understanding before asking the student to do the skill again. Tutors should also be taught how to give feedback to their students about skill performance. Verbal feedback consists of positive general, positive specific, and corrective statements. Nonverbal feedback consists of such things as high fives, thumbs up, or a pat on the back. Positive feedback is given after the student executes a skill correctly, and corrective feedback is given after the student executes a skill incorrectly. For more information on peer tutoring, see appendix B.

Step 6: Use Scenarios to Aid in Teaching

During the tutor training program, it is essential that the instructor utilize real-life scenarios to check for understanding (Houston-Wilson, Lieberman, et al. 1997). For example, if the peer tutor is teaching a child a throwing skill and the child does not understand the instructions, the tutor is asked, "What should you do now?" The peer tutor would have to say or show a demonstration of the activity for the correct answer. If the student then exhibits the appropriate behavior, the peer tutor should give appropriate feedback.

The instructor should give at least 5 to 10 different scenarios to make sure the peer tutor understands what he or she is being asked to do within the parameters of the program. If the tutor participates in the scenario incorrectly, the instructor should go over the concept again until the tutor fully understands what is expected.

Step 7: Test for Understanding

A peer tutor test can be given as part of the peer tutor training program (Houston-Wilson, Lieberman, et al. 1997). The test should consist of any information directly relevant to the particular program. Things to consider include: (1) the type of disability (signs for a child who is deaf, techniques for physical assistance for a child with cerebral palsy, or a behavior modification program for a child with a behavior problem), (2) the unit of instruction (cooperative games, basketball, swimming, or others), and (3) the goals of the program (teamwork, improvement of skills, improvement of fitness, socialization, or other goals). Instructors should decide what skills would be considered necessary for the tutor to be able to articulate and develop written or oral exams to test this knowledge.

The tutor should be able to score at least 90 percent or better to continue in the peer tutor program. If the child does not meet this standard, then he or she should be instructed in the weak areas and given the test again. Appendix B contains a complete peer tutor program including application procedures and tests.

Step 8: Monitoring Progress

It is important that progress of all the students, including those involved in the peer tutor program, is documented. Just as the instructor makes use of assessment data, the peer tutor can also learn how to effectively collect data. After data are collected, the instructor should check on progress and observe the tutors periodically to make sure data are being collected accurately. There are several ways peer tutors can collect data. The first is through the use of a *process checklist* (see p. 85). A process checklist contains a breakdown of skills into component parts, also known as *task analysis*. The peer tutor can observe the student executing the skill and check off the components that were done correctly. The second way to collect data is through the use of *rubrics* (Block, Lieberman, and Conner-Kuntz 1998). The peer tutor can mark off which level the student reaches during each class period. A third way to collect data is by simply *tallying opportunities*. The student must execute a skill such as push-ups, kicking, walking across a beam, moving through an obstacle course, or running laps around the gymnasium. Each time the student accomplishes a task that can be tallied, the tutor makes a hash mark. This system allows instructors to note how often the student

Process Checklist

Peer Tutoring Rating Scale

Skill: Dribbling

Tutor: Follow these steps.

1. Tell your partner to complete Task #1.

2. While your partner completes the task, rate his or her dribbling by placing a checkmark in the category that best describes his or her performance ("Always," "Sometimes," or "Never").

3. Move on to the next task and repeat step 2 until all the tasks are finished.

Task #1: Dribble while standing stationary.

Skills	Always	Sometimes	Never
Uses fingertips			
Looks forward, not at the ball			
Knees are bent			
Dribbles at waist level			
Has control of the ball			
Can use both hands			

Task #2: Dribble while walking.

Skills	Always	Sometimes	Never
Uses fingertips			
Looks forward, not at the ball			
Knees are bent			
Dribbles at waist level			
Has control of the ball			
Can use both hands			

Task #3: Dribble while running.

Skills	Always	Sometimes	Never
Uses fingertips			
Looks forward, not at the ball			
Knees are bent			
Dribbles at waist level			
Has control of the ball			
Can use both hands			

Lieberman, Houston-Wilson, Brock, Aldrich, and Kolb 2000.

* Created by Sheri Brock, PhD.

is engaged in activity. For those skills that cannot be tallied, tracking *time on task,* or how long the student is engaged in the activity, is another way to collect data.

It is also important to monitor progress of the peer tutors. This can be done informally through feedback, meetings before or after class, or in between units. The process can also be more formalized with the utilization of a peer tutor evaluation form (see p. 87). This form can be filled out during the program, at the end of the program, or both, to give the tutor feedback on his or her performance.

Step 9: Behavior Programs (If Necessary)

Peer tutors should also be aware of any behavior plans that are in place for the child they are tutoring. The peer tutor, however, should not be responsible for implementing the behavior plan. It is up to the teacher or assigned paraprofessional to handle any behavior problems that may occur during the class.

Teachers today are extremely busy with duties, planning, assessments, and often coaching. Some of the biggest questions asked are, "How long will this take?" and "When can I do the training?" These are good questions.

Possible Time Periods for Peer Tutoring

During recess

Before school

After school

During a portion of the lunch period

Superintendent Days

Study halls

A portion of the physical education class

Other

Lieberman, Houston-Wilson, and Aiello 2001.

The basic peer tutor program takes about one hour, or two 30-minute sessions. When the instructor adds information relating to disability, unit of instruction, or program goals, the training time increases. The training time should be short (15 to 30 minutes) but within a close time frame. If the peer tutors can be trained within a two-week period, they will be better able to retain and utilize the information. Also, peer tutors and students should periodically arrive at class a few minutes early to discuss the lesson for the day. This way the student can choose equipment, the peer tutor can plan instructional strategies, and questions can be asked and answered with no interruptions or distractions.

Support Personnel

Like peer tutors, support personnel are there to facilitate a more successful inclusive environment. Support personnel may be teacher's aides or assistants, educational assistants, paraprofessionals, parents, or one-to-one aides. Because children with severe disabilities benefit from one-to-one instruction, these individuals are important in appropriate inclusive environments. Some teacher's

Peer Tutor Evaluation Checklist

Name: _____ Date: _____

Evaluator: _____ Period: _____

Name of tutee: _____

Code marks		
* Good	✓ Progressing	- Needs work

Tutor Performance Assessment

___ Ability to cue appropriately

___ Ability to model appropriately

___ Ability to physically assist as needed

___ Ability to maintain data

___ Ability to work well and cooperatively with teacher and peers

Comments:

_____

_____

_____

_____

_____

_____

Suggestions for improvement:

_____

_____

_____

_____

_____

_____

Signature of peer tutor:_____ Date:_____

Signature of teacher: _____ Date:_____

aides may expect to have the period of physical education as a break or planning period like the teacher's, but this is not acceptable (Block 2000). If a class or a child needs a teacher's aide in the classroom, it is likely that they will need the aide even more in physical education.

According to Mach (2000), it would be helpful if support personnel had training in emergency procedures as well as an orientation session to the physical education program in which they will be working. Support personnel may be used in several ways. Such people assist in teaching at a station or with a small group including the child with a disability. They could shadow the child with the disability and the child's peer tutor, giving feedback and support for the pair. They could also facilitate appropriate behavior by the children and assist off-task children in getting back on task. Support personnel can collect data as well as assist with evaluation and group instruction (Mach 2000). Support personnel can be the physical support for the instructor in tasks such as toileting, changing clothes, and adjustment of adapted materials and mobility (Mach 2000). If the unit is not conducive to peer tutoring, or if tutoring is not beneficial to the child with a disability, support personnel could also work one on one with the child. If this is the case, social interactions with other students in the class should be encouraged. As mentioned earlier, Block (1998) recommends that students with disabilities who are assigned a one-to-one aide be provided with as many social interactions with other students as possible, because the one-to-one relationship can be a limiting factor in social interactions in physical education. Teachers who work with support personnel should be clear in terms of expectations and should give appropriate direction and guidance so that the support is useful. Failure to make expectations clear can lead to frustration for the teacher and the paraprofessional. Training support personnel in the same or similar fashion as peer tutors would be ideal.

Supplemental Instruction

Students with disabilities benefit from additional practices in the functional setting as well as one-to-one instruction. The following sections: using homework to fill in the gaps, making the most of community resources, use of grandparents, use of university or community college professional preparation students, use of community facilities, and use of role models will be helpful in setting up successful programming.

Using Homework to Fill the Gaps

Many children with disabilities will be behind their same-age peers in motor skills, fitness, and development. When the developmental delay or limited level of fitness becomes significant enough, it is difficult for the child with a disability to keep up with his or her same-age peers. In this case, the typical scheduling of physical education two times per week will not be enough to be truly effective in meeting the child's educational objectives. It is perfectly acceptable—in fact, preferred—to give the child (or the class) homework to improve skills or level of fitness. The following

Two siblings jump rope together as part of their homework assignment.

list presents suggestions for setting up a homework program in physical education.

1. Send a copy of the class objectives or an individual rubric home with the class to help the families understand what is expected.

2. The family and the teacher should have a physical education communication notebook in which they keep data on each lesson.

3. If the child does not have the appropriate equipment at home (scarves for juggling, hula hoops, jump ropes, softball gloves, lacrosse sticks, in-line skates, or other items), allow the child to sign out equipment each night and bring it back the next day. This policy will facilitate appropriate practice and may provide the parents guidance on buying age-appropriate and enjoyable equipment.

4. If the child shows a genuine interest in a certain activity and the family does not have the equipment at home, send a copy of the equipment catalog or the phone number of the company where the item can be purchased. For example, Irma is a child with a developmental delay who had a hard time with the skill of kicking. Her physical education teacher sent home a ball on a string so that she could practice kicking with her brother. She enjoyed the ball on the string so much that her parents bought the ball from *Sportime* for her next birthday.

Give positive feedback to families who implement the homework. Encourage them to continue what they have been doing, and document the additional parent involvement on the IEP.

This high school student weight trains with university student supervision.

Making the Most of Community Resources

There is a powerful movement toward utilizing the community in teaching children with disabilities. The following section will assist teachers in pinpointing effective ways to incorporate community personnel and facilities in maximizing instructional adaptations and variations.

Use of Grandparents

As mentioned earlier in this chapter, instruction for individuals with disabilities is best when it is one-to-one. Many schools have limited resources to employ support personnel, leaving the instructor with the responsibility of teaching the students with and without disabilities and the feeling that no one's needs are being met. One often-overlooked resource is grandparents. More and more people today are retiring at the ages of 62 to 65 with plenty of energy and enthusiasm left to contribute to society. Grandparents, whether they have children with disabilities or not, are readily available to assist the physical educator in a variety of ways. They can contribute in the same ways mentioned earlier for support personnel, and they can be trained in a similar fashion as peer tutors. They can help create and adapt equipment, improve time on task, and evaluate. Grandparents who are former teachers may need very little training.

You can find grandparents to assist in physical education by sending letters home, recruiting on open school night, making phone calls upon suggestion of the parents, or putting notices up at senior centers. Any way you look at it, this is a win-win situation for everyone involved, especially for children with disabilities!

A student bowls in a community bowling alley.

Use of University or Community College Professional Preparation Students

University or community college students are another resource that is not tapped often enough. The teacher, again, does not have to struggle to meet the needs of all children. Most university programs in special education, physical education, adapted physical education, counseling, or communication have practicum requirements for their students. Many universities have a hard time placing the large number of students who need these hours. These students can be used and trained in the same way as peer tutors or grandparents.

You can acquire university students to assist in physical education by calling or writing letters to relevant departments at local universities. The physical education teacher will need to find out the requirement for each specific department and create a proposal that would allow the university student to meet his or her requirement. The physical educator could ask for the syllabus to ensure the student is meeting the objectives for the class within the physical education class. This will encourage the college or university to send students to the school in future semesters. Again, this is definitely a win-win situation.

Use of Community Facilities

Use of community facilities is a necessary function to ensure a high quality of life after school age. For individuals with and without disabilities, this practice doe not have to wait until age 21. In fact, currently there is a trend to include individuals with disabilities in general community recreation swimming program (Block 2000; Conatser, Block, and Lepore 2000). Utilizing community facilitie such as pools, ice-skating rinks, parks, health clubs, and climbing walls can facilitate a variety of physical education and transition goals. These goals include such diverse skills as communication, socialization, activities of daily living, physical activity, improved motor skills, and even banking and budgeting.

A few minor barriers to community involvement may be attitudes of community personnel, transportation to and from school, and time missed from a core subject area. The benefits of community involvement far outweigh the drawbacks of time spent setting up the program or time missed from classes. In fact, many of the goals and objectives taught in core classes can be embedded into the community recreation program. For example, students can meet speech and language goals by communicating with personnel at health clubs; they can meet physical therapy goals by participating in rock climbing; and they can meet math goals by calculating the distance of a hike.

Use of Role Models

Children without disabilities often have role models in sport. There is now a myriad of role models, male and female, to choose from in dozens of sports. Role models foster motivation, goal setting, and inspiration.

For children with disabilities, this is not often the case. A child with spina bifida does not always know another person with spina bifida, especially one that is involved in sport. A great example of a role model with spina bifida is Jean Driscoll. She won the wheelchair marathon in the 2000 Paralympics in Sydney, Australia, with a time of 1 hour and 51 minutes! It is important for the instructor to assist the child in finding role models with similar disabilities. Places to find role models are described in the following section.

Where to Find Role Models Who Have Disabilities

Internet

WeMedia.com

Disability sport Web sites (see appendixes E and G)

Adapted physical education and sport journals

Local support groups for specific disabilities

Other

The following list offers various ways that instructors can utilize role models.

How to Incorporate Role Models in the Program

Posters on the wall

Short biographical papers on role models

Interviews with role models

Field trips to a competition or tournament

Guest speakers (either in class or during halftime of a sporting event)

A role model's participation with the class in sport or activity

The preceding section provided some creative ways to utilize the community to improve instruction and gain the most out of inclusive physical education. With some simple planning and good networking the community can help make each child a winner!

Question Review and Summary

1. Amanda should have spoken to her peers so that they would better understand her.

   As a new student, Amanda probably found it difficult to talk to peers she was unfamiliar with. Teachers should play a role in facilitating communication among and between students.

2. Amanda's parents should have gone to the school and educated the teachers and her peers about her skills, abilities, and potential modification needs.

   Although Amanda's parents were free to schedule additional meetings with staff to assist in the inclusion process, parents should not be held responsible for calling such meetings. Again, teachers should play a role in facilitating communication between parents and staff.

3. Amanda should have been in a separate physical education class if her peers did not accept her.

   Peer acceptance does not determine a child's placement in physical education classes. Class placement is determined by the needs of the student. Amanda should not have been placed in a separate physical education class.

4. Mr. Aiello should be commended for his efforts toward the disability awareness program, because most teachers have no time to do "extra" work.

   Yes, his work is truly commendable.

5. The peers should be more sensitive toward others. They should know better than to ignore a child just because she is different.

   Children as well as adults need to go through the levels of awareness to be accepting of those different from themselves.

Ideally, when all components—from IEPs to assessments and adaptations to understanding—work together, students achieve at much higher levels and are empowered to strive to meet even higher expectations. The scenario in part II highlights the inclusion strategies discussed throughout this book. It presents the steps necessary to successfully include children of all abilities in a classroom setting and gives concrete ideas for teachers facing the challenge of preparing an inclusive environment. It is a true model of what is possible with understanding, cooperation, communication, and creativity.

STRATEGIES FOR INCLUSION

Jose is a sixth grader who has a spinal cord injury. He uses a wheelchair to get around, but he can walk slowly with a walker. He also uses Lofstrand crutches for game situations, but he can only stand with them for short periods. In the past, Jose received separate, small-group adapted physical education. In September, his district decided to have the adapted physical educator serve as a consultant instead of a teacher. Jose will now receive his adapted physical education program in an inclusive class.

Mrs. O'Connor, the general physical education teacher, was worried about how she was going to include Jose and the other three children from his previous separate class into the general physical education program. She searched for a variety of resources to guide her, but her search was unsuccessful.

This book has been created to help Mrs. O'Connor and others in similar situations to successfully plan programs that include students with disabilities in physical education environments. Following are the steps Mrs. O'Connor took to plan effectively to include Jose in the general physical education class.

1. *Complete the Ability Description Form.* The first step Mrs. O'Connor took was to find out everything she could about Jose's disability. She copied the Ability Description Form from her inclusion book and filled out what she could. Then,

95

for the rest of the information, she asked Jose's mother and his previous class-room teacher. To complete the adaptations/modification part, she asked his previous adapted physical education teacher for information.

Mrs. O'Connor could then determine what special adaptations in instruction, rules, environment, or equipment Jose might need to be more actively involved in her various units of instruction. Mrs. O'Connor made an appointment with the IEP team leader and sat down and reviewed the IEP. This information helped in her planning process and also supported the information on her Ability Description Form. Mrs. O'Connor also reviewed Jose's previous IEP goals and objectives that had been developed by his adapted physical education teacher. She utilized these goals and objectives initially until she was able to assess Jose and develop her own goals and objectives. Jose's previous IEP goals were as follows: Increase standing and walking endurance, increase upper-body strength, and improve fundamental motor skills. During the fall she conducted a formal fitness assessment, using the Brockport Physical Fitness Test (Winnick and Short 1999) and an informal assessment of his sports skill abilities, to get a present level of performance for the new year. She determined that the current IEP goals were still appropriate and decided to incorporate these goals into her units.

2. *Develop inclusion strategies.* Jose originally had a part-time teacher's aide assigned to accompany him during his physical education class. Mrs. O'Connor discussed this option with Jose and found that he preferred to have a peer tutor. Mrs. O'Connor read chapter 5 and appendix B of this book. This reading gave her step-by-step information on setting up a peer tutor program. Mrs. O'Connor started by asking his peers who would like to be a peer tutor for Jose. She received more than 20 applications (see chapter 5) and chose five children to be trained as peer tutors for Jose. She then obtained permission (see chapter 5) from all parents, as well as administrative permission for the program.

The peer tutors came during their 20-minute recess, four times over two weeks. She taught them how to give instructions, feedback, and physical assistance if Jose needed it. She also taught them how to evaluate performance using a variety of checklists. During the last training session, Mrs. O'Connor brought in Jose for simulations, discussions, and practice. She worked with the peer tutors until they could all teach, give feedback, and evaluate Jose effectively.

Mrs. O'Connor also utilized disability awareness activities with the class, based on the unit of instruction. For example, if Jose needed to use his wheelchair to more easily navigate his environment, Mrs. O'Connor would allow other students in the class to participate in the unit while using a wheelchair. This proved to be a very helpful strategy because, as children experienced what Jose faced, they were more willing to incorporate rule adjustments.

3. *Choose units of instruction.* Mrs. O'Connor then examined her curriculum and developed a plan for units of instruction throughout the year. The first unit chosen was tennis. With the information she obtained from the Ability Description Form and the IEP, Mrs. O'Connor was beginning to formulate how she would approach teaching Jose in her inclusive class. She reviewed the information about authentic assessment and chose to implement a rubric to determine Jose's (as well as the class') present level of performance. She decided to use the full tennis rubric and to have the children work in partners to assist one another in their

progressions. This would also facilitate the peer tutoring program that had already been established.

Adaptation Choices

Mrs. O'Connor examined the adaptations to tennis in part II of the book and chose which ones best suited Jose. She discussed the adaptations with him to be sure he was comfortable with each one. The subsequent list describes the adaptations Mrs. O' Connor used to successfully include Jose in the tennis unit.

1. Equipment modifications
   - Use of wheelchair rather than crutches
2. Rule modifications
   - Two-bounce rule
   - Unlimited serves
   - Shorter serving distance
3. Environmental modifications
   - Installation of ramp to give Jose access to the courts
   - Chalk line to distinguish Jose's territory
4. Instructional modifications
   - Task analysis of the strokes
   - Physical assistance when necessary
   - Peer tutoring
5. Use of rubric (tennis)
   - Rubric within a rubric

Mrs. O'Connor decided that Jose would work on his progressions for forehand, backhand, and serve. He needed each task to be slower and task analyzed, but he could still move up the progressions of the rubric with his peers. He started out at the yellow rubric, and he wanted to be at the brown level for forehand and backhand and at the green level for serving. He worked hard in class with his peers, but he also worked on the progressions at home with his younger sister.

6. Homework

Mrs. O'Connor wanted to be sure Jose improved and achieved the goal of reaching the brown rubric. She sent him home with a copy of the rubric and a bag of tennis balls. In addition, she gave him some short cues to help him in remembering to follow through and to continue moving. For serving, she gave him the cue of the "Y" (both arms up) and extend to help him be more consistent in getting the ball over the net. She wrote these cues in his homework communication notebook so that he could remember which ones he was supposed to work on.

7. Posttesting

To posttest the unit, Mrs. O'Connor again assessed the children by using the tennis rubric. She used the already developed rubric from this book to assess forehand and serving skills during game play. She also developed her own rubric for the backhand and assessed the students with her rubric. She documented

Jose's process skills in forehand, backhand, and serving. After the unit, Jose added his rubrics and evaluation checklist to his portfolio. He had documentation of all his units from the year in his portfolio as well as a video of the dance show that culminated the dance unit. He had a few certificates in the portfolio from his fitness testing and a picture of himself and his peer tutors. Mrs. O'Connor also used Jose's scores from the rubric to write his quarterly progress report, and she used his overall performance in the unit to update his IEP goals and objectives. An example of the quarterly progress report has been included here.

Tennis Unit

1. Jose can hit a forehand with proper form during a game situation and get the ball over the net 7 times out of 10 (brown level).
2. Jose can serve the ball with proper form from the service line during a game situation and get the ball over the net 7 times out of 10 (brown level).
3. Jose can participate in a game of tennis, use the forehand, backhand, drop shot, and overhand smash shots correctly 75 percent of the time, and he can get the ball over the net 50 percent of the time (blue level).

Jose's parents and teachers understood these assessments, and Jose found them challenging. He fit right in with his class and he felt good about his performance.

Mrs. O'Connor utilized this book to set up a challenging yet successful environment for Jose, a student with a disability who was in an inclusive physical education class. She used the support strategies of peer tutors; she evaluated skills using current assessment tools; and she adapted the rules, instruction, and environment for Jose. She also used the results of Jose's performance from the rubrics assessments to write progress reports and IEP goals and objectives. Part II of this book gives the reader 38 unit adaptations and more than 52 rubrics. Teachers are encouraged to utilize these resources and to develop and create their own to successfully include all students in physical education.

The purpose of part II is to give physical educators like Mrs. O'Connor ideas for adaptations, assessment through rubrics (see chapter 2 for information on rubrics), and specific ways to document individual performance. It is important to keep in mind that part II consists only of selected ideas and is not a total curriculum. The purpose is to give the instructor examples as a starting point for developing more ideas. The instructor is encouraged to look at several specific areas before starting:

1. Skills and abilities of the child (or children) with disabilities
2. Unit of instruction
3. Goals and objectives of the class

After the instructor assesses these three areas, this curriculum guide may be used.

▉ Unit Adaptations

The adaptations part of the curriculum is broken into four sections. Each section gives the instructor a variety of variables to choose from. Although the unit may be soccer, a fourth-grade teacher may be playing keep-away or small-sided games and may use specific adaptations and instructional modifications to meet the goals and objectives of the soccer unit for that age group. The instructor must assess the students' abilities and the goals and objectives of the unit. The instructor can share the adaptations part of this book so that the child knows what variables are available. The child will be more likely to be invested and motivated in each unit if some ownership of variable selection is provided. If the child does not know what to do, the instructor can choose from the variables presented in this section and try a combination that may prove to be successful. If the instructor has tried a variable, it should be marked with an O.

If the attempted modification works well, the instructor should put a check and the date next to it so that the multidisciplinary team knows which adaptations were used and for how long. If an adaptation was chosen and it was unsuccessful or was discontinued, then a dated O with a line through it should be used. This allows future teachers to know what has been tried, what worked, and what did not work.

The final report on the child's IEP would include which adaptations were used and which were successful. If there is a change to the adaptations used, a note should be made on the master sheet.

The following are two examples of two different units. The authors give a few examples of how this system works.

■ JUMP ROPE

Potential Modifications/Adaptations

Equipment	Rules	Environment	Instruction
__ Light rope	__ Roll over rope	__ Lay rope on floor	__ Physical assistance
__ Heavier rope	__ Crawl over rope	__ Student holds one	__ Jump with arms
__ Shorter rope	✓O Step over rope 10/1	side of rope	✓O Peer tutor
__ Longer rope	__ Leap over rope	__ Student holds both	✓⊘ Peer holds one side 10/3 *standing
__ Velcro glove	✓⊘ Jump forward over rope 10/3	sides of rope	__ Command style
__ Bells on rope	__ Jump sideways over rope	✓O Student wheelchair	__ 1:1 assistance
__ Bright rope	__ Swing rope and step over	rolls over rope while	✓O Task analyze 10/1
✓O Handled	__ Swing rope and jump over	holding rope 10/3	__ Slow down
rope 10/1	__ Swing rope and jump	__ Music	__ Demonstrate
__ Cloth rope	consecutively	__ Limit situation	__ Feedback
✓O Plastic	__ Swing rope and jump	__ Increase stimulation	__ Braille
rope 10/1	double	__ Cushioned floor	__ Homework
__ No rope	__ Swing rope and jump	__ Place student on	__ Guided discovery
__ Rope cut 1/2	crossed in front	trampoline	
__ Glove for hand	__ Swing rope and jump		
padding	back & double back		
	__ Rope can slide		
	__ Jumps don't need to be		
	consecutive		

Note: Jose can jump over the rope with peers holding the rope but prefers to roll over the rope in the wheelchair.

■ SOCCER ▓▓▓▓▓▓▓▓▓▓▓▓▓▓▓▓▓▓▓

Potential Modifications/Adaptations

Equipment	Rules	Environment	Instruction
__ Auditory balls	__ Ground pass	__ Bright boundaries	✓○ Peer tutor entire unit
__ Bright balls	__ Timed dribble	__ Carpet squares	__ Physical assistance
__ Tactile balls	__ Undefended	__ Shooting line	__ Hand signals
__ Bell balls	__ Time limitations	__ Tactile lines	__ Verbal cues
✓⊘ Nerf balls	__ Boundary limitations	__ Auditory lines	__ Close proximity
stuck under	__ Free shooting	✓ Cones	__ Signs
wheelchair	__ Throw-ins	__ Ropes	__ Brailling
10/21	__ Walk with ball	__ Clap behind goal	__ Bright clothing
__ Bells on net	__ Run with ball	__ Limit mobility	__ Discovery learning
__ Buzzer on net	✓○ Cooperation vs. competition	✓○ Smooth surface	✓○ Task analyze 10/23-11/2
__ Radio	10/28	entire unit	used rubrics
__ Fan	__ Peer place ball	✓⊘ Can be goalie 10/30	__ Slow down
__ Wheelchair	__ Free kicks	*bored	__ Demonstrate
✓○ Front bumper 10/21	__ Stay in assigned area	__ Music	__ Feedback
__ Smaller goal	✓○ Hands used for protection	__ Watch film	__ Indirect
__ Assigned area	10/28	__ Modify field size	__ Direct
✓○ Ball size larger 10/23	✓○ Pass to everyone	__ Cones in front of net	✓○ Task style
__ Soft ball	__ 5 passes	✓○ Stations 10/21-25	__ Problem solving
__ Wider goals	__ Space as a defender	__ Decrease distractions	__ Lane soccer
__ Bright goals	__ No heading		✓○ Smaller groups
__ Flags	__ 5 dribbles		10/28-11/2
✓○ Pinnies 10/28	__ Do defense for 5 sec.		cooperative games
__ Cones	__ Pass before goal		__ Small sided games
__ Whistle	__ Shooting zone/score		
__ Bigger nets	__ Minimum 3 passes		
__ Shin guards			
__ Flip cards			
__ Ball on string			

■ Assessment Through Rubrics

The next part of this curriculum is the use of rubrics. For each unit we offer at least one rubric on which to base additional rubrics. For most of the units in the book, the instructor will need to create additional rubrics to use for an entire unit. For example, the soccer unit has only dribbling, passing, and game rubrics. The teacher will need to create additional rubrics for defense and other game skills. This section is meant to give the instructor a starting point for creating additional rubrics for each unit in this book and the ability to create new rubrics for additional units.

The rubrics fit into the assessment process by documenting the level at which the child performs. The elementary rubrics are broken into seven levels, each a different color of the rainbow. For the elementary section, the rubrics begin with red, the simplest, and move through the rainbow to violet, which is the most difficult. The sports, recreation, and fitness rubrics are broken into different levels signified by martial arts colors, with white being simplest and black being most difficult. The *task descriptions* are what skill or game the student is asked to execute for the authentic assessment. The *scale components* are what the child is being evaluated on during the lesson.

Examples are as follows:

Soccer

Task	Sport games: soccer, dribbling
Task description	Student can dribble using both inside and outside of the foot against a defender
Scale components	Type and velocity of performance, radius of direction change, with or without defenders
Rubric level & color	**Rubric descriptors**
1-white	Attempts to dribble with dominant and nondominant foot
2-yellow	Dribbles with inside of each foot, through 10 cones set 7 feet apart, up and back, without losing the ball
3-orange	Dribbles fast with outside of each foot, through 10 cones set 7 feet apart, up and back, without losing the ball
4-green	Dribbles fast with inside and outside of each foot, through 10 cones set 5 feet apart, up and back without losing the ball
5-blue	Student can dribble against a defender with inside and outside of the foot for 30 yards
6-brown	Student can dribble against a defender, through 10 cones set 5 feet apart, up the field, without losing the ball
7-black	Student can dribble against 2 defenders, for 30 seconds, within a 20-yard radius, using the inside and outside dribble, without losing the ball
Task	**Sport games: soccer, passing**
Task description	Student can perform an exact pass using the inside and outside of the foot to a standing and moving partner
Scale components	Type and number of performances, from stationary pass to passing while in motion
Rubric level & color	**Rubric descriptors**
1-white	Attempts to pass with dominant and nondominant foot
2-yellow	Student can pass with inside of the foot to a partner standing 10 feet away, using each foot, 10 times
3-orange	Student can pass with outside of the foot to a partner standing 10 feet away, using each foot, 10 times
4-green	Student can pass with inside and outside of the foot to a partner standing 20 feet away, using each foot, 10 times

(continued)

(continued)

Rubric level & color	Rubric descriptors
5-blue	Student can pass using only the inside of the foot to a partner, moving up and down the field, without losing control
6-brown	Student can pass using only the outside of the foot to a partner, moving up and down the field, without losing control
7-black	Student can pass to a partner 20 yards up the field, leading the receiver on the run, within 5 feet of the foot, 8 times out of 10

Jump Rope

Task	Jump rope
Task description	Student can perform the act of rolling, walking, hopping, or jumping over a rope at any height
Scale components	From one time over, one way, to jumping forward and backward once or twice around

Rubric level & color	Rubric descriptors
1-red	Student will crawl, roll, walk, or jump over a rope placed up to 1 foot off the floor
2-orange	Student will step or jump forward over a rope, placed 1 foot off the ground, either stationary or swinging
3-yellow	Student will bring rope over head with arms and step or roll over rope once
4-green	Student will bring rope over head with arms and step or roll over rope 2-20 times
5-blue	Student will jump rope, swinging rope over head backward, 1-20 times
6-indigo	Student will jump rope to music, forward, backward, crisscross, for 1-5 minutes
7-violet	Student will jump rope to music, either alone or with a partner, for 6-20 minutes

■ Documenting Individual Performance

The next step the instructor takes is recording the individual student's performance on the section titled "Individual Performance Report." The instructor records the child's current performance qualitatively. In other words, a description of the child's performance is recorded, such as a task analysis, or the process of performance is documented. Second, the product scores must be recorded, such as number of times executed, speed, distance, or accuracy. Next, any specific adaptations used from the unit adaptation guide should be recorded. From this information the teacher can then record the future goals and short-term objectives for that unit. An example of this can be found in the following record sheet.

Record Sheet

Current performance: _____

_____

Product scores: _____

Adaptations: _____

Future goals: _____

Short-term objectives: _____

_____

Derek is a fourth grader who has spina bifida. He can walk with crutches and also uses a wheelchair when necessary. His physical education teacher, Ms. Duncan, was working on a soccer unit. The class worked on basic skills such as dribbling with control, passing, shooting, and defense. At the end of the unit Ms. Duncan set up four games of keep-away. Derek needed some modification in order to be successful, and he could then participate fully in the class' goals and objectives, as well as utilize the existing rubric assessments. The following is a description of his Record Sheet.

Record Sheet for Derek H.

Current performance: Derek currently kicks with proper form using his crutches. Dribbles with inside of each foot, through 10 cones set 7 feet apart, up and back, without losing the ball. Can pass with inside and outside of the foot to a partner standing 20 feet away, using each foot.

Product scores: Derek kicks with proper form 8 out of 10 times. He dribbles through cones without losing the ball 4 out of 5 times. Derek passes with the inside and outside of his foot, to a partner 20 feet away, 8 out of 10 times. Derek can participate in a game of keep-away on a one-quarter-size field, using his crutches, for 8 to 10 minutes at a time.

Adaptations: Derek uses his crutches for skilled practice and games. He uses a Nerf soccer ball, and during practice he uses a peer tutor (reciprocal) for demonstrations, feedback, and help with ball retrieval.

Future goals: Derek will be able to kick with proper form, 10 out of 10 times, hitting an 8-foot target 10 feet away, 3 out of 5 times. He will be able to dribble through 10 cones set 5 feet apart, without losing the ball, 5 out of 5 times. Derek will pass with the inside and outside of his foot, to a partner 20 feet away, 10 out of 10 times. Derek will participate in a game of keep-away on a half-size field, using his crutches, for 10 to 12 minutes at a time.

Short-term objectives: Derek will be able to kick with proper form 10 out of 10 times. He will be able to dribble through 10 cones set 7 feet apart, without losing the ball, 5 out of 5 times. Derek will pass with the inside and outside of his foot, to a partner 20 feet away, 9 out of 10 times. Derek will participate in a game of keep-away on a one-quarter-size field, using his crutches, for 10 to 12 minutes at a time.

This entire unit summary, or the Record Sheet alone, can be placed directly in the child's IEP. This will give parents some great feedback on what their child can do and what modifications need to be made.

No matter what the unit or level of ability, any child can participate in this assessment process. The instructor is encouraged to create his or her own rubrics and add to the existing list of adaptation variables when necessary. With careful planning and preparation, all your students will maintain a lifelong passion for physical activity!

6 Basic Skills

*P*urpose: The importance of fundamental motor skills cannot be overlooked in elementary physical education. These are the prerequisite skills for more advanced movement skills, sports, and recreation. Introducing these skills at the appropriate developmental level is essential for successful performance in middle and high school.

Unit adaptations: There are many ways of adapting the curriculum for children with disabilities. It is imperative that the modifications for each child be specific to his or her needs. For example, if a child has athetoid cerebral palsy and moves more slowly than his peers, the instructor could slow down the activity, use a different teaching style to focus on individual movement, or utilize a technique that would slow down the movement of the child's peers.

Assessment options: In this section, rubrics that evaluate the process or product of movements have been provided for each unit. The instructor can also use the Test of Gross Motor Development (see chapter 2), or the I CAN curriculum.

■ BALANCE

Potential Modifications/Adaptations

Equipment	Rules	Environment	Instruction
__ Balance beam	__ Holding objects	__ Play stations	__ Peer tutor
__ High beam	__ Forward	__ Sequence centers	__ Verbal command
__ Low beam	__ Backward	__ Give and get	__ Problem solving
__ Narrow beam	__ Dodging	__ Stations	__ Brailling
__ Wide beam	__ One foot	__ Boundaries	__ Indirect
__ Balance board	__ Two feet	__ Small space	__ Physical assistance
__ Bean bags	__ Hands free	__ Large space	__ Task style
__ Jump ropes	__ Sideways	__ Obstacle	__ Enlarged task cards
__ Mat	__ Step over		__ Guided discovery
__ Ladder	__ Step through		__ Close proximity
__ Chair	__ Step in		
__ Tilt board	__ Step out		
__ Bench	__ Moving		
__ Lines	__ Stations		
__ Rebounder			
__ Steps			
__ Tires			
__ Hula hoops			

Example 1: Balance Beam

Task	Balance beam
Task description	Student can balance and walk forward and backward on standard high beam (__ ft long, __ ft high from floor, __ inches wide)
Scale components	(a) assistance, (b) task difficulty; (c) base of support
Rubric level & color	**Rubric descriptors**
1-red	Student will balance with assistance on low beam (__ inches high from floor)
2-orange	Student will walk sideways with assistance on low beam
3-yellow	Student will walk forward with assistance on low beam
4-green	Student will walk backward with assistance on low beam
5-blue	Student will walk forward without assistance on low beam
6-indigo	Student will walk backward without assistance on low beam
7-violet	Student will walk forward/backward without assistance on high beam
Specific adaptations	

Individual Performance Report

Name: _____ Date: _____

Current performance: _____

_____

_____

_____

_____

Product scores: _____

_____

_____

_____

_____

Adaptations: _____

_____

_____

_____

_____

Future goals: _____

_____

_____

_____

_____

Short-term objectives: _____

_____

_____

_____

■ BODY AWARENESS

Potential Modifications/Adaptations

Equipment	Rules	Environment	Instruction
__ Gym	__ Disability awareness	__ Group activities	__ Peer tutor
__ Mats	__ Gender rule	__ Team activities	__ Visual aids
__ Gymnastic apparatus	__ Use all body parts	__ Mirrors	__ Picture cards
__ Obstacle course	__ Follow instructions	__ Sections	__ Verbal cues
__ Music	__ Personal space	__ Mats	__ Feedback
__ Bean bags	__ Gender space	__ Line on floor	__ Demonstrate
__ Balloons	__ Work with others	__ Spots	__ Physical assistance
__ Sticks	__ Keep hands to self	__ Music	__ Learning
__ Ropes	__ Cooperation	__ Small area	__ Guided discovery
__ Award	__ Work in all directions	__ Large area	__ Mirroring
__ Beach balls	__ Clockwise	__ Indoor/outdoor	__ Task analysis
__ Whistle	__ Counterclockwise	__ Neat and clean	__ Clap when changing
__ Carpet squares	__ Draw peers	__ Flags	__ Partial participation
__ Cones	__ Trace partner	__ Cones	__ Problem solving
__ Footprints	__ Use partner when balancing	__ Stations	__ Balance
__ Fun mirrors	__ 3 different shapes	__ Different surfaces	__ Command teaching
__ Chalk	__ Small to large progression	__ Quiet	__ Brailling
__ Paper	__ Name shapes made	__ Padded walls	__ Positive reinforcement
__ Balance beam	__ 2 arm lengths apart	__ Uncluttered	__ Increase time
__ Skeleton	__ Use tactile mirroring	__ Pictures	
__ Bright balls	__ Roll balls over body		
__ Varying weights			
__ Flash cards			

Example 1: Body Awareness

Task	Body awareness
Task description	Student can name and perform actions (stabilize, manipulate, and move) with the body and its parts
Scale components	(a) from comprehension to action, (b) from body to environmental cues, (c) from self to external pacing
Rubric level & color	**Rubric descriptors**
1-red	Student will name body parts, laterality, and directions of movement
2-orange	Student will imitate, mirror examples related to body parts and limb movements
3-yellow	Student will perform on verbal command actions related to body parts and limb movements
4-green	Student will imitate, mirror examples related to movements crossing body midline (i.e., twisting, bending, rolling, and swinging)

Rubric level & color	Rubric descriptors
5-blue	Student will perform on verbal command complex movements in space including limb movements, movements crossing midline, and locomotion
6-indigo	Student will counteract actions of peers trying to enter personal space, (i.e., blocking, defending)
7-violet	Student will collaborate with peer to perform complex movements in space, including limb movements, movements crossing midline, and locomotion
Specific adaptations	

Individual Performance Report

Name: _____ Date: _____

Current performance: _____

_____

Product scores: _____

Adaptations: _____

Future goals: _____

Short-term objectives: _____

◼ HULA HOOPS

Potential Modifications and Adaptations

Equipment	Rules	Environment	Instruction
__ Hula hoops	__ Don't hit with hoops	__ Plenty of room	__ Use whole body
__ Sponge balls	__ To time limit	__ Each student has	__ Partner work
__ Bean bags	__ Do what everyone is doing	own boundaries	__ Jump rope with
__ Football	__ Stay in own space	__ Throw ball through	hoop
__ Tape	__ Throw with partner	hoop	__ Problem solving
__ Solid design on hoop	__ Start/stop signal	__ Work on accuracy	__ Stations
__ Adjustable hoops	__ *L* test	__ Large areas	__ Use names
__ Cones	__ 2 feet or 2 hands	__ Mirrors	__ Feedback
__ Balloons	__ Airplane space	__ Music	__ Command
__ Poly spots	__ Personal time	__ Lines	__ Physical assistance
__ Carpet squares	__ Gender rule	__ Lights on or off	__ Brailling

(continued)

(continued)

Equipment	Rules	Environment	Instruction
__ Whistle	__ Shapes	__ Different levels	__ Guided discovery
__ Scarves	__ In or out rule	__ Mats	__ Increase time
__ Smaller hoops	__ Don't bang hoops	__ Indoors or outdoors	__ Demonstrate
__ Lighter hoops	__ Don't touch others	__ Ropes	__ Task analyze
__ Brighter hoops	__ Feet, hands, waist	__ Small groups	__ Peer tutor
__ Thicker hoops	__ Over, under, through	__ In pool	__ Visual aids
__ Mats	__ Swim through hoop	__ Cooperative	__ Indirect
__ Jump ropes	__ Make noise with hoop	environment	
	__ Free time to explore	__ Quiet	
	__ Use signals	__ Bright lighting	
	__ Progress to activities	__ Tactile boundaries	
	__ No throwing hoops	__ Flat surface	
		__ Circuit	
		__ Audio stimulated	
		__ Visually stimulated	

Example 1: Hula Hoops

Task	Hula hoop
Task description	Student can maintain rhythm with hula hoop around hips, leg, wrists, arms, or foot for specific periods of time
Scale components	(a) assistance, (b) task difficulty, (c) momentum of hoop

Rubric level & color	Rubric descriptors
1-red	Student will walk or crawl in and out of hoop placed on floor
2-orange	Student will create circular motion on floor with foot inside hoop
3-yellow	Student will, with arms out and hoop around the elbow, create a circular motion with the hoop
4-green	Student will, with leg out and hoop around the knee, create a circular motion with the hoop
5-blue	Student will, with hoop around the waist, create a circular motion with hoop
6-indigo	Student will, with arms out and hoop around the wrist, create a circular motion with the hoop
7-violet	Student will meet a challenge (How long can you maintain the momentum with each body part? 5 seconds? 30 seconds? 2 minutes?)
Specific adaptations	

Individual Performance Report

Name: _____ Date: _____

Current performance: _____

_____

Product scores: _____

Adaptations: _____

Future goals: _____

Short-term objectives: _____

■ JUMP ROPE

Potential Modifications and Adaptations

Equipment	Rules	Environment	Instruction
__ Light rope	__ Roll over rope	__ Lay rope on floor	__ Physical assistance
__ Heavier rope	__ Crawl over rope	__ Student holds one	__ Jump with arms
__ Shorter rope	__ Step over rope	side of rope	__ Peer tutor
__ Longer rope	__ Leap over rope	__ Student holds both	__ Peer holds one side
__ Velcro glove	__ Jump forward over rope	sides of rope	__ Command style
__ Bells on rope	__ Jump sideways over rope	__ Student wheelchair	__ 1:1
__ Bright rope	__ Swing rope and step over	rolls over rope while	__ Task analyze
__ Handled rope	__ Swing rope and jump over	holding the rope	__ Slow down
__ Cloth rope	__ Swing rope and jump	__ Music	__ Demonstrate
__ Plastic rope	consecutively	__ Limit situation	__ Feedback
__ No rope	__ Swing rope and jump	__ Increase stimulation	__ Braille
__ Rope cut 1/2	double	__ Cushioned floor	__ Homework
__ Glove for hand	__ Swing rope and jump	__ Place student on	__ Guided discovery
padding	crossed in front	trampoline	
	__ Swing rope and jump		
	backward & double time		
	__ Rope can slide		
	__ Jumps don't need to be		
	consecutive		

Example 1: Jump Rope

Task	Jump rope
Task description	Student can perform the act of rolling, walking, hopping, or jumping over a rope at any height
Scale components	(a) number of jumps, (b) direction of jumps
Rubric level & color	**Rubric descriptors**
1-red	Student will crawl, roll, walk, jump over a rope placed up to 1 foot off the ground
2-orange	Student will step or jump forward over a rope placed 1 foot off the ground, either stationary or swinging
3-yellow	Student will bring rope over head with arms and step or roll over rope once
4-green	Student will bring rope over head with arms and step or roll over rope 2-20 times
5-blue	Student will jump rope, swinging rope over head backward, 1-20 times
6-indigo	Student will jump rope to music forward, backward, crisscross, for 1-5 minutes
7-violet	Student will jump rope to music, either alone or with a partner, for 6-20 minutes
Specific adaptations	

Individual Performance Report

Name: _____ Date: _____

Current performance: _____

_____

Product scores: _____

Adaptations: _____

Future goals: _____

Short-term objectives: _____

■ LOCOMOTOR SKILLS ▨

Potential Modifications and Adaptations

Equipment	Rules	Environment	Instruction
__ Cones	__ Fast	__ Boundaries/tactile	__ Physical assistance
__ Scooters	__ Slow	(ropes taped on floor)	__ Mirroring
__ Footprints	__ Directions	__ Small space	__ Peer tutor
__ Dots	__ Rhythm	__ Large space	__ Task analyze
__ Ropes	__ Holding objects	__ Cones	__ Demonstrate
__ Hoops	__ Left	__ Secluded	__ Feedback
__ Tires	__ Right	__ Use music	__ Brailling
__ Mats	__ Up	__ No music	__ Verbal cues
__ Tunnel	__ Down	__ Play stations	__ Partial participation
__ Stairs	__ Low	__ Sequence centers	__ Small groups
__ Sound source	__ Move in own space	__ Give and get	__ Problem solving
__ Video	__ Constant movement	__ Guided discovery	__ Shaping
__ Wheelchair	__ Play favorite music	__ Bright lines	__ Extensions
__ Walker	__ To time restriction	__ Gymnasium	__ Progressions
__ Wall bar	__ Start/stop with music	__ Outside	__ One-to-one
__ Ramps	__ Head up	__ Track	__ Auditory cues
__ Visual aids	__ At own speed	__ Pool	__ Kidnastics
__ Soft basketballs	__ 3-second rule	__ Classroom	__ Inclusion
__ Foam balls	__ Animal walk	__ Carpet squares	__ Direct
__ Balloons	__ Shadow shake	__ Targets	__ Indirect
__ Scarves	__ Follow leader	__ Mirrors	__ Task cards
__ Smaller hoops	__ Simon says	__ Indoors or outdoors	__ Explanation
__ Rails	__ Walk to music	__ Task cards on floor	
__ Noodles	__ Stop on whistle	__ Posters on wall	
__ Sticks	__ Locomotor skills	__ Uncluttered	
	__ Cooperation	__ Well spaced	
	__ Different levels	__ Padded	
	__ Pick movement	__ Flat	
	__ Blindfolded	__ Elevated	
	__ Freeze	__ Angled	
	__ No bumping others	__ Quiet	
	__ No sliding	__ Auditory lines	
		__ Hard surface	

Example 1: Running

Task	Running
Task description	Student will run from one side of the gymnasium to the other (50 feet) with best form
Scale components	(a) flight phase, (b) arm opposition, (c) back leg bent 90 degrees, (d) heel-toe placement

Rubric level & color	Rubric descriptors
1-red	Student will run from one end of gymnasium to cone 50 feet away
2-orange	Student will run from one end of gymnasium to cone 50 feet away, with flight phase at least 4 rotations
3-yellow	Student will run with flight phase and arm opposition during at least 4 rotations
4-green	Student will run with flight phase, arm opposition, and back leg bent at least 90 degrees during at least 4 rotations
5-blue	Student will run with flight phase, arm opposition, back leg bent at least 90 degrees, and feet landing heel-toe, during at least 4 rotations
6-indigo	Student will run with flight phase, arm opposition, back leg bent at least 90 degrees, and feet landing heel-toe, a distance of 50 feet, 3 out of 5 times
7-violet	Student will run with proper form consistently for 50 feet
Specific adaptations	

Individual Performance Report

Name: _____ Date: _____

Current performance: _____

_____

Product scores: _____

Adaptations: _____

Future goals: _____

Short-term objectives: _____

LOW-ORGANIZED AND TAG GAMES

Potential Modifications and Adaptations

Tag Games

Equipment	Rules	Environment	Instruction
___ Poly spots	___ Have spots on floor	___ Constant movement	___ Make student calm self
___ Soft, long objects	___ Must use soft object	___ Bright boundaries	before starting
___ Time-out chair	___ Same locomotor activity	___ Rough boundaries	___ Peer tutoring
___ Pinnies	___ Use first names	___ Check understanding	___ "It" students do different
___ Scarves	___ Everybody is "it"	___ Big smile to class	skill
___ Sponge balls	___ Steal teammates' scarves	___ Ice arena	___ Direct
___ Cones	___ If tagged, 5 push-ups	___ Mats	___ Indirect
___ Whistle	___ Gender rule	___ Flat surface	___ Small group
___ Carpet squares	___ Touch rule	___ Mirrors	___ Physical assistance
___ Scooters	___ Bumpers up	___ Remove leg rest	___ Feedback
___ Radio	___ Airplane space	___ Large area	___ Positive role model
___ Hula hoops	___ Partner tag	___ Boundaries	___ Demonstration
___ Pillow polo stick	___ Animal walk	___ Circles	___ Verbal cues
___ Bean bags	___ 10-second rule	___ Lines	___ Brailling assistance
___ Hard scarves	___ Start/stop signal	___ Music	___ Nonverbal cues
___ Different size balls	___ Activity book	___ Smaller lines	___ Quality movement
___ Bright color objects	___ After tag do a skill	___ Smaller distance	___ Stress cooperation
___ Tagging objects	___ More than 1 person	___ Flags	___ Instruction feedback
___ Wands	___ Practice moving safely	___ Safety zone	___ Proximity
___ Nerf balls	___ Use soft stick to tag	___ Goals	___ Verbal cues
___ Tape	___ Clap 4 times then run	___ Groups for tag	___ Peer runners
___ Wiffle balls	___ Partner is "it"	___ Uncluttered	___ Command style
	___ Walk, no running	___ No confusing sounds	___ No time factor
	___ Tag on body parts	___ Good lighting	___ Task analyze
	___ Blindfold partner	___ Level surface	___ Speak naturally
	___ Change locomotion	___ Large movement	___ Braille tags
	___ Run on balls of feet	___ Movement friendly	___ Preorient child
	___ Tag softly	___ Outside on grass	___ Utilize all senses
	___ Don't throw at face	___ Cooperative	___ Guided discovery
	___ Freeze when tagged		
	___ Follow the leader		

Example 1: Cooperative Games

Task	Cooperative game
Task description	Student can interact with large groups of peers and adults (more than 6) for periods of 45 minutes
Scale components	(a) attention span, (b) group size, (c) leadership
Rubric level & color	**Rubric descriptors**
1-red	Student can start and stop on command repeatedly (4-6 times)
2-orange	Student can follow a set of instructions for 10-15 minutes
3-yellow	Student can adhere to a cooperative task (such as passing balls) in a small group (less than 7 participants)
4-green	Student can adhere to a cooperative task (such as passing balls) in a large group (more than 6 participants)
5-blue	Student can assist, follow, and support peers most of the time
6-indigo	Student can adhere to a cooperative task even if offended by peer
7-violet	Student can provide positive feedback and constructive instructions to peers without getting into major conflicts
Specific adaptations	

Individual Performance Report

Name: _____ Date: _____

Current performance: _____

_____

Product scores: _____

Adaptations: _____

Future goals: _____

Short-term objectives: _____

■ MANIPULATIVE SKILLS

Potential Modifications and Adaptations

Equipment	Rules	Environment	Instruction
__ Large beach balls	__ Kick for distance	__ Indoors	__ Specific instruction
__ Nerf ball	__ Kick for height	__ Outdoors	__ Partial participation
__ Nerf soccer ball	__ Kick for accuracy	__ Smaller playing area	__ Peer tutor
__ Large racket face	__ Throw for accuracy	__ Smaller teams	__ Visually demonstrate
__ Larger ball in dribbling	__ Throw for distance	__ Closer shooting line	__ Task analyze
__ Lower net in volleyball	__ Catch ball with hands	__ Closer passing area	__ Good speed of ball
__ Large ball	__ Pull ball toward chest	__ Decrease distance	__ Modeling
__ Smaller ball	__ Return serve	__ Stations	__ Guided discovery
__ Smaller target	__ Utilize accuracy	__ Groups of 2	__ Feedback
__ Lighter balls	__ Dribble with 1 hand	__ Different surfaces	__ Task cards
__ Lower baskets	__ Get ball over net	__ Different seasons	
__ Wider goals	__ One push, one ride	__ Bright lights	
__ Bigger mitt	__ Bounce before catch	__ Nets	
__ Bigger, lighter bat	__ Walk with ball		
__ Flags	__ Unlimited strikes		
__ Wands	__ Not throwing objects		
__ Lummi sticks	__ Freeze		
__ Bean bags	__ Personal space		
__ Scooters	__ Stop, look, listen		
__ Fuzzy balls	__ Kick against wall		
__ Cones	__ Kicking under control		
__ Hoops			
__ Noodles			

Example 1: Kicking

Task	Kicking
Task description	Student can kick a stationary ball
Scale components	(a) three-step approach, (b) trunk inclined backward during contact, (c) forward swing of opposite arm, (d) follow-through
Rubric level & color	**Rubric descriptors**
1-red	Student will kick stationary ball with any form
2-orange	Student will kick stationary ball with a three-step approach, walking or running during most kicks
3-yellow	Student will kick stationary ball with a three-step approach and trunk inclined backward during contact during most kicks

(continued)

(continued)

Rubric level & color	Rubric descriptors
4-green	Student will kick stationary ball with a three-step approach, trunk inclined backward during contact, and forward swing of opposite arm during most kicks
5-blue	Student will kick stationary ball with a three-step approach, trunk inclined backward during contact, and forward swing of opposite arm during 3 out of 5 kicks
6-indigo	Student will kick stationary ball with a three-step approach, trunk inclined backward during contact, forward swing of opposite arm, and follow-through, propelling the ball 30 feet
7-violet	Student will kick stationary ball with a three-step approach, trunk inclined backward during contact, forward swing of opposite arm, and follow-through, propelling the ball 30 feet
Specific adaptations	

Individual Performance Report

Name: _____ Date: _____

Current performance: _____

_____

Product scores: _____

Adaptations: _____

Future goals: _____

Short-term objectives: _____

■ OBJECT CONTROL SKILLS

Potential Modifications and Adaptations

Equipment	Rules	Environment	Instruction
__ Large balls	__ Varied distance	__ Nonstimulatory	__ Physical assistance
__ Small balls	__ Against a wall	__ Boundaries	__ Guided discovery
__ Auditory balls	__ With 1 hand	__ Small space	__ Peer tutor
__ Yarn ball	__ With 2 hands	__ Large space	__ Task analyze
__ Wiffle ball	__ Dominant hand	__ Cones	__ Demonstrate
__ Tactile ball	__ Nondominant hand	__ Secluded	__ Feedback
__ Heavy ball	__ Dominant foot	__ Use music	__ Brailling
__ Light balls	__ Nondominant foot	__ No music	__ Verbal command
__ Bright balls	__ Underhand	__ Play stations	__ Problem solving
__ Ball on a rope	__ Overhand	__ Sequence centers	__ Indirect
__ Hockey puck	__ Sidearm	__ Give and get	__ Small group
__ Rackets	__ Stationary	__ Bat into panel mat	
__ Bats	__ Traveling	__ Choice of balls	
__ Paddles	__ Pass ball w/ partner	__ Indoor/outdoor	
__ Tee	__ Bat the Wiffle ball	__ Use bright balls	
__ Hockey stick	__ Bean bag toss	__ Have volleyball nets up	
__ Bean bags	__ Catch balls	to play all positions	
__ Sponges	__ Keep eyes on ball	__ Flat surface	
__ Baskets	__ Bat for points	__ Mirrors	
__ Buckets	__ Bounce rule	__ Large area	
__ Goals	__ Lower target	__ Railing assistance	
__ Bases	__ Closer target	__ Ropes	
__ Auditory bases	__ 10-second rule	__ Remove leg rest	
__ Soft bats	__ Touch rule	__ Attach ball to string	
__ Gloves	__ Gender rule		
__ Bouncy balls			
__ Basketballs			
__ Volleyball			
__ Football			
__ Panel mats			
__ Beach ball			
__ Deflated balls			
__ Velcro balls			
__ Balloons			
__ Shoe on stick			

Example 1: Underhand Throw

Task	Underhand throw
Task description	Student will throw underhand to peer
Scale components	(a) step with opposite foot, (b) release in front, (c) weight shift forward, (d) follow-through
Rubric level & color	**Rubric descriptors**
1-red	Student will attempt to throw a bean bag underhand to peer standing 10 feet away
2-orange	Student will throw a bean bag underhand, stepping with the opposite foot most of the time.
3-yellow	Student will throw a bean bag underhand, stepping with the opposite foot and releasing in front of the body most of the time
4-green	Student will throw a bean bag underhand, stepping with the opposite foot, releasing in front of the body, and shifting weight forward during the throw most of the time
5-blue	Student will throw a bean bag underhand, stepping with the opposite foot, releasing in front of the body, shifting weight forward during the throw, and following through most of the time
6-indigo	Student will throw a bean bag underhand, stepping with the opposite foot, releasing in front of the body, shifting weight forward during the throw, and following through, to a partner 10 feet away
7-violet	Student will throw a bean bag underhand, stepping with the opposite foot, releasing in front of the body, shifting weight forward during the throw, and following through to hit an 8-foot square target, 15 feet away, 3 out of 5 times
Specific adaptations	

Example 2: Locomotor Skills

Task	Locomotor skills (run, skip, leap, horizontal jump, slide)
Task description	Student can perform basic skill with all qualitative components characterizing adult action
Scale components	Follow TGMD and I CAN; use a separate rubric for each skill

See following example of separate rubric:

Task	Object control skill: bounce
Task description	Student can perform basic skill with all qualitative components characterizing adult action
Scale components	(a) qualitative elements, (b) "flow"
Rubric level & color	**Rubric descriptors**
1-red	Student will bounce and catch small physio-ball (diameter 30-40 cm) with 2 hands, 1 time
2-orange	Student will bounce and catch small physio-ball (diameter 30-40 cm) with 1 hand, 3-4 times
3-yellow	Student will bounce small physio-ball in front of the body repeatedly without losing ball
4-green	Student will control height of bounce by keeping small physio-ball at hip level
5-blue	Student will perform bounce with volleyball or small basketball (No. 5) with proper hand joint control
6-indigo	Student will perform bounce while moving in space with volleyball or small basketball (No. 5) without losing ball
7-violet	Student will perform bounce while moving quickly in space with volleyball or small basketball (No. 5) without losing ball
Specific adaptations	

Individual Performance Report

Name: _____ Date: _____

Current performance: _____

_____

Product scores: _____

Adaptations: _____

Future goals: _____

Short-term objectives: _____

■ PARACHUTE

Potential Modifications and Adaptations

Equipment	Rules	Environment	Instruction
__ Large parachute	__ Limit range of motion	__ Smooth surface	__ Explanation
__ Small parachute	__ Increase range of motion	__ Grass	__ Physical assistance
__ Towel	__ Change objective	__ Mats	__ Routines to music
__ Straps on chute	__ Limit number of shakes	__ Lighting (dim or bright)	__ Guided discovery
__ Ace bandage around	__ Increase number of shakes	__ Stimulating	__ Partners
hand	__ Limit amount of movement	__ Consistency	__ Problem solving
__ Bells on chute	__ Parachute chair height	__ Open area	__ Demonstration
__ Balls on chute	__ All balls in parachute	__ Indoors or outdoors	__ Proximity
(bright or auditory)	__ Keep parachute moving	__ Lines	__ Group instruction
__ Parachute bright	__ Stop/start	__ Circles	__ Peer tutor
__ Parachute tactile	__ Gender rule	__ Target	__ Certified personnel
__ Foam balls	__ 2 hands on parachute	__ Different levels	__ Command style
__ Rag balls	__ Color change	__ Boundaries	__ Parent
__ Beach balls	__ Airplane space	__ Quiet	__ Feedback
__ Gymnasium	__ Big waves	__ Limit distractions	__ Verbal cues
__ Wrist wraps	__ Loud/quiet	__ Large space	__ Visual aids
__ Tennis balls	__ Walking rule	__ Tactile boundaries	__ History of parachute
__ Bean bags	__ Name game	__ Roped boundaries	
__ Scarves	__ Animal game	__ Cooperative	
__ Whistle	__ Don't pull on chute	__ Cushioned	
__ Music	__ Verbal cues for start	__ Welcoming area	
__ Mirrors	__ Call out names while	__ Fun environment	
__ Poly spots	changing positions		
__ Wiffle balls	__ Run in place		
__ Ping-Pong balls	__ Mushroom parachute		
__ Nerf balls	__ Sit down on whistle		
__ Basketballs	__ Move in direction		
__ Jump ropes	__ Don't let go		
__ Fuzzy balls			
__ Mats			

Example 1: Parachute

Task	Parachute
Task description	Student will progress from maintaining one level to being able to change levels to a rhythm
Scale components	Able to change levels at any time from low to medium to high, according to the rhythm

Rubric level & color	Rubric descriptors
1-red	Student will be able to hold on to parachute at a medium level using any grip (with or without assistance)
2-orange	Student will be able to hold on to a parachute at a medium level using an overhand grip
3-yellow	Student will be able to hold on to a parachute at a medium level using an overhand grip, and to take his or her part of the parachute to a low level and back to a medium level
4-green	Student will be able to hold on to a parachute at a medium level using an overhand grip, and to take his or her part of the parachute to a high level and back to a medium level
5-blue	Student will be able to hold on to parachute at a medium level using an overhand grip, and to take his or her part of the parachute to any level, on cue
6-indigo	Student will be able to hold on to parachute at a medium level using an overhand grip, and to take his or her part of the parachute to any level, in rhythm and on cue
7-violet	Student will be able to hold on to parachute at a medium level using an overhand grip, and to take his or her part of the parachute to any level, in rhythm and on cue, for the duration of a song
Specific adaptations	

Individual Performance Report

Name: _____ Date: _____

Current performance: _____

_____

Product scores: _____

Adaptations: _____

Future goals: _____

Short-term objectives: _____

◼ RHYTHMS ▨▨▨▨▨▨▨▨▨▨▨▨▨▨▨▨▨▨

Potential Modifications and Adaptations

Equipment	Rules	Environment	Instruction
___ Music (radio)	___ Animal walks	___ Mirrors	___ Visual aids
___ Scarves	___ Start/stop signal	___ Lines	___ Verbal cues
___ Bean bags	___ *L* test	___ Flat surface	___ Direct
___ Balls	___ Mimicking	___ Small groups	___ Indirect
___ Balloons	___ Sub–upper body	___ Boundaries	___ Peer tutor
___ Rubber chicken	___ Locomotor	___ Circles	___ Feedback
___ Cones	___ Use peers	___ Mats	___ Demonstration
___ Wrist bands	___ Link arms	___ Targets	___ Physical assistance
___ Lummi sticks	___ Bounce to beat	___ Small boxes	___ Counting beats
___ Sticks	___ Toss to beat of music	___ Smaller feet position	___ Slow movement
___ Poly spots	___ Have peer toss ball	___ Slower tempo	___ Mirroring
___ Footprints	___ Shorter time on task	___ Smaller line	___ Proximity
___ Different size balls	___ Dance in groups	___ Smaller circles	___ Teach with or without music
___ Bright wands	___ Change partners	___ Small groups	___ Task analyze
___ Tambourines	___ Can lie or sit	___ Small dance area	___ Command style
___ Maracas	___ Braille movements	___ Happy environment	___ Brailling
___ Drums	___ Create own steps	___ Bright posters	
___ Keyboards	___ Movements to music	___ Quiet when music is on	
___ Boxes	___ Start/stop music	___ No clutter	
	___ Time limitations	___ Well lit	
	___ Hand clap on beats	___ Tactile lines	
		___ Obstacle course	
		___ Acoustic	
		___ Colorful	
		___ Cooperative	

Example 1: Developing Rhythmic Skills

Task	Rhythmic skills
Task description	Student will march and clap to a beat, and clap and side-step to a beat
Scale components	(a) clap to 1/4-and 1/8-count beat, (b) march to 1/4-and 1/8-count beat, (c) side-step to the beat while clapping
Rubric level & color	**Rubric descriptors**
1-red	Student will clap to a rhythmic song (1/4-count beats)
2-orange	Student will march to a rhythmic song (1/4-count beats)
3-yellow	Student will clap and march to a rhythmic song (1/4-count beats)
4-green	Student will clap to a rhythmic song (1/8-count beats)

Rubric level & color	Rubric descriptors
5-blue	Student will clap and march to a rhythmic song (1/8-count beats)
6-indigo	Student will clap and side-step to a rhythmic song (1/8-count beats)
7-violet	Student will clap and side-step to an entire rhythmic song (1/8-count beats) * Optional—be the leader in front of the class and have them follow
Specific adaptations	

Individual Performance Report

Name: _____ Date: _____

Current performance: _____

_____

Product scores: _____

Adaptations: _____

Future goals: _____

Short-term objectives: _____

■ SCOOTER BOARD

Potential Modifications and Adaptations

Equipment	Rules	Environment	Instruction
__ Scooter boards	__ Use all general space	__ Gym	__ Task analysis
__ Radio	__ Must pass end lines	__ Boundaries	__ Verbal cues
__ Bean bags	__ Use feet or hands to	__ End line boundaries	__ Large groups
__ Soccer balls	dribble while moving	__ Flags mark end lines	__ Small groups
__ Soft foam balls	__ Use hands or feet to move	__ Volleyball court	__ One-to-one
__ Soft balls	__ Down and back 2 times	__ Basketball court	__ Teacher help
__ Hula hoops	before switch	__ Parking lot	__ Direct
__ Scarves	__ Lower target	__ Lines on floor	__ Indirect
__ Whistle	__ 10-second rule	__ Cones	__ Guided discovery
__ Music	__ Touch rule	__ Ropes	__ Shaping
__ Poly spot	__ Sharing	__ Large area	__ Peer tutor
__ Pinnies	__ Gender rule	__ Railing assistance	__ Feedback
__ Ropes	__ Start/stop signal	__ Flat surface	__ Visual aid
__ Pillow polo sticks	__ Bumpers up	__ Different surface	__ Demonstration

(continued)

(continued)

Equipment	Rules	Environment	Instruction
___ Small scooters	___ Airplane space	___ Small boundaries	___ Stress safety
___ Cones	___ Partner tag	___ Safety zone	___ Peer work
___ Hoops	___ Time rule	___ Flags	___ Increase time
___ Mats	___ Use partner	___ Mats on walls	___ Utilize all senses
___ Jump ropes	___ Pull with string	___ Quiet while instructing	___ Brailling
___ Alternate boards	___ One pushes, one pulls	___ Padded walls	___ In pairs
___ Bright cones	___ Have 2 pull one	___ Personal space	___ Relay races
___ Bright balls	___ Make train	___ Use peer guides	___ Modeling
___ Textured balls	___ Group work	___ Different positions	
___ Soft sticks	___ Direction	___ Support body parts	
___ Noodles	___ Speed	___ Obstacles	
	___ Mode of movement	___ Circuit obstacles	
	___ Sitting or lying down		

Example 1: Scooter Board

Task	Scooter board
Task description	Student will demonstrate the ability to pull him or herself prone on a scooter
Scale components	(a) pulling motion, (b) distance, (c) speed (optional)
Rubric level & color	**Rubric descriptors**
1-red	Students will pull themselves, prone on a scooter, up a rope with intermittent knots tied vertically to the wall, for 5 feet
2-orange	Students will pull themselves, prone on a scooter, up a rope with intermittent knots tied vertically to the wall, for 10 feet
3-yellow	Students will pull themselves, prone on a scooter board, through 4 cones placed 5 feet apart, once
4-green	Students will pull themselves, prone on a scooter board, through 4 cones placed 5 feet apart, twice
5-blue	Students will pull themselves, prone on a scooter board, through 8 cones placed 5 feet apart, twice
6-indigo	Students will pull themselves, prone on a scooter board, through a 50-foot obstacle course consisting of around, through, and over, once
7-violet	Students will pull themselves, prone on a scooter board, through a 50-foot obstacle course consisting of around, through, and over, at least 2 times * Optional—practice this for time

Individual Performance Report

Name: _____ Date: _____

Current performance: _____

_____

Product scores: _____

Adaptations: _____

Future goals: _____

Short-term objectives: _____

■ SPATIAL AWARENESS ▨▨▨▨▨▨▨▨▨▨

Potential Modifications and Adaptations

Equipment	Rules	Environment	Instruction
__ Mats	__ Personal space	__ Visual boundaries	__ Peer tutor
__ Bean bags	__ Control speed	__ Sequence centers	__ Guided discovery
__ Balls	__ Right	__ Play stations	__ Proximity
__ Ropes	__ Left	__ Give and get	__ Feedback
__ Tunnels	__ Up	__ Exploration	__ Physical assistance
__ Hoops	__ Down	__ No music	__ Orientation
__ Scooters	__ Don't touch others	__ Limit noise	__ Verbal cues
__ Tires	__ Stay in boundaries	__ Solid colored walls	__ Brailling
__ Yarn balls	__ Mirror child's action	__ Large space	__ Stations
__ Balloons	__ Run around boundaries	__ Small area	__ Demonstration
__ Poly spots	__ Change positions	__ Bars	__ Explanation
__ Tape on floor	__ Airplane space	__ Steps	__ Small group
__ Sponge balls	__ Directionality	__ Tires	__ Problem solving
__ Flags	__ Make shapes	__ Different levels	__ Verbal command
__ Lined fields	__ Blindfolded	__ Lines on floor	__ Tactile discovery
__ Cones	__ Crawling	__ Indoors or outdoors	__ Intervener assistance
__ Beach balls	__ Staying on mats	__ Lights on or off	__ Cognitive cues
__ Whistle	__ Dribble low	__ Texture	__ Task cards
__ Music	__ Jump rope	__ Flags	__ Stations close
__ Pictures	__ Gender rule	__ Cones	__ Increase time
__ Mirrors	__ Changing direction	__ Equipment close together	__ Circuit stations
__ Carpet squares	__ Different levels	__ Uncrowded	__ Command

(continued)

(continued)

Equipment	Rules	Environment	Instruction
___ Footprints ___ Wands ___ Knee or elbow pads ___ Hula hoops ___ Scarves	___ Zigzag run ___ Run around bags ___ Group or individual ___ Limit number of steps ___ Fast or slow movement ___ Stay on spots ___ Stop on whistle ___ Stay arm length away	___ Mats for boundaries ___ Alter surfaces ___ Stations ___ Obstacle course ___ Little star in space	___ Hand guided ___ Shaping

Example 1: Body Awareness

Task	Spatial awareness
Task description	Obstacle course completion
Scale components	Show understanding of up, down, in, out, around, through, on, right, left, fast, slow, close, far, and others
Rubric level & color	**Rubric descriptors**
1-red	Student will participate in an obstacle course with 2 components, such as in (a hula hoop) and around (cones)
2-orange	Student will participate in an obstacle course with 4 components, such as in (a hula hoop), around (cones), on (a mat), and through (a tunnel)
3-yellow	Student will participate in an obstacle course with 6 components, such as those mentioned previously, up (steps), and down (wedge mat)
4-green	Student will participate in an obstacle course with 8 components, such as those mentioned previously, fast (over a swinging jump rope), and slow (over a balance beam)
5-blue	Student will participate in an obstacle course with 10 components, such as those mentioned previously, right (on a scooter board), and left (on a carpet square)
6-indigo	Student will participate in an obstacle course with at least 8 concepts, and name each one as completed (Can you do it with a partner?)
7-violet	Student will participate in an obstacle course with at least 10 concepts and name each one as completed (Can you do it with a partner?)
Specific adaptations	

Individual Performance Report

Name: _____ Date: _____

Current performance: _____

_____

Product scores: _____

Adaptations: _____

Future goals: _____

Short-term objectives: _____

■ TUMBLING

Potential Modifications and Adaptations

Equipment	Rules	Environment	Instruction
__ Mats	__ Two tumble mats	__ Gym floor	__ Guided discovery
__ Hula hoops	__ No boundaries	__ Covered with mats	__ Cognitive cues
__ Light medicine ball	__ No time restriction	__ No boundaries	__ Peer tutor
__ Radio	__ Start or stop with music	__ Stay on mats	__ One-to-one
__ Bean bags	__ Use general space	__ Limit distractions	__ Auditory cues
__ Balloons	__ Cooperation	__ Gymnasium	__ Small groups
__ Beach balls	__ Personal space	__ Smooth surface	__ Visual cues
__ Wedge mats	__ Use safely	__ Inside surface	__ Verbal cues
__ Railings	__ L test	__ Mirrors	__ Demonstration
__ Awards	__ No touching	__ Ropes	__ Physical assistance
__ Cones	__ Use all body parts	__ Railings	__ Shaping
__ Music	__ Spotting	__ Large boundaries	__ Task analyze
__ Poly spots	__ Gender rule	__ Color indicators	__ Small group
__ Carpet squares	__ Bumpers up	__ Equipment spread out	__ Direction
__ Scarves	__ Unlimited time	__ Mats around equipment	__ Indirect
__ Soft small balls	__ Animal walk	__ Elevated	__ Spotting
__ Ropes	__ Side roll/no forward	__ Bright boundaries	__ Task cards
__ Hoops	__ Balance	__ Tactile boundaries	__ Problem solving
__ Incline mats	__ Stunts with partner	__ Quiet	__ Brailling
__ Safety mats	__ Choose tumble area	__ Bright lights	
__ Ramps	__ Blindfold sighted	__ Padded walls	
__ Balls	__ Vary level of skills	__ Circuit	
__ Balance beams	__ Assist in skills	__ Obstacle	
__ Accordion tunnel	__ One person	__ Constructive	
__ Poles	__ Wait for turn	__ Colorful	
__ Tape	__ No pushing		
__ Sticks			

Example 1: Handstand

Task	Simple tumble: handstand
Task description	Student will perform a stable handstand in combination with different gymnastic elements
Scale components	(a) level of support (spotting, wedge mat), (b) type of performance, (c) number of performances
Rubric level & color	**Rubric descriptors**
1-red	Student will attempt a handstand with support, legs lifted off ground less than 90 degrees
2-orange	Student will perform a handstand, with a spot or wedge mat, for any amount of time, legs vertically above head
3-yellow	Student will perform a handstand, hold 1-5 seconds, against a wall, without a spot or wedge mat
4-green	Student will perform the handstand and hold 1 second, without a spot, wall, or wedge mat
5-blue	Student will perform a handstand or headstand, hold 3 seconds, and turn into a forward roll
6-indigo	Student will perform a headstand or handstand for 3-10 seconds independently
7-violet	Student will perform a headstand or handstand for 3-10 seconds independently, and will attempt to take one or more steps
Specific adaptations	

Individual Performance Report

Name: _____ Date: _____

Current performance: _____

_____

Product scores: _____

Adaptations: _____

Future goals: _____

Short-term objectives: _____

◼ TWISTER

Potential Modifications and Adaptations

Equipment	Rules	Environment	Instruction
__ Bed sheet __ Blanket __ Raised shapes __ Shapes in different textures __ Different colors __ Numbers in rows __ Letters in rows __ Braille spinner __ Large print spinner __ Tactile spinner	__ Use only hands __ Use only feet __ Use right and left __ Count number found __ Play with partner __ Change rules __ Limit space or objects to touch __ Add space or objects to touch __ Commands written __ Increase time allotted	__ Limit space __ Add space __ Limit distractions __ Add support staff __ Give commands on a board __ Lighting dim or bright __ Limit sound distractions __ Cues given (for example, light for right and left)	__ Demonstration __ Brailling __ Peer tutor __ Problem solving __ Teach signs for shapes, colors, and textures

Example 1: Twister

Task	Twister
Task description	Student will put hands and feet on correct shape or color using the correct laterality
Scale components	Twister from one hand only to using all four limbs on the correct placements consistently right hand on red, green, yellow, or blue; left hand same, right foot same, left foot same

Rubric level & color	Rubric descriptors
1-red	Student can correctly (right hands and feet, on correct shape, on command) play twister with verbal and physical assistance
2-orange	Student can place right hand on shape, on command, most of the time
3-yellow	Student can place right and left hands on correct shape, on command, most of the time
4-green	Student can place right and left hands and right foot on correct shape, on command, most of the time, without assistance
5-blue	Student can place right and left hands and right and left feet on correct shape, on command, most of the time, without assistance
6-indigo	Student can correctly place any body part on shape, on command, 4 out of 5 times
7-violet	Student can correctly play twister with peers, and can consistently assist others when they are having trouble understanding what to do in the game

Example 2: Twister

Task	Twister
Task description	Student will show range of motion of the shoulder girdle of more than 45 degrees in both directions
Scale components	(a) rotation, (b) right and left

Rubric level & color	Rubric descriptors
1-red	Student can turn shoulder girdle to either the right or left, less than 10 degrees
2-orange	Student can turn shoulder girdle to either the right or left, less than 15 degrees but more than 10 degrees
3-yellow	Student can turn shoulder girdle to both the right and left, less than 15 degrees
4-green	Student can turn shoulder girdle to both the right and left, less than 25 degrees but more than 15 degrees
5-blue	Student can turn shoulder girdle to both the right and left, less than 35 degrees but more than 25 degrees
6-indigo	Student can turn shoulder girdle to both the right and left, less than 45 degrees but more than 35 degrees
7-violet	Student can show range of motion of the shoulder girdle of greater than 45 degrees in both directions

Individual Performance Report

Name: _____ Date: _____

Current performance: _____

_____

Product scores: _____

Adaptations: _____

Future goals: _____

Short-term objectives: _____

7 *Sport Skills and Teamwork*

*P*urpose: The importance of sports and teamwork cannot be undervalued in secondary physical education. This framework of sportsmanship, basic skill, and problem solving will help students not only in class, but also in the world of work. Introducing these skills at the appropriate developmental level is essential for successful performance in adulthood.

Unit adaptations: There are many ways of adapting the curriculum for children with disabilities. It is imperative that the modifications for each child be specific to the child's needs. For example, if a child has spina bifida and uses a wheelchair, the skills would be adapted according to his needs, such as more bounces in tennis, more hits in volleyball, a bigger ball for soccer, or different rules for badminton.

Assessment options: In this section, rubrics have been provided for each unit, which evaluate the process or product of movements. The instructor can create his or her own rubrics in addition to using the rubrics given to enhance each unit. Instructors can also create checklists and rating scales and have students keep journals. These can all be included in student portfolios (see chapter 2).

■ BADMINTON

Potential Modifications and Adaptations

Equipment	Rules	Environment	Instruction
__ Larger racket	__ Points for landing in certain area	__ Wider net	__ Task analysis
__ Bright birdie	__ Use nondominant hand	__ Wider court	__ Feedback
__ Wiffle ball	__ Play to 5 or 7 points	__ Lower net	__ Demonstration
__ Tetherball	__ Unlimited bounces	__ Use music	__ Visual aids
__ Beeping birdie	__ Sign for stopping	__ Stations	__ Routine
__ Remove arm rests	__ Peer tutor helps child hit birdie	__ Proximity	__ Peer tutor
__ Balloons	__ Points awarded for hitting birdie	__ Reduce court size	__ Verbal cues
__ Fleece balls		__ Positive atmosphere	__ Physical assistance
__ Smaller racket	__ Shorter service line	__ Bright lights	__ Command style
__ Shuttlecocks	__ Shorter back line	__ Short, simple cues	__ Universal signs
__ Flip cards	__ 2 serves	__ Shorter court	__ Hand signals
__ Lower net	__ Rally points	__ Narrower sidelines	__ Reciprocal
__ No net	__ 2-hit rule	__ Short visual aids	__ Direct instruction
__ Shorter racket	__ No service box	__ Lighting	__ Repetition of strokes
__ Head	__ Alternate serve	__ Boundaries	__ In front of students
__ Colored birdies	__ Time limit	__ Markers of placement	__ Comfortable
__ Bigger birdies	__ Play games to 7	__ Change light accordingly	
__ Many birdies	__ Shuttle can't hit floor	__ Indoors or outdoors	
__ Shuttle	__ Only hit once	__ Decrease distractions	
__ Whistle	__ Stay in bounds	__ Small groups	
__ Strap racket to hands	__ Use sign language		

Example 1: Forehand

Task	Badminton: forehand shot
Task description	Student will hit a forehand shot in a badminton game situation
Scale components	(a) form, (b) number of performances, (c) placement
Rubric level & color	**Rubric descriptors**
1-white	Student will hit, with a forehand shot, a birdie thrown from 6 feet away
2-yellow	Student will hit a thrown birdie with contact out in front of body most of the time
3-orange	Student will hit a thrown birdie with contact out in front of body and a distinct weight shift forward, most of the time
4-green	Student will hit a thrown birdie with contact out in front of body, a distinct weight shift forward, and follow-through, most of the time

Rubric level & color	Rubric descriptors
5-blue	Student will hit a forehand, with proper form, from a toss, and get birdie over the net, 8 out of 10 times
6-brown	Student will hit a forehand, with proper form, during a game situation, and get birdie over the net, 7 out of 10 times
7-black	Student will hit a forehand, with proper form, during a game situation, and get birdie over the net, 9 out of 10 times
Specific adaptations	

Example 2: Serve

Task	Badminton: serve
Task description	Student will hit a serve in a badminton game situation
Scale components	(a) form, (b) number of performances, (c) success

Rubric level & color	Rubric descriptors
1-white	Student will serve the birdie from half-court
2-yellow	Student will serve the birdie from half-court, with contact out in front of the body most of the time
3-orange	Student will serve the birdie from half-court, with contact out in front of body and a distinct weight shift forward, most of the time
4-green	Student will serve the birdie from half-court, with contact out in front of body, a distinct weight shift forward, and follow-through, most of the time
5-blue	Student will serve the birdie from half-court, with proper form, and get birdie over the net, 8 out of 10 times
6-brown	Student will serve the birdie, with proper form, from the service line, during a game situation, and get birdie over the net, 7 out of 10 times
7-black	Student will serve the birdie, with proper form, from the service line, during a game situation, and get birdie over the net, 9 out of 10 times
Specific adaptations	

Example 3: Badminton Game Play

Task	Badminton: game play
Task description	Student will participate in a game of badminton
Scale components	(a) choice of shots, (b) percentage of successful shots

(continued)

(continued)

Rubric level & color	Rubric descriptors
1-white	Student will participate in a game of badminton, using the forehand and backhand shots correctly, 50 percent of the time
2-yellow	Student will participate in a game of badminton, using the forehand, backhand, drop shot, and overhand smash shot correctly, 50 percent of the time
3-orange	Student will participate in a game of badminton, using the forehand, backhand, drop shot, and overhand smash shot correctly, 75 percent of the time
4-green	Student will participate in a game of badminton, using the forehand, backhand, drop shot, and overhand smash shot correctly, 75 percent of the time, and getting the birdie over the net 50 percent of the time
5-blue	Student will participate in a game of badminton, using the forehand, backhand, drop shot, and overhand smash shot correctly, 75 percent of the time, and getting the birdie over the net 75 percent of the time
6-brown	Student will participate in a game of badminton, using the forehand, backhand, drop shot, and overhand smash shot correctly, 90 percent of the time, and placing the birdie in the desired spot 50 percent of the time
7-black	Student will participate in a game of badminton, using the forehand, backhand, drop shot, and overhand smash shot correctly, 95 percent of the time, and placing the birdie in the desired spot 75 percent of the time
Specific adaptations	

Individual Performance Report

Name: _____ Date: _____

Current performance: _____

_____

Product scores: _____

Adaptations: _____

Future goals: _____

Short-term objectives: _____

■ BASEBALL AND SOFTBALL

Potential Modifications and Adaptations

Equipment	Rules	Environment	Instruction
__ Beep ball	__ Set number of strikes	__ Guide rails	__ Peer tutor
__ Auditory balls	__ Set number of trials	__ Shooting	__ Physical assistance
__ Bright balls	__ 5 people in outfield	__ Carpet squares	__ Write out lesson
__ Tactile balls	__ Hit off tee	__ Shooting line	__ Verbal cues
__ Bell balls	__ Hit off ground	__ Tactile line	__ Proximity
__ Nerf balls	__ No tag-outs	__ Auditory lines	__ Universal signs
__ Wiffle balls	__ Tag-outs on bases	__ Cones	__ Brailling
__ Bells on bases	__ Ground pass	__ Ropes	__ Bright clothing
__ Buzzer on bases	__ Time limitations	__ Clap behind goal	__ Instructor in front
__ Radio	__ Boundary limitations	__ Bright lines	__ One-to-one
__ Fan	__ Throw ball out	__ Open space	__ Task analyze
__ Tee	__ Cooperation versus	__ Success-oriented	__ Slow down
__ Light bats	competition	__ Increase stimulation	__ Demonstration
__ Flat bases	__ Peer places ball	__ Intervener gives	__ Feedback
__ Very soft ball	__ Peer runs	continuous explanation	__ Indirect
__ Big ball	__ 2 bases only	__ On pavement	__ Direct
__ Light balls	__ Limited space	__ Number of players	__ Tandem run
__ Colored balls	__ Hit hanging ball	__ Shorter base distance	__ Play-by-play action
__ Gloves-mitt	__ Out in air or on bounce	__ More infield players	__ Sign language
different sizes,	__ No double play	__ Music	__ Task style
and textures	__ Play all positions	__ Number of bases	__ Trunk rotation
__ Smaller mitt	__ Basic rules	__ Shorter base path	__ Hand signals
__ Softer ball	__ Bat around	__ Closer pitcher's mound	__ Students not hitting,
__ Lighter ball	__ Tee ball	__ Shorter fence	work on catching
__ Velcro balls	__ 5-strike rule	__ Small space	__ Constant shaping
and gloves	__ Undefended	__ White baseline	__ Problem solving
__ Tether balls	__ 2 extra tosses to field players	__ Markers indicate base	__ Use first names
__ Bigger glove	__ All attempt activity	__ Indoors or outdoors	__ Shadow
__ Bigger bases	__ No strikeout	__ Use batting cages	
__ Safety base	__ 3 swings, not strikes	__ Sun not in eyes	
__ Helmet	__ Safety rules	__ Decrease distractions	
	__ Must pass ball	__ Eye contact	
	__ Use sign for score		
	__ Use flip cards		

Example 1: Ball Throw

Task	Baseball and softball: ball throw
Task description	Student will throw the ball from shortstop to first base
Scale components	(a) form of throw, (b) distance, (c) accuracy

(continued)

(continued)

Rubric level & color	Rubric descriptors
1-white	Student can throw ball from shortstop position to second base most of the time
2-yellow	Student can throw ball with opposite-foot step, weight shift, hip rotation, and a follow-through across the body, from shortstop position to second base, most of the time
3-orange	Student can throw a ball, with proper form, from shortstop position to second base, 75 percent of the time
4-green	Student can throw a ball, with proper form, from shortstop position to first base, 75 percent of the time
5-blue	Student can throw a ball, with proper form, from shortstop position to first base, 85 percent of the time
6-brown	Student can throw a ball, with proper form, from shortstop position to first base, so first base player can catch the ball, 85 percent of the time
7-black	Student can throw a ball, with proper form, from shortstop position to first base, so first base player can catch the ball, 95 percent of the time
Specific adaptations	

Example 2: Fielding

Task	Baseball and softball: fielding
Task description	Student will show proper form and skill in fielding the ball
Scale components	(a) proper form, (b) percent of stopped balls

Rubric level & color	Rubric descriptors
1-white	Students know ready position in the field and can show this 100 percent of the time
2-yellow	Students will keep knees bent and eyes on the ball most of the time the ball is hit to them
3-orange	Students will keep knees bent, eyes on the ball, and glove down on the ground, most of the time the ball is hit to them
4-green	Students will keep knees bent, eyes on the ball, glove down on the ground, body behind the ball, and non-glove hand covering the ball, most of the time the ball is hit to them
5-blue	Students will use proper form for fielding a ball, and will slide right or left to field any ball near them most of the time
6-brown	Students will use proper form for fielding a ball, will slide right or left to field any ball near them 75 percent of the time, and will stop at least 50 percent of the balls that come near them

Rubric level & color	Rubric descriptors
7-black	Student will use proper form for fielding a ball, will slide right or left to field any ball near them 95 percent of the time, and will stop at least 95 percent of the balls that come near them
Specific adaptations	

Example 3: Batting

Task	Baseball and softball: batting
Task description	Student will bat a ball from a tee and off a pitch
Scale components	(a) form, (b) hitting percentage
Rubric level & color	**Rubric descriptors**
1-white	Student can hit a ball off a tee, with shoulder to outfield and nondominant foot forward, most of the time
2-yellow	Student can hit a ball off a tee, with shoulder to outfield, nondominant foot forward, and weight shift to front foot, most of the time
3-orange	Student can hit a ball off a tee, with shoulder to outfield, nondominant foot forward, weight shift to front foot, ball contact in front of front foot, and follow-through with the bat, most of the time
4-green	Student can hit a ball off a tee, with shoulder to outfield, nondominant foot forward, weight shift to front foot, ball contact in front of front foot, and follow-through with the bat, 90 percent of the time
5-blue	Student can bat a ball, with proper form, from a pitch, contacting the ball 50 percent of the time
6-brown	Student can bat a ball, with proper form, from a pitch, contacting the ball 75 percent of the time
7-black	Student can bat a ball, with proper form, from a pitch, contacting the ball 75 percent of the time, and hit in desired direction 50 percent of the time
Specific adaptations	

Individual Performance Report

Name: _____ Date: _____

Current performance: _____

_____

Product scores: _____

Adaptations: _____

Future goals: _____

Short-term objectives: _____

■ BASKETBALL

Potential Modifications and Adaptations

Equipment	RulesEnvironment		Instruction
__ Auditory balls	__ Bounce pass	__ Bright boundaries	__ Peer tutor
__ Bright balls	__ Double dribble	__ Carpet squares	__ Physical assistance
__ Tactile balls	__ Undefended	__ Shooting line	__ Task cards
__ Bell balls	__ Time limitations	__ Tactile lines	__ Verbal cues
__ Buzzer basket	__ Boundary limitation	__ Auditory lines	__ Proximity
__ High basket	__ Free shooting	__ Cones	__ Write out lesson plan
__ Low basket	__ Throw-ins	__ Ropes	__ Brailling
__ Bright basket	__ Walk with ball	__ Clap under basket	__ Bright clothing
__ Whistle	__ Run with ball	__ Halve court space	__ Cognitive cues
__ Ball size	__ Cooperation versus	__ Surface adaptations	__ One-to-one
__ Ball texture	competition	__ Change 3-point line	__ Task analyze
__ Ball color	__ Space limit	__ Number of players	__ Slow down
__ Visual aid	__ Keep away	__ Smaller base line	__ Demonstration
__ Bigger rim	__ Vary bounces	__ Narrower court	__ Feedback
__ Softer ball	__ Different points for	__ Bright lights	__ Indirect
__ Cones	scoring at different	__ Colorful setting	__ Direct
__ Task cards	baskets	__ Use first names	__ Task style
__ Flip cards	__ Everyone touch ball	__ Low noise	__ Stop if wheelchair tips
__ Colored jerseys	__ Bounce before score	__ Boundaries	__ Problem solving
	__ Number of steps per pass	__ Nerf hoops and balls	__ Shadowing
	__ Extra step on layup	__ Gymnasium	
	__ 10-foot cushion	__ More than one game	
	__ At least 4 passes		
	__ Must pass ball to score		
	__ Nondominant dribble		
	__ Pass to buddy		
	__ 5 seconds for defense		
	__ "Go" cues start		
	__ No double dribble		
	__ 5 fouls, you're out		

Example 1: Dribbling

Task	Basketball: dribbling
Task description	Student will dribble a basketball around cones and inactive defensive players
Scale components	(a) form, (b) control
Rubric level & color	**Rubric descriptors**
1-white	Student will dribble in place, using fingertips at waist height, with ball contacting floor in front of (or to the outside of) foot on the side of the hand being used, most of the time.
2-yellow	Student will dribble while walking around 8 cones placed 5 feet apart, using fingertips at waist height, with ball contacting floor in front of (or to the outside of) foot on the side of the hand being used, most of the time
3-orange	Student will dribble with proper form, while walking around 8 cones placed 5 feet apart, controlling the ball 50 percent of the time
4-green	Student will dribble with proper form, while jogging around 8 cones placed 5 feet apart, controlling the ball 50 percent of the time
5-blue	Student will dribble with proper form, while jogging around 8 cones placed 5 feet apart, controlling the ball 75 percent of the time
6-brown	Student will dribble with proper form, while jogging around 8 cones placed 5 feet apart, controlling the ball 75 percent of the time with dominant hand and 50 percent of the time with nondominant hand
7-black	Student will dribble with proper form, while jogging around 8 stationary defenders placed 5 feet apart, controlling the ball 75 percent of the time with dominant hand and 50 percent of the time with nondominant hand
Specific adaptations	

Example 2: Foul Shot

Task	Basketball: foul shot
Task description	Student will shoot foul shots from the foul line
Scale components	(a) form, (b) accuracy
Rubric level & color	**Rubric descriptors**
1-white	Student will attempt to shoot foul shot from 5 feet in front of the foul line
2-yellow	Student will face the basket from 5 feet in front of the foul line, knees bent, dominant hand palm up under ball, and nondominant hand supporting ball from side, most of the time

(continued)

(continued)

Rubric level & color	Rubric descriptors
3-orange	Student will face the basket from 5 feet in front of the foul line, knees bent, dominant hand palm up under ball, nondominant hand supporting ball from side, with knee and arm extension during the shot, most of the time
4-green	Student will shoot foul shot with proper form from the foul line
5-blue	Student will shoot foul shot, with proper form, from the foul line, and hit the rim most of the time
6-brown	Student will shoot foul shot, with proper form, from the foul line, and make 7 out of 10 baskets
7-black	Student will shoot foul shot, with proper form, from the foul line, and make at least 8 out of 10 baskets
Specific adaptations	

Example 3: Game Play

Task	Basketball: game play
Task description	Student will be evaluated on offensive skills during game play
Scale components	(a) use of passes, dribbling, and shooting, (b) ability to retain ball on offensive side or to score

Rubric level & color	Rubric descriptors
1-white	Student will properly use bounce pass and chest pass during game play
2-yellow	Student will properly use the triple threat, by obtaining possession and then dribbling, passing, or shooting, according to the appropriate option, 50 percent of the time
3-orange	Student will use the triple threat, by obtaining possession and then dribbling, passing, or shooting, according to the appropriate option, 75 percent of the time
4-green	Student will dribble around defenders and retain possession, complete passes, and shoot accurately, 50 percent of the time
5-blue	Student will dribble around defenders and retain possession, complete passes, and shoot accurately, 75 percent of the time
6-brown	Student will assist others in shooting by passing off for the shot 75 percent of the time
7-black	Student will properly use triple threat and display appropriate skills 95 percent of the time, with accuracy at least 50 percent of the time
Specific adaptations	

Individual Performance Report

Name: _____ Date: _____

Current performance: _____

_____

Product scores: _____

Adaptations: _____

Future goals: _____

Short-term objectives: _____

■ FOOTBALL (FLAG)

Potential Modifications and Adaptations

Equipment	Rules	Environment	Instruction
__ Bright Nerf ball	__ 2 flags on chair	__ Indoors or outdoors	__ Peer tutor
__ Longer flags	__ 3-foot cushion area	__ Small environment	__ Command style
__ 3 completions to get first down	__ More points for running	__ Wider field	__ Universal signs
	__ 10 seconds before rushing	__ Use cones	__ Demonstration
__ Bright cones	__ Rotate positions	__ Boundaries	__ Task analyze
__ Bright flags	__ Have to pass ball	__ Everybody included	__ Visual aids
__ Larger football	__ Basic rules	__ Shorter field	__ One-to-one
__ Pass patterns	__ No late hitting	__ Shorter goal post	__ Proximity
__ Whistle	__ Certain number of time-outs	__ Narrower field	__ Teach signs
__ Shorter flags		__ Closer goal post	__ Direct
__ Only one flag	__ Cooperation	__ Low noise	__ Small group work
__ Helmet	__ Alternate running	__ Surfaces proper	__ Lesson plan on board
__ Mouth guard	__ Must get both flags	__ No distractions	__ Clear explanation
__ Beeper balls	__ Blindfold half class	__ Sun not in eyes	
__ Velcro balls	__ Buddy catches		
__ Bright pinnies	__ 3 time-outs		
__ Soft balls	__ Smaller-sided games		
__ Task cards			
__ Flip cards			

Example 1: Defense

Task	Football: defense
Task description	Student will defend opponent in game of flag football
Scale components	(a) form, (b) proximity, (c) interceptions

Rubric level & color	Rubric descriptors
1-white	Student will slide sideways, run forward, run backward, and then slide again, for the distance of one football field
2-yellow	Student will practice guarding opponent by shadowing through zigzag drills at half speed, staying with opponent most of the time
3-orange	Student will practice guarding opponent by shadowing through zigzag drills at 3/4 speed, staying with opponent most of the time
4-green	Student will practice guarding opponent by shadowing through zigzag drills at full speed, staying with opponent 75 percent of the time
5-blue	Student will stay within 8 feet of opponent 75 percent of the time during flag football game
6-brown	Student will stay with opponent 75 percent of the time and intercept 75 percent of the balls that come near him or her during flag football game
7-black	Student will stay with opponent 80 percent of the time and intercept 75 percent of the balls that come near him or her during flag football game
Specific adaptations	

Example 2: Passing

Task	Flag football: passing
Task description	Student will pass to teammate while running
Scale components	(a) form, (b) distance, (c) accuracy

Rubric level & color	Rubric descriptors
1-white	Student can throw with proper form (step with the opposite foot, shift weight, rotate hip, and follow through) most of the time
2-yellow	Student can throw 10 feet, with proper form, spiraling the football, most of the time
3-orange	Student can throw 10 feet, with proper form, spiraling the football, to a stationary teammate, most of the time
4-green	Student can throw 10 feet, with proper form, spiraling the football, to a teammate running toward her most of the time

Rubric level & color	Rubric descriptors
5-blue	Student can throw 10 feet, with proper form, spiraling the football, to a running teammate 50 percent of the time
6-brown	Student can throw 10 feet, with proper form, spiraling the football, to a running teammate, 75 percent of the time
	Stick with descriptors of running toward and away for objectivity and clarity
7-black	Student can throw 10 feet, with proper form, spiraling the football, to a running teammate with a defender, 75 percent of the time
Specific adaptations	

Individual Performance Report

Name: _____ Date: _____

Current performance: _____

_____

Product scores: _____

Adaptations: _____

Future goals: _____

Short-term objectives: _____

■ GOLF

Potential Modifications and Adaptations

Equipment	Rules	Environment	Instruction
__ Larger heads	__ Limit distance	__ Uncluttered (no sand or ponds)	__ Explanation
__ Larger balls	__ Add distance	__ Limit distractions	__ Demonstration
__ Auditory balls	__ Count every other or every third hit	__ Predictable	__ Physical assistance
__ Brighter balls			__ Visual aids
__ Larger grip	__ Move ball to preferred spot	__ Braille description of course	__ Peer tutor
__ Shorter club	__ Pair up with buddy	__ Consistent	__ Command style
__ Hockey stick	__ Play in teams	__ Play on cloudy day	__ First names
__ String tied to ball and club	__ Play for fun with no score		__ Task style
	__ Frisbee golf		__ Problem solving

(continued)

(continued)

Equipment	Rules	Environment	Instruction
__ Golf cart with driver __ Lighter clubs __ Beeper balls __ Flags __ Plastic balls __ Larger shaft __ Small basket for hole	__ Make up own course __ At own pace __ Wait for command __ Points for certain area __ Take any number of shots __ No out of bounds __ Student not required to perform __ Mulligan redo __ Add 2 strokes __ 2 swings at hazard __ Shorter green flags __ Larger number for par __ Be quiet __ Personal space	__ Play at night with bright ball __ Practice at a range __ Supportive __ Music __ Directional arrows __ Targets are marked __ Positive atmosphere __ Short instruction __ Shorter fairways __ Closer tees __ Open field __ Cage __ Nets __ Larger holes __ Make smaller __ Decrease distractions __ Sun not in eyes	__ Allow practice __ Diagram course __ Task analyze __ Cooperative games __ Brailling __ Feedback __ Reciprocal __ Shaping __ Universal signs

Example 1: Drive

Task	Golf: drive
Task description	Student will drive a golf ball
Scale components	(a) form, (b) distance

Rubric level & color	Rubric descriptors
1-white	Student will attempt a drive shot with proper club
2-yellow	Student will attempt a drive shot, standing with shoulder to desired direction, feet shoulder-width apart, and knees bent
3-orange	Student will attempt a drive shot, standing with shoulder to desired direction, feet shoulder-width apart, knees bent, and holding club with the ten-finger grip, most of the time
4-green	Student will attempt a drive shot, standing with shoulder to desired direction, feet shoulder-width apart, knees bent, holding club with the 10-finger grip, shifting weight, and following through, most of the time
5-blue	Student will hit a drive shot, with proper form, 10-20 feet, most of the time
6-brown	Student will hit a drive shot, with proper form, 10-20 feet, in desired direction, 8 out of 10 times

Rubric level & color	Rubric descriptors
7-black	Student will hit a drive shot, with proper form, at least 20 feet, in desired direction, 8 out of 10 times
Specific adaptations	

Example 2: Putt

Task	Golf: putt
Task description	Student will putt a golf ball
Scale components	(a) form, (b) accuracy

Rubric level & color	Rubric descriptors
1-white	Student will attempt a putt, choosing the proper club 3 out of 5 times
2-yellow	Student will attempt a putt, choosing the proper club all the time, and standing with shoulder to desired direction, feet shoulder-width apart, and knees bent
3-orange	Student will attempt a putt, standing with shoulder to desired direction, feet shoulder-width apart, knees bent, and holding club with reverse overlap grip (index finger of the top hand overlaps between the little finger and the ring finger of the bottom hand; bottom hand palm covers the top hand thumb on the shaft) most of the time
4-green	Student will attempt a putt, standing with shoulder to desired direction, feet shoulder-width apart, knees bent, holding club with reverse overlap grip, shifting weight, and following through, most of the time
5-blue	Student will hit a putt, with proper form, 5-10 feet, most of the time
6-brown	Student will hit a putt, with proper form, 10-20 feet, in desired direction, 8 out of 10 times
7-black	Student will hit a putt, with proper form, at least 10-20 feet, in desired 5-foot square area, 8 out of 10 times
Specific adaptations	

Individual Performance Report

Name: _____ Date: _____

Current performance: _____

_____

Product scores: _____

Adaptations: _____

Future goals: _____

Short-term objectives: _____

■ GYMNASTICS

Potential Modifications and Adaptations

Equipment	Rules	Environment	Instruction
__ Mats all sizes	__ Cooperation	__ Lower bars	__ Spotting
__ Beam	__ Rubrics	__ Lower rings	__ Shaping
__ Horse	__ Have partner	__ Lower equipment	__ Peer tutor
__ Rings	__ Adequate space	__ Wider beam	__ Demonstration
__ Parallel bars	__ No shoes on mats	__ Music	__ Problem solving
__ Uneven bars	__ Loose-fitting clothing	__ Pictures	__ Face students
__ Ribbons	__ Spring board	__ Use names	__ Visual aids
__ Short horse	__ Varied distance	__ Shorter approach	__ Task analyze
__ Wedge mats	__ Physical assistance	__ Smaller space	__ Feedback
__ Safety at all times	__ Less floor events	__ Boundaries	__ Direct
__ Trampoline	__ Attempt all activities	__ Low noise level	__ Indirect
__ Balls	__ No activity without tutor	__ Large mat area	__ Clear
__ Whistle	__ Challenge by choice	__ Break down skill	__ Braille
	__ Personal best	__ Bright equipment	__ Independence
	__ No horseplay	__ Small groups	__ Verbal cues
	__ No flipping		__ Hand signs
	__ One at a time		__ Write out class plans
			__ Orientation

Example 1: Cartwheel

Task	Gymnastics: cartwheel
Task description	Student can perform side and front cartwheels 2 times in a row to each side, in combination with other gymnastic elements
Scale components	(a) support (spotting), (b) type of cartwheel, (c) number of performances
Rubric level & color	**Rubric descriptors**
1-white	Student will attempt a side or front cartwheel with limited success
2-green	Student will perform one of the cartwheels with or without support
3-orange	Student will perform both cartwheels without a spot
4-blue	Student will perform both cartwheels 2 times in a row

Rubric level & color	Rubric descriptors
5-brown	Student will perform both cartwheels 2 times in a row to nondominant side
6-black	Student will combine each of the cartwheels with other gymnastic elements in a series

Example 2: Handstand

Task	Gymnastics: handstand
Task description	Student can perform a stable handstand in combination with different gymnastic elements
Scale components	(a) support (spotting, wedge mat), (b) type of performance, (c) number of performances

Rubric level & color	Rubric descriptors
1-white	Student will attempt a handstand with limited success
2-yellow	Student will perform the handstand with a spot or wedge mat
3-orange	Student will perform the handstand and hold for 1 second without a spot or wedge mat
4-green	Student will perform the handstand, hold for 3 seconds, and turn into a forward roll
5-blue	Student will perform the handstand over into a bridge, with controlled step out (one leg over at a time), and hold for 2 seconds
6-brown	Student will perform a handstand, turning into a forward roll, in a pike position
7-black	Student will perform a backward roll into a handstand position and hold for 2 seconds

The latter rubrics are based on skill levels of nondisabled children, and on *milestones* usually required for skill development. However, what happens if the child does not fit into this scheme? We had a secondary school child with spastic CP and tetraplegia, with whom the teacher developed a gymnastic series of basic elements combined together with music to a final exercise. These elements included the knee-and-handstand, the kneestand, and the side roll. Here is an example of a rubric for one of these elements.

Example 3: Balance Tasks

Task	Gymnastics: knee-and-handstand for child with spastic CP and tetraplegia
Task description	Student can control balance on hands and knees while raising some body parts
Scale components	(a) laterality, (b) number of body parts raised

Rubric level & color	Rubric descriptors
1-white	Student will stand, stable, with both knees and hands on the mat
2-yellow	Student can raise less-affected arm and hand without losing balance

(continued)

(continued)

Rubric level & color	Rubric descriptors
3-orange	Student can raise less-affected knee and foot without losing balance
4-green	Student can raise more-affected arm and hand without losing balance
5-blue	Student can raise more-affected knee and foot without losing balance
6-brown	Student can raise the hand or arm and knee or foot of the less-affected side, without losing balance
7-black	Student can raise the hand or arm and knee or foot of the more-affected side, without losing balance
7-red	Student can raise the hand or arm and knee or foot of the opposite sides of the body, without losing balance
Specific adaptations	

Example 4: Squat Vault

Task	Gymnastics: squat vault
Task description	Student will perform a squat vault, landing with both feet, with good balance
Scale components	(a) form

Rubric level & color	Rubric descriptors
1-white	Student will stand on spring board, with hands 1 foot away on horse, jump 3 times, land on horse in squat position, and jump off horse on two feet
2-yellow	Student will repeat above skill with only one quick touch on top of the horse with feet before jumping down
3-orange	Student will take a running start with medium speed, jump from spring board 1 foot away to top of horse, land on feet, and jump down onto both feet, with control
4-green	Student will run from end of runway at moderate speed, jump on springboard 1 foot away from horse, squat over horse without touching, and land on both feet
5-blue	Student will run from end of runway at full speed, jump on springboard 2 feet away from horse, squat over horse without touching, and land on both feet
6-brown	Student will run from end of runway at full speed, jump on springboard 2 feet away from horse, squat over horse without touching, land on both feet, with control, and raise hands over head for finish
7-black	Student will run from end of runway at full speed, jump on springboard 2-3 feet away from horse, squat over horse without touching, land on both feet, with control, raising hands over head for finish, 4 out of 5 times attempted
Specific adaptations	

Individual Performance Report

Name: _____ Date: _____

Current performance: _____

_____

Product scores: _____

Adaptations: _____

Future goals: _____

Short-term objectives: _____

■ SOCCER

Potential Modifications and Adaptations

Equipment	Rules	Environment	Instruction
___ Auditory balls	___ Ground pass	___ Bright boundaries	___ Peer tutor
___ Bright balls	___ Timed dribble	___ Carpet squares	___ Physical assistance
___ Tactile balls	___ Undefended	___ Shooting line	___ Hand signals
___ Bell balls	___ Time limitations	___ Tactile lines	___ Verbal cues
___ Nerf balls	___ Boundary limitations	___ Auditory lines	___ Proximity
___ Bells on net	___ Free shooting	___ Cones	___ Signs
___ Buzzer on net	___ Throw-ins	___ Ropes	___ Brailling
___ Radio	___ Walk with ball	___ Clap behind goal	___ Bright clothing
___ Fan	___ Run with ball	___ Limit mobility	___ Discovery learning
___ Wheelchair	___ Cooperation vs. competition	___ Smooth surface	___ Task analyze
___ Front bumper	___ Peer place ball	___ Can be goalie	___ Slow down
___ Smaller goal	___ Free kicks	___ Music	___ Demonstration
___ Assigned area	___ Stay in assigned area	___ Watch film	___ Feedback
___ Ball size	___ Hands used for protection	___ Modify field size	___ Indirect
___ Soft ball	___ Pass to everyone	___ Cones in front of net	___ Direct
___ Wider goals	___ 5 passes	___ Stations	___ Task style
___ Bright goals	___ Space as a defender	___ Decrease distractions	___ Problem solving
___ Flags	___ No heading		___ Lane soccer
___ Pinnies	___ 5 dribbles		___ Smaller groups
___ Cones	___ Do defense for 5 sec.		___ Small sided games
___ Whistle	___ Pass before goal		
___ Bigger nets	___ Shooting zone equals score		
___ Shin guards	___ Minimum 3 passes		
___ Flip cards			
___ Ball on string			

Example 1: Dribbling

Task	Soccer: dribble
Task description	Student can dribble using both inside and outside of the foot against a defender
Scale components	(a) form, (b) velocity of performance, (c) radius of direction change, (d) number of defenders
Rubric level & color	**Rubric descriptors**
1-white	Student attempts to dribble with dominant and nondominant foot
2-yellow	Student dribbles with inside of each foot, through 10 cones set 7 feet apart, up and back, without losing the ball
3-orange	Student dribbles fast, with outside of each foot, through 10 cones set 7 feet apart, up and back, without losing the ball
4-green	Student dribbles fast, with inside and outside of each foot, through 10 cones set 5 feet apart, up and back, without losing the ball
5-blue	Student dribbles against a defender, with inside and outside of foot, for 30 yards
6-brown	Student dribbles against a defender, through 10 cones set 5 feet apart, up the field without losing the ball
7-black	Student dribbles against 2 defenders, for 30 seconds, within a 20-yard radius, using the inside and outside dribble, without losing the ball
Specific adaptations	

Example 2: Passing

Task	Soccer: pass
Task description	Student can perform an exact pass using the inside and outside of the foot to a standing and moving partner
Scale components	(a) form, (b) number of performances, (c) motion
Rubric level & color	**Rubric descriptors**
1-white	Student attempts to pass with dominant and nondominant foot
2-yellow	Student passes with inside of the foot, to a partner standing 10 feet away, using each foot 10 times
3-orange	Student passes with outside of the foot, to a partner standing 10 feet away, using each foot 10 times
4-green	Student passes with inside and outside of the foot, to a partner standing 20 feet away, using each foot 10 times

Rubric level & color	Rubric descriptors
5-blue	Student passes using only the inside of the foot, to a partner moving up and down the field, without losing control
6-brown	Student passes using only the outside of the foot, to a partner moving up and down the field, without losing control
7-black	Student passes to a partner 20 yards up field, leading the receiver on the run, keeping ball within 5 feet of the foot, 8 out of 10 times
Specific adaptations	

Example 3: Game Play

Task	Soccer: game play
Task description	Student can play and be an active participant in a soccer game
Scale components	(a) dribbling, (b) passing, (c) defense, (d) shooting (all performed consistently during a scrimmage or game situation)

Rubric level & color	Rubric descriptors
1-white	Student participates in a small game of 3-on-3, can demonstrate a dribble and a pass when on offense, and shows knowledge of defense when team is on defense
2-yellow	Student participates in a small game of 3-on-3, can consistently demonstrate a dribble and a pass when on offense, and consistently shows knowledge of defense when team is on defense
3-orange	Student participates in a 5-on-5 scrimmage, can consistently demonstrate a dribble and a pass when on offense, and consistently shows knowledge of defense when team is on defense
4-green	Student demonstrates all previous skills, can cut for a pass, and can shoot on goal when the shot is available
5-blue	Student demonstrates all previous skills, can consistently cut for a pass, and can consistently shoot on goal when the shot is available
6-brown	Student participates in a full-field game of soccer, with consistent offensive and defensive skills, for at least 10 minutes
7-black	Student participates in a full-field game of soccer, with consistent offensive and defensive skills, for at least 15 minutes
Specific adaptations	

Individual Performance Report

Name: _____ Date: _____

Current performance: _____

_____

Product scores: _____

Adaptations: _____

Future goals: _____

Short-term objectives: _____

■ TENNIS ▬▬▬▬▬▬▬▬▬▬▬▬▬▬▬▬▬▬▬▬▬

Potential Modifications and Adaptations

Equipment	Rules	Environment	Instruction
___ Larger rackets	___ More than 1 bounce	___ Like racquetball court	___ Peer tutor
___ Larger balls	___ Smaller court	___ Smaller play area	___ Smaller
___ Bells in balls	___ Bounce ball	___ Against wall	___ One-to-one
___ Bright colors	___ Modified serve	___ Music	___ Physical assistance
___ Lighter balls	___ Nondominant hand	___ Boundaries	___ Universal signs
___ Lower net	___ Points only to 5	___ Stations	___ Feedback
___ Straps for racket	___ Points for accuracy	___ Shorter court	___ Task analyze
___ Tether ball	___ 2 bounces	___ Cones	___ Verbal cues
___ Balloons	___ 2-step serve	___ Shorter net	___ Routine warm-up
___ Wiffle balls	___ Unlimited steps	___ No net	___ Task cards
___ Shorter racket	___ Bounce serve	___ Proper surface	___ Proximity
___ Smaller ball	___ Buddy stops ball	___ Doubles lines	___ In front of students
___ Brighter balls	___ Hit off tee for serve	___ Indoors or outdoors	___ Use names
___ Bigger ball	___ Slow down game	___ Sun not in eyes	___ Demonstration
___ Visual aids	___ Serve from back	___ Decrease distractions	___ Partner work
___ Lighter racket	___ Play only one set	___ Large space	___ Brailling
___ Whistle	___ No collisions		___ Goal of instruction
	___ Flip cards for score		___ Many verbal cues

Example 1: Forehand

Task	Tennis: forehand shot
Task description	Student will hit a forehand shot in a tennis game
Scale components	(a) form, (b) number of performances, (c) placement
Rubric level & color	**Rubric descriptors**
1-white	Student will hit a tennis ball, thrown with a bounce from 6 feet away, with a forehand shot
2-yellow	Student will hit ball thrown with a bounce, body turned sideways, making contact in front of body, most of the time
3-orange	Student will hit ball thrown with a bounce, body turned sideways, making contact in front of body, and distinctly shifting weight forward, most of the time
4-green	Student will hit thrown ball, body turned sideways, making contact in front of body, shifting weight forward, and following through, most of the time
5-blue	Student will hit a forehand, with proper form, from a toss, and get ball over the net 8 out of 10 times
6-brown	Student will hit a forehand, with proper form, during a game situation, and get ball over the net 7 out of 10 times
7-black	Student will hit a forehand, with proper form, during a game situation, and get ball over the net 9 out of 10 times
Specific adaptations	

Example 2: Serve

Task	Tennis: serve
Task description	Student will hit a serve in a tennis game
Scale components	(a) form, (b) number of performances, (c) success
Rubric level & color	**Rubric descriptors**
1-white	Student will serve the tennis ball from half-court
2-yellow	Student will serve the ball from half-court with shoulder facing the net, proper toss above head, and contact out in front of the body, most of the time
3-orange	Student will serve the ball from half-court with shoulder facing the net, proper toss above head, contact out in front of the body, weight shift, and follow-through, most of the time

(continued)

(continued)

Rubric level & color	Rubric descriptors
4-green	Student will serve the ball from half-court with shoulder facing the net, proper toss above head, contact out in front of the body, weight shift, and follow-through, and get ball over the net 5 out of 10 times
5-blue	Student will serve the ball from half-court, with proper form, and get ball over the net 8 out of 10 times
6-brown	Student will serve the ball from the service line, with proper form, during a game situation, and get ball over the net 7 out of 10 times
7-black	Student will serve the ball from the service line, with proper form, during a game situation, getting ball over the net 9 out of 10 times and in the proper service box 5 out of 10 times
Specific adaptations	

Example 3: Tennis Game Play

Task	Tennis: game play
Task description	Student will participate in a game of tennis
Scale components	(a) choice of shots, (b) percentage of successful shots

Rubric level & color	Rubric descriptors
1-white	Student will participate in a game of tennis using the forehand and backhand shots correctly 50 percent of the time
2-yellow	Student will participate in a game of tennis using the forehand, backhand, drop shot, and overhand smash shot correctly 50 percent of the time
3-orange	Student will participate in a game of tennis using the forehand, backhand, drop shot, and overhand smash shot correctly 75 percent of the time
4-green	Student will participate in a game of tennis using the forehand, backhand, drop shot, and overhand smash shot correctly 75 percent of the time, and getting the ball over the net 50 percent of the time
5-blue	Student will participate in a game of tennis using the forehand, backhand, drop shot, and overhand smash shot correctly 75 percent of the time, and getting the ball over the net 75 percent of the time
6-brown	Student will participate in a game of tennis using the forehand, backhand, drop shot, and overhand smash shot correctly 90 percent of the time, and placing the ball in the desired spot 50 percent of the time

Rubric level & color	Rubric descriptors
7-black	Student will participate in a game of tennis using the forehand, backhand, drop shot, and overhand smash shot correctly 95 percent of the time, and placing the ball in the desired spot 75 percent of the time
Specific adaptations	

Individual Performance Report

Name: _____ Date: _____

Current performance: _____

_____

Product scores: _____

Adaptations: _____

Future goals: _____

Short-term objectives: _____

■ TRACK & FIELD

Potential Modifications and Adaptations

Equipment	Rules	Environment	Instruction
__ Bright lane lines	__ Set number of trials	__ Bright boundaries	__ Peer tutor
__ Auditory start	__ Time limitations	__ Carpet squares	__ Physical assistance
__ Soft hurdles	__ Boundary limitations	__ Throwing line	__ Eye contact
__ Low hurdles	__ Guide runner	__ Tactile lines	__ Verbal cues
__ Ropes	__ Cooperation versus	__ Auditory lines	__ Proximity
__ Tethers	competition	__ Cones	__ Sign language
__ Sand pit	__ Limited space	__ Ropes	__ Brailling
__ Auditory jump	__ Clap in target areas	__ Jumping line	__ Bright clothing
boards	__ Form versus time	__ Success-oriented	__ Cognitive cues
__ Tactile jump	__ Look before throwing	__ Limited distractions	__ One-to-one
boards	__ Clear surface	__ Open and friendly	__ Slow down
__ Auditory high	__ Warm up	__ Safe, clean surface	__ Demonstration
jump	__ Help others	__ Water is accessible	__ Feedback
__ Various throwing	__ Wait for others	__ Long distance	__ Direct
objects	to finish	__ Short distance	__ Tandem run

(continued)

(continued)

Equipment	Rules	Environment	Instruction
___ Track	___ No jumping with shunts	___ Chalk lines instead of hurdles	___ Play-by-play action
___ Batons	___ Bigger ring for shot put	___ Wide vector	___ Inclusive
___ Mats	___ Throw in any manner	___ Obstacle course	___ Task style
___ Shot put	___ Lines closer to target	___ Indoors or outdoors	___ Command
___ Discus	___ Shorter fly zone	___ Music	___ Sequential
___ Weights	___ Adjust times	___ Controlled group	___ Activity analysis
___ Whistles	___ Shorter approach	___ Divided for safety	___ Guided discovery
___ Lanes	___ Head start	___ Larger lane lines	___ Use of first name
___ Score sheets	___ Checklist of activities	___ Smoother surface	___ Brailling
___ Bean bags	___ Ability grouping		___ Task analysis
___ Soft shot	___ Run time, not distance		
___ Task cards	___ No time on field events		
___ Soft discus	___ Throw with good technique		
___ Small shot put	___ Hand signals		
___ Light shot put	___ Run at own pace		
___ Whistle	___ No high jump bar		
___ Parachute for training			
___ Lighter disc			
___ Visual aids			
___ Tape measure			
___ Timing device			

Example 1: High Jump (Flop Approach)

Task	Track & field: high jump (flop approach)
Task description	Student will perform a high jump with moderate speed on the approach, obvious flow from the approach to the jump, leading the jump with the shoulders and head, all other body parts following, and landing on the upper back/shoulder area, over a 3-foot pole
Scale components	(a) flow, (b) form, (c) speed, (d) height

Rubric level & color	Rubric descriptors
1-white	Student utilizes slow speed on the approach and obvious nonflow from the approach to the actual jump, leads the jump with the side or feet, all other body parts following, and lands on a 2-foot-high pit mat
2-yellow	Student utilizes medium speed on the approach and obvious nonflow from the approach to the actual jump, leads the jump with the side or feet, all other body parts following, and lands on a 2-foot-high pit mat
3-orange	Student utilizes moderate speed on the approach and obvious flow from the approach to the actual jump, leads the jump with the side or feet, all other body parts following, and lands on a 2-foot-high pit mat

Rubric level & color	Rubric descriptors
4-green	Student utilizes moderate speed on the approach and obvious flow from the approach to the actual jump, leads the jump with the side or feet, all other body parts following, and lands on a 2-foot-high pit mat most of the time
5-blue	Student utilizes moderate speed on the approach and obvious flow from the approach to the actual jump, leads the jump with the shoulders or head, all other body parts following, and lands on a 2-foot-high pit mat (pole at the 2-foot mark)
6-brown	Student utilizes previous approach with the pole at the 2 1/2-foot mark
7-black	Student utilizes previous approach with the pole at the 3-foot mark
Specific adaptations	

Example 2: Hurdles

Task	Track & field: hurdles
Task description	Student will jump over regulation height hurdles using proper form
Scale components	(a) form, (b) height, (c) speed (optional)

Rubric level & color	Rubric descriptors
1-white	Student runs flat-footed during pre-flight, uses arms and legs on the same side to initiate flight, jumps over a plastic pole 1 foot high, and lands unbalanced
2-yellow	Student runs with mature form during pre-flight, uses arms and legs on same side to initiate flight, leads with one distinct foot, jumps over a plastic pole 1 foot high, and lands unbalanced
3-orange	Student runs with mature form during pre-flight, uses arms and legs on opposite sides to initiate flight, leads with one distinct foot, jumps over a plastic pole 1 foot high, and lands balanced
4-green	Student runs with mature form during pre-flight, uses arms and legs on opposite sides to initiate flight, leads with one distinct foot, jumps over a plastic pole 2 feet high, and lands balanced
5-blue	Student successfully jumps 1 regulation hurdle with mature form
6-brown	Student successfully jumps 5 regulation hurdles with mature form
7-black	Student successfully runs a hurdle race at 3/4 speed with mature form
Specific adaptations	

Individual Performance Report

Name: _____ Date: _____

Current performance: _____

_____

Product scores: _____

Adaptations: _____

Future goals: _____

Short-term objectives: _____

■ VOLLEYBALL ▨▨▨▨▨▨▨▨▨▨▨▨▨▨▨

Potential Modifications and Adaptations

Equipment	Rules	Environment	Instruction
__ Volleyball	__ No change	__ Tactile boundaries	__ Physical assistance
__ Larger ball	__ 1 bounce	__ Visual boundaries	__ Teach signs
__ Smaller ball	__ 2 bounce	__ Limit distractions	__ Peer tutor
__ Lighter ball	__ Play volleyball with a	__ Success-oriented	__ One-to-one
__ Beach ball	catch instead of hitting	__ Limit space	__ Task analyze
__ Balloon	the ball (also known	__ 1 game at a time	__ Slow down
__ Heavier ball	as newcomb)	__ People out of the way	__ Demonstration
__ Trainer ball	__ Walk with ball	__ All students help	__ Feedback
__ Raise the net	__ 3 passes	__ Communication	__ Task style
__ Auditory ball	__ 4 passes	__ Stations	__ Certified personnel
__ Wheelchair	__ Unlimited passes	__ Wall volleyball	__ Universal signs
__ Bright net	__ Serve closer to net	(Wallyball)	__ Model
__ Wall	__ Limited space	__ Nice flat surface	__ Constant encouraging
__ Spike machine	responsibility	__ Use videos	__ Command style
__ Remove arm	__ Cooperation versus	__ Decrease boundaries	__ Cognitive cues
rests	competition	__ Racquetball court	__ Verbal explanation
__ Rope	__ More than 1 hit	__ Keep on inside surface	__ Comfortable
__ Bench	__ Everyone must serve	__ Textured floor markings	__ Shadowing
__ Colored ball	__ Modify serve	__ Make signs or banners	__ Problem solving
__ Bright colored	__ Less skilled in front	__ Indoors or outdoors	__ Direct
tape	__ No rotation	__ Many games at a time	__ Verbal analysis
__ Flip cards for	__ Call name before		__ Indirect
score	passing ball		__ Reciprocal

Equipment	Rules	Environment	Instruction
__ Whistle __ Task cards	__ No jumping for people with shunts __ No-spike rule __ No-block rule __ Shorter service line __ Tutor may catch __ As many hits as want __ No-carry rule __ No punching ball __ Serve from anywhere __ Overhand or underhand __ Pay attention		__ Inclusive

Example 1: Serve

Task	Volleyball: serve
Task description	Student will hit a serve in a volleyball game
Scale components	(a) form, (b) number of performances, (c) success
Rubric level & color	**Rubric descriptors**
1-white	Student will serve the volleyball from half-court
2-yellow	Student will serve the ball from half-court, with shoulder facing the net, proper position of ball (held in nondominant hand in front of front foot), and contact out in front of the body, most of the time
3-orange	Student will serve the ball from half-court, with shoulder facing the net, proper position of ball, contact out in front of the body, weight shift, and follow-through, most of the time
4-green	Student will serve the ball from half-court, with shoulder facing the net, proper position of ball, contact out in front of the body, weight shift, and follow-through, getting ball over the net 5 out of 10 times
5-blue	Student will serve the ball from half-court, with proper form, getting ball over the net 8 out of 10 times
6-brown	Student will serve the ball from the service line, with proper form, during a game situation, getting ball over the net 7 out of 10 times
7-black	Student will serve the ball from the service line, with proper form, during a game situation, getting ball over the net 9 out of 10 times and in the desired area 5 out of 10 times
Specific adaptations	

Example 2: Bump

Task	Volleyball: bump
Task description	Student will hit a bump shot in a volleyball game
Scale components	(a) form, (b) number of performances, (c) success
Rubric level & color	**Rubric descriptors**
1-white	Student will bump a volleyball tossed underhand by a peer 8 feet away
2-yellow	Student, with both palms up, one hand lying on the other, and arms out straight, will bump a volleyball tossed underhand by a peer 8 feet away, most of the time
3-orange	Student, with both palms up, one hand lying on the other, arms out straight, and knees bent, will bump a volleyball tossed underhand by a peer 8 feet away, most of the time
4-green	Student, with both palms up, one hand lying on the other, arms out straight, knees bent, contact in front of the body, and follow-through, will bump a volleyball tossed underhand from a peer 8 feet away, most of the time
5-blue	Student, with proper form, will bump a volleyball tossed underhand by a peer from half-court, getting the ball over the net or to a setter 8 out of 10 times
6-brown	Student, with proper form, will move to bump a volleyball tossed anywhere on the court by a peer on the opposite side of the net, getting the ball back over the net or to a setter 8 out of 10 times
7-black	Student, with proper form, will bump a volleyball from anywhere on the court during a scrimmage situation, getting the ball successfully over the net or to a setter 7 out of 10 times
Specific adaptations	

Example 3: Volleyball Game Play

Task	Volleyball: game play
Task description	Student will participate in a game of volleyball
Scale components	(a) choice of shots, (b) percentage of successful shots
Rubric level & color	**Rubric descriptors**
1-white	Student will participate in a game of volleyball using the bump and set shot correctly 50 percent of the time
2-yellow	Student will participate in a game of volleyball using the bump, set, overhead smash, and dig shot correctly 50 percent of the time
3-orange	Student will participate in a game of volleyball using the bump, set, overhead smash, and dig shot correctly 75 percent of the time

Rubric level & color	Rubric descriptors
4-green	Student will participate in a game of volleyball using the bump, set, overhead smash, and dig shot correctly 75 percent of the time, and getting the ball over the net 50 percent of the time
5-blue	Student will participate in a game of volleyball using the bump, set, overhead smash, and dig shot correctly 75 percent of the time, and getting the ball over the net 75 percent of the time
6-brown	Student will participate in a game of volleyball using the bump, set, overhead smash, and dig shot correctly 90 percent of the time, and placing the ball in the desired spot 50 percent of the time
7-black	Student will participate in a game of volleyball using the bump, set, overhead smash, and dig shot correctly 95 percent of the time, and placing the ball in the desired spot 75 percent of the time
Specific adaptations	

Individual Performance Report

Name: _____ Date: _____

Current performance: _____

_____

Product scores: _____

Adaptations: _____

Future goals: _____

Short-term objectives: _____

■ WRESTLING

Potential Modifications and Adaptations

Equipment	Rules	Environment	Instruction
__ Head equipment	__ Different time	__ Bright boundaries	__ Task analyze
__ Visual aids	__ Levels of skill match	__ Stations	__ Demonstration
__ Mats of all sizes	__ Skill utilization	__ Soft surface	__ Guided discovery
__ No prosthetics	__ Pin counts as 1	__ Decrease boundaries	__ Cognitive cues
__ No wheelchairs	__ No shunts	__ Gymnasium	__ Problem solving

(continued)

(continued)

Equipment	Rules	Environment	Instruction
___ Wrestling shoes	___ No spinal injuries	___ Bright lights	___ Minimize instruction
___ Soft mat	___ Control position	___ Short, simple cues	___ Verbal cues
___ Shorter ropes	___ 5-count equals a pin	___ Technique posters	___ Small groups
___ Shorter jump ropes	___ No half nelson	___ Safety procedures	___ Physical assistance
___ Smaller stationary	___ No fireman's carry	posted	___ Personal cues
bike	___ 2 points	___ Cones	___ Brailling
___ Blindfold	___ Large number cards	___ Lesser-load work	___ Command style
___ Tackle dummy	___ Time limit	___ Padded wall	___ Shaping
___ Use videos	___ Slow down pace	___ Proper clothing	___ Reciprocal
___ TV and VCR	___ Contain no inner circle	___ Clear boundaries	___ Peer tutor
___ Elbow and	___ Have peer tutor	___ Warmer room	___ Inclusive
knee pads	___ No body slamming	___ Lower ceiling	
___ Whistle	___ No choke holds	___ Mirrors	
___ Timer	___ No arm bars		
___ Task cards	___ Stop when told		
___ Flip cards	___ No "trash talking"		

Example 1: Arm-Bar Takedown (Bottom Position)

Task	Wrestling: arm-bar takedown from bottom position
Task description	From the kneeling position, the wrestler makes a two-handed wrist lock on the top person's right hand, brings the opponent into the body, wraps right arm over opponent's arm, uses body weight in opposition to the opponent's, rolls to the right side, and maintains grip on the wrist throughout (done within 5 seconds)
Scale components	(a) weight transfer, (b) weight opposition, (c) rolling, (d) speed
Rubric level & color	**Rubric descriptors**
1-white	From the kneeling position, the student makes a two-handed wrist lock on the top person's right hand, uses body weight in opposition to the opponent's, and rolls to the right side
2-yellow	From the kneeling position, the student makes a two-handed wrist lock on the top person's right hand, uses body weight in opposition to the opponent's, rolls to the right side, and maintains grip throughout
3-orange	From the kneeling position, the student makes a two-handed wrist lock on the top person's right hand, brings arm into the body, uses body weight in opposition to the opponent's, rolls to the right side, and maintains grip throughout
4-green	From the kneeling position, the student makes a two-handed wrist lock on the top person's right hand, brings arm into the body, wraps right arm over opponent's, uses body weight in opposition to the opponent's, rolls to the right side, and maintains grip throughout

Rubric level & color	Rubric descriptors
5-blue	Student performs a proper takedown in less than 15 seconds
6-brown	Student performs a proper takedown in less than 10 seconds
7-black	Student performs a proper takedown in less than 5 seconds
Specific adaptations	

Individual Performance Report

Name: _____ Date: _____

Current performance: _____

_____

Product scores: _____

Adaptations: _____

Future goals: _____

Short-term objectives: _____

8 Health and Fitness

P*urpose:* The importance of fitness skills and activities cannot be overlooked at any age. A basic fitness level is vital to enjoyment of physical activity and sport. In addition, possessing adequate fitness will ward off heart disease, high cholesterol, the potential for diabetes, and obesity. Introducing fitness skills at the appropriate developmental level is essential for successful performance throughout life.

Unit adaptations: There are many ways of adapting the fitness curriculum for children with disabilities. It is imperative that the modifications for each child be specific to his or her current fitness needs. For example, if a child is blind, he may use a guidewire or guide with a tether when running, a tandem bike when riding, and a long pole with a ball on the end (*bonker*) to signal the end of a lane when swimming.

Assessment options: In this section, rubrics that evaluate the process or product of movements are provided for each unit. The instructor can also use the Brockport Physical Fitness Test for assessment (see chapter 2).

AEROBICS

Potential Modifications and Adaptations

Equipment	Rules	Environment	Instruction
__ Lower steps	__ Shorter movements	__ Flat surface	__ Repetition
__ Light weights	__ Keep moving	__ Accessible	__ Peer tutor
__ Modify weights	__ Cooperation	__ Least restrictive	__ Partner up
__ Stereo	__ Grades based on	environment	__ Demonstration
__ Lines on floor	effort	__ Inclusive	__ Command
__ Poly spots	__ Go at own pace	__ Space	__ Physical assistance
__ Ribbon	__ Modify movements	__ Bright boundaries	__ Cardio workout
__ Scarves	__ Be creative	__ Spots mark places	__ Visual aids
__ Television	__ Work together	__ Large room	__ Shadowing
__ Stretch bands	__ 4 beats	__ Quiet	__ Verbal cues
__ Step on mat	__ Change complexity	__ Close to instructor	__ Task analyze
__ Matless	__ Slower beat	__ Closed gym	__ Brailling
__ Task cards	__ Low impact	__ Scheduled	__ Feedback
__ Mirrors	__ Number of steps	__ Slower steps	__ One-to-one
__ Lights	__ Time	__ Slower tempo	__ Reinforce
	__ 8-count beat	__ Smaller group	__ Lesson plan on board
	__ Work side by side	__ Steps by the wall	
	__ Respect classmates	__ Limit distractions	
		__ Indoors or outdoors	
		__ Blinking lights to beat	

Example 1: Basic Aerobic Workout

Task	Aerobics: basic workout
Task description	Student will participate in a 30- to 45-minute aerobics class
Scale components	(a) ability to execute the skill that is demonstrated, (b) keeping up a 1/8 beat, (c) duration of continuous exercise
Rubric level & color	**Rubric descriptors**
1-white	Student will be able to execute 3-4 aerobic moves with no music, as demonstrated by the instructor
2-yellow	Student will be able to execute 5-8 aerobic moves with no music, as demonstrated by the instructor
3-orange	Student will be able to execute at least 8 aerobic moves with music, as demonstrated by the instructor, to a 1/4 count, for 10 minutes continuously
4-green	Student will be able to execute at least 10 aerobic moves with music, as demonstrated by the instructor, to a 1/4 count, for 15 minutes continuously

Rubric level & color	Rubric descriptors
5-blue	Student will be able to execute at least 10 aerobic moves with music, as demonstrated by the instructor, to a 1/8 count, for 20 minutes continuously
6-brown	Student will be able to execute any number of moves with music, as demonstrated by the instructor, to a 1/8 count, for 20-30 minutes continuously
7-black	Student will be able to execute any number of moves with music, as demonstrated by the instructor, to a 1/8 count, for 30-45 minutes continuously * Optional—student could lead all or part of the workout
Specific adaptations	

Individual Performance Report

Name: _____ Date: _____

Current performance: _____

_____

Product scores: _____

Adaptations: _____

Future goals: _____

Short-term objectives: _____

■ AQUATICS AND SWIMMING

Potential Modifications and Adaptations

Equipment	Rules	Environment	Instruction
__ Pool	__ General space	__ Boundaries	__ Guided discovery
__ Hula hoops	__ Respect others	__ Shallow end of pool	__ Braille out strokes
__ Kickboards	__ No rough play	__ Limit distractions	__ Peer tutors
__ Buoys	__ Listen to music	__ Mark off deep end	__ One-to-one
__ Fins	__ Large or small groups	__ Small space	__ Task analyze
__ Personal flotation	__ Cooperation versus competition	__ Large space	__ Physical assistance
__ Lane lines	__ All strokes	__ Lane assignments	__ Clear instruction
__ Deck rings	__ Floating	__ Tactile	__ Brailling
__ Inner tubes	__ Diving	__ Auditory	__ Proximity
__ Rafts	__ Surface diving	__ Bright tape	__ Demonstration
__ Mats	__ Breath control	__ Roped areas	__ Feedback
		__ Padding	__ Task style

(continued)

(continued)

Equipment	Rules	Environment	Instruction
___ Bright balls	___ Propulsion	___ Lights brighter or dimmer	___ Small group
___ Bell balls	___ Kicking	___ Warm water	___ Verbal cues
___ Radio	___ Arm stroke games	___ Clean deck	___ Visual aids
___ Extension pole	___ Object control skills	___ Bright room	
___ Whistle	___ Swim for time, not distance	___ Music	
___ Beach ball	___ No diving in shallow	___ Supervised out of water	
___ Rescue tube	___ Lifeguard on duty	___ No obstacles	
___ Waist floaties	___ No diving	___ Quiet	
___ Transfer device	___ No running	___ Keep deck dry	
___ Safety devices	___ No jewelry	___ Side of pool	
___ Flippers	___ Long hair pulled back	___ Positive	
___ Sinking objects	___ Learn first aid	___ Indoors or outdoors	
___ Chair lift	___ Buddy system		
___ Goggles	___ Make shapes		
___ Aqua gloves	___ No splashing		
___ Aqua jogger	___ No gum		
___ Snorkels	___ Supine position		
___ Aqua socks	___ Peer help for 10 minutes		
___ Noodles	___ Time differences		
___ Bonker	___ Hands to oneself		

*For aquatics assessment, please see appendix D.

Example 1: Distance Swim

Task	Aquatics and swimming: distance swim
Task description	Student will swim and increase distance as much as possible
Scale components	(a) distance, (b) timing (optional)
Rubric level & color	**Rubric descriptors**
1-white	Student will swim 200 yards with any stroke, stopping when necessary
2-yellow	Student will swim 250 yards with any stroke, stopping when necessary
3-orange	Student will swim 300 yards with any stroke, stopping when necessary
4-green	Student will swim 350 yards with any stroke, stopping when necessary
5-blue	Student will swim 400 yards with any stroke, stopping when necessary
6-brown	Student will swim 450 yards with any stroke, stopping when necessary
7-black	Student will swim at least 500 yards with any stroke, stopping when necessary * Optional—time decreases with practice of 500 yards
Specific adaptations	

Individual Performance Report

Name: _____ Date: _____

Current performance: _____

_____

Product scores: _____

Adaptations: _____

Future goals: _____

Short-term objectives: _____

◼ CROSS-COUNTRY SKIING

Potential Modifications and Adaptations

Equipment	Rules	Environment	Instruction
___ Skis	___ Pulled in sled	___ Different trails	___ Relays
___ Poles	___ Stay in groups	___ Flags at trails	___ Timed effort
___ Sled	___ Help others	___ Wish for snow	___ Discuss hypothermia
___ Rollerblades	___ Follow trails	___ Use gyms if no snow	___ Use signs
___ Scooters	___ No snowball fights	___ Go for distance	___ Small groups
___ Sit skis	___ Move slowly	___ Stations	___ Demonstration
___ NordicTrack	___ Everyone skis	___ Flat or smooth	___ Proximity
___ Cones	___ Peer buddy	___ Already made tracks	___ Command style
___ Shorter poles	___ Alternative trail	___ Slight decline	___ Follow leader
___ Shorter skis	___ Half distance	___ Length of trails	___ Peer tutor
___ Tow rope	___ Head start	___ Different snow	___ Physical assistance
___ Lighter skis	___ Time constraints	___ Open space	___ Progression
___ Proper clothing	___ Group leader	___ Time of day	___ Braille
___ Sunglasses	___ Personal space	___ Smaller hills	___ Guided discovery
___ Ski tip attachment	___ Bells on skis	___ Shorter trails	___ Direct
___ Ski boots	___ Work at own ability	___ Trail markers	___ Indirect
___ Screwdriver	___ Not too fast	___ Auditory environment	___ Inclusive
___ Task cards	___ Peer tutor help	___ Not too cold	___ Task analyze
	___ No jumping		___ Problem solving
	___ Stay on trails		

Example 1: Cross Country Traditional Stride

Task	Cross country skiing: traditional stride
Task description	Student will ski traditional stride for at least 20 feet consecutively without falling
Scale components	(a) form, (b) control
Rubric level & color	**Rubric descriptors**
1-white	Student can stand with poles in ground and move legs back and forth 1-5 times without losing balance
2-yellow	Student can step with left foot and a right-pole push and glide on both skis one time with control
3-orange	Student can step with left foot and a right-pole push and glide, then step with right foot and a left-pole push and glide, on both skis, one time, each with control
4-green	Student can continue stepping and gliding on flat surface for 10 feet with control
5-blue	Student can continue stepping and gliding on flat surface for 100 yards with control
6-brown	Student can continue stepping and gliding routine on slightly inclined surface for 100 yards with control
7-black	Student can continue stepping and gliding routine on a varied inclined surface for at least 100 yards with control
Specific adaptations	

Example 2: Cross Country Ski for Distance

Task	Cross country ski: distance
Task description	Student will cross country ski for distance
Scale components	(a) distance, (b) time (optional)
Rubric level & color	**Rubric descriptors**
1-white	Student can ski on a flat surface for 1/4 mile
2-yellow	Student can ski on a flat surface for 1/2 mile
3-orange	Student can ski on a slightly inclined terrain up to 1 mile
4-green	Student can ski on a slightly inclined terrain up to 1.5 miles
5-blue	Student can ski on a slightly hilly terrain with a few turns up to 2 miles
6-brown	Student can ski on a slightly hilly terrain with a few turns up to 2.5 miles

Rubric level & color	Rubric descriptors
7-black	Student can ski on a hilly terrain with a few turns up to 3.1 miles (5 kilometers) *Optional—student tries to decrease time on course
Specific adaptations	

Individual Performance Report

Name: _____ Date: _____

Current performance: _____

_____

Product scores: _____

Adaptations: _____

Future goals: _____

Short-term objectives: _____

■ FITNESS GAMES

Potential Modifications and Adaptations

Equipment	Rules	Environment	Instruction
__ Jump ropes	__ Freeze on number	__ Bright environment	__ Command style
__ Hula hoops	__ Use stair steppers	__ Solid color	__ Partner work
__ Sponge balls	__ Have times stations	__ Equipment setup	__ Group work
__ Bean bags	__ Follow instructor	__ Boundaries for each	__ Stations
__ Stair steps	__ No touching others	group	__ Guided discovery
__ Carpet squares	while in pool	__ Indoors or outdoors	__ Modeling
__ Poly spots	__ As many reps as possible	__ Level	__ Demonstration
__ Numbers on	__ Large personal space	__ Uncluttered	__ Aerobic
the floor	__ Blindfold sighted kids	__ Quiet	__ Peer tutor
__ Kick boards	__ Water breaks	__ Music	__ Braille
__ Life vests		__ Large space	__ Physical assistance
__ Running vests		__ Bright lights	__ Follow beat
__ Cones		__ Circuit training	__ Direct
__ Mats			__ One-to-one
__ Balls			
__ Dyna bands			

Example 1: Fitness Activities

Task	Fitness: timed activity
Task description	Student will participate in an aerobic activity such as biking, jump rope, step aerobics, weight circuit, or aerobic obstacle course for time
Scale components	(a) time (Heart rate can be monitored by use of heart rate monitors, taking pulse, or level of perceived exertion.)
Rubric level & color	**Rubric descriptors**
1-white	Student will continuously sustain 65-75 percent of target aerobic heart rate for 10 minutes
2-yellow	Student will continuously sustain 65-75 percent of target aerobic heart rate for 15 minutes
3-orange	Student will continuously sustain 65-75 percent of target aerobic heart rate for 20 minutes
4-green	Student will continuously sustain 65-75 percent of target aerobic heart rate for 25 minutes
5-blue	Student will continuously sustain 65-75 percent of target aerobic heart rate for 30 minutes
6-brown	Student will continuously sustain 65-75 percent of target aerobic heart rate for 35 minutes
7-black	Student will continuously sustain 65-75 percent of target aerobic heart rate for at least 40 minutes
Specific adaptations	

Individual Performance Report

Name: _____ Date: _____

Current performance: _____

_____

Product scores: _____

Adaptations: _____

Future goals: _____

Short-term objectives: _____

■ WEIGHT TRAINING

Potential Modifications and Adaptations

Equipment	Rules	Environment	Instruction
__ Enough space	__ No max weight	__ Accessible	__ Demonstration
__ Accessible	__ Replace equipment	__ Music	__ Peer tutor
__ Modified bars	__ Warm up	__ Video on proper technique	__ Command style
__ Hand grips	__ Proper breathing	__ Bright atmosphere	__ Buddy system
__ Weight belt	__ Follow own plans	__ Positive feedback	__ Shadowing
__ Equip-weights	__ Spotter	__ Padding on floor	__ Test standards
__ Towel	__ Proper form	__ Wheelchair accessible	__ Hand signs
__ Sneakers	__ Stretch	__ Acceptance	__ Visual aids
__ Bars and weights	__ Cool down	__ Safety rules	__ Verbal cues
__ Wooden weights	__ Isometric	__ Posters	__ Small groups
__ Light weights	__ Isotonic	__ Muscles used	__ Direct
__ Rubber weights	__ Isokinetic	__ Cushioned areas	__ Task analyze
__ No weights	__ Own pace	__ Texture of walls	__ Guided discovery
__ Stretch bands	__ Half sets	__ Large area	__ Correct technique
__ Gloves	__ Number of body parts	__ Minimize distractions	__ Problem solving
__ Straps	__ Always with partners	__ Welcoming atmosphere	__ Physical assistance
__ Shorter benches	__ Stop if it hurts	__ Indoors or outdoors	__ Brailling
__ Smaller machines	__ Personal space	__ Positive environment	__ One-to-one
__ Padded benches	__ Respect others		__ Shaping
__ Ankle weight			
__ Bright weights			
__ Carpets			
__ Nautilus			
__ Use of everyday objects			
__ Task cards			
__ Flags			
__ Stations			

Example 1: Bench Press

Task	Weight training: bench press
Task description	Student will lift the weight bar during a bench press, increasing the maximum amount of weight on the bench press by percentage of initial pretest maximum
Scale components	(a) weight increase
Rubric level & color	**Rubric descriptors**
1-white	Student will lift weight equal to pretest maximum
2-yellow	Student will lift weight 1-3 percent heavier than pretest maximum

(continued)

(continued)

Rubric level & color	Rubric descriptors
3-orange	Student will lift weight 4-6 percent heavier than pretest maximum
4-green	Student will lift weight 7-9 percent heavier than pretest maximum
5-blue	Student will lift weight 10-12 percent heavier than pretest maximum
6-brown	Student will lift weight 13-15 percent heavier than pretest maximum
7-black	Student will lift weight more than 15 percent heavier than pretest maximum
Specific adaptations	

Individual Performance Report

Name: _____ Date: _____

Current performance: _____

_____

Product scores: _____

Adaptations: _____

Future goals: _____

Short-term objectives:

CHAPTER 9

Recreation and Life Skills

Purpose: The importance of recreation skills cannot be overlooked at any age. Recreation and the ability to participate in enjoyable leisure-time activities are imperative for quality of life at school age and beyond.

Unit adaptations: There are many ways of adapting the recreation curriculum for children with disabilities. It is imperative that the recreation modifications for each child be specific to his or her needs. For example, a 13-year-old child with mild mental retardation was going to an in-line skating party. He had never done in-line skating before. With some physical assistance from his physical educator and slow, small steps using teaching cues, he became proficient enough to be independent at the birthday party!

Assessment options: In this section, rubrics that evaluate the process or product of movements are provided for each unit. The instructor can also use checklists, rating scales, and journals. These can all be included in the student's portfolio.

▪ BACKPACKING AND HIKING ▬▬▬

Potential Modifications and Adaptations

Equipment	Rules	Environment	Instruction
___ Smaller bags	___ Stay with group	___ Nature	___ Orientation
___ Maps	___ Know environment	___ Gym	___ Scavenger hunt
___ Compasses	___ No running	___ Fields	___ Progression
___ Water	___ Know basic first aid	___ Short distance	___ Clear instructions
___ Camp gear	___ Know what to do when lost	___ Shorter time	___ Peer tutoring
___ Bright flags	___ Don't touch plants	___ Accessible trails	___ Small group
___ First aid kit	___ No alternative trails	___ Shorter trails	___ Guided discovery
___ Extra medical	___ Drink or rest when needed	___ Daytime hours	___ Physical assistance
equipment	___ Peer tutor available	___ Nice weather	___ Brailling
___ Change of clothes	___ Half pace	___ Smaller hills	___ Safety
___ Plenty of fluids	___ Half course	___ Groomed trails	___ Task analysis
___ Nourishment	___ Short pack carrying	___ Shorter map table	___ Direct
___ Hiking boots	___ Buddy assistance	___ Boundaries	___ Indirect
___ Water bottle	___ Stay on path	___ Different trails	___ Compass reading
___ Proper clothing	___ Free hands	___ Ropes to guide	___ Problem solving
___ Lighter packs	___ No littering	___ No dangerous area	___ Group work
___ Walking stick	___ Identify poison ivy	___ Smooth walking path	___ Universal signs
___ Visual aids	___ Don't eat anything	___ Markers to guide	___ Verbal cues
___ Ropes		___ Rails on side of path	___ Demonstration
___ Whistle		___ Indoors or outdoors	___ Feedback
___ Toilet paper		___ Sun not in eyes	___ Map reading
___ Proper footwear		___ Decrease distractions	
___ Bright flags			
___ Trail markers			

Example 1: Backpacking and Hiking

Task	Backpacking and hiking
Task description	Student will hike with or without a pack
Scale components	(a) distance, (b) terrain, (c) weight and distance with a pack (optional)
Rubric level & color	**Rubric descriptors**
1-white	Student will walk on a flat trail in the woods with few roots and rocks for 1/2 mile
2-yellow	Student will walk on a flat trail in the woods with few roots and rocks for 1 mile
3-orange	Student will walk moderate hills with some roots and rocks for 1 mile
4-green	Student will walk moderate hills with some roots and rocks for 2 miles
5-blue	Student will walk terrain with 250- to 500-foot elevation with some roots and rocks for 2 miles

Rubric level & color	Rubric descriptors
6-brown	Student will walk terrain with 250- to 500-foot elevation with some roots and rocks for 3 or more miles * Optional: 10- to 25-pound pack
7-black	Student will walk terrain with 250- to 1000-foot elevation with abundant roots and rocks for 3 or more miles * Optional: 20- to 40-pound pack
Specific adaptations	

Individual Performance Report

Name: _____ Date: _____

Current performance: _____

_____

Product scores: _____

Adaptations: _____

Future goals: _____

Short-term objectives: _____

■ BOWLING ■

Potential Modifications and Adaptations

Equipment	Rules	Environment	Instruction
__ Bumper bowling	__ More tries	__ Directional arrow	__ Physical assistance
__ Plastic ball	__ Two hands if needed	__ Shorter distance	__ Hand signals
__ Rails	__ Can cross line	__ More pins	__ Use first names
__ Colored pins	__ Use proper steps	__ Keep scoring	__ Universal sign
__ Lighter balls	__ Throw 3 times	__ Guide rails	__ Modeling
__ Brighter balls	__ Spare equals strike	__ Ramps to roll ball	__ Verbal cues
__ Lighter pins	__ 2-hand roll	__ Bright lights	__ Brailling
__ Softer ball	__ Any number of steps	__ Short instruction	__ Peer tutor
__ Ramps	__ Partner games	__ Automatic scoring	__ Slow down
__ Lighter colored ball	__ Tutor recovers ball	__ Shorter lanes	__ Indirect
__ Balloons	__ Stand at line	__ Wider lanes	__ Demonstration
	__ 1-step approach	__ Sloped lanes	__ Shaping

(continued)

(continued)

Equipment	Rules	Environment	Instruction
__ Visual aid __ Task cards	__ No finger hole __ 10 frames __ Groups of 3	__ Have only 1 ball in ball return rack __ Boundaries __ Group setting __ Minimize distractions __ 1 person bowl at a time __ Indoors or outdoors __ Set up in gym	__ Feedback __ Command style

Example 1: Bowling

Task	Bowling
Task description	Student will bowl a bowling ball in a game
Scale components	(a) form, (b) accuracy

Rubric level & color	Rubric descriptors
1-white	Student attempts to roll the bowling ball
2-yellow	Student uses the 3-step approach and steps with the opposite foot most of the time
3-orange	Student uses the 3-step approach, swings ball from back to front, and steps with the opposite foot most of the time
4-green	Student uses the 3-step approach, swings ball from back to front, steps with the opposite foot, and releases the ball out front with a smooth transition most of the time
5-blue	Student uses proper form with a smooth release and hits the pins without rolling the ball in the gutter, 5 out of 10 times
6-brown	Student uses proper form with a smooth release and hits the pins without rolling the ball in the gutter, 8 out of 10 times
7-black	Student uses proper form and hits at least 3 pins, 8 out of 10 times
Specific adaptations	

Individual Performance Report

Name: _____ Date: _____

Current performance: _____

_____

Product scores: _____

Adaptations: _____

Future goals: _____

Short-term objectives: _____

■ CANOEING ■

Potential Modifications and Adaptations

Equipment	Rules	Environment	Instruction
__ Wider canoe	__ Know canoe	__ Water	__ Break down strokes
__ Paddles	__ First aid needed	__ Gym	__ Lifelong activity
__ Life preservers	__ Refer to swimming	__ Pool	__ Demonstration
__ Canoe pads	__ Safety from sun	__ Number of students	__ Small groups
for seat	__ Paddle on one side	in canoe	__ Orientation
__ Bathing suits	__ 2 people paddle	__ Calm pool	__ Relay races
__ Rowboat	__ No rocking boat	__ Acceptance	__ Direct
__ Water bottle	__ Gunneling	__ Accessibility	__ Peer tutoring
__ Flotation devices	__ Third man	__ Bright lighting	__ Brailling
__ Size of boat	__ Physical assistance	__ Time of day	__ Short instruction
__ Size of paddle	__ Alternate responsibility	__ Up or downstream	__ Feedback
__ Harness	__ Never leave buddy	__ Seat belt strap	__ Safety
__ Helmets	__ Never stand up	__ Boundaries	__ Guided discovery
__ Cushion	__ No splashing	__ Ponds	__ Reciprocal
__ Double-sided	__ No horseplay	__ Streams	__ Task analysis
paddle	__ No jumping	__ Sun not in eyes	__ Shaping
__ Sunscreen		__ Decrease distractions	__ Visual aids
__ Bigger handle			__ Command style
__ Task cards			__ Problem solving
__ Red flags			__ Universal signs
__ Rescue tubes			__ Verbal cues
__ Boundary markers			
__ Benches			

Example 1: Canoeing

Task	Canoeing
Task description	Student will enter canoe, paddle using two different strokes, and control direction of canoe in calm water
Scale components	(1) entry, (2) form, (3) control

Rubric level & color	Rubric descriptors
1-white	Student can enter and leave canoe safely from a dock or landing with some physical and verbal assistance
2-yellow	Student can paddle forward on one side
3-orange	Student can paddle forward on both sides
4-green	Student can paddle forward in beat with partner and attempt the J stroke
5-blue	Student can paddle forward in beat with partner and successfully use the J stroke
6-brown	Student can point and steer the canoe in the desired direction most of the time
7-black	Student can show control of the canoe by performing a controlled zigzag through the water
Specific adaptations	

Individual Performance Report

Name: _____ Date: _____

Current performance: _____

_____

Product scores: _____

Adaptations: _____

Future goals: _____

Short-term objectives: _____

■ DANCING

Potential Modifications and Adaptations

Equipment	Rules	Environment	Instruction
__ Wheelchair	__ Stay in own space	__ Flat surface	__ Peer tutor
__ Walker	__ Change beat count	__ Dry area	__ Move up and down
__ Cone	__ Adapt standards	__ Nothing on floor	levels with the dance
__ Forearm crutches	__ Boundary	__ Smaller dance floor	__ Task analyze
__ Floor mats	__ Cooperation	__ Music of choice	__ Direct
__ Wall mats	__ 4 count	__ Same-size partner	__ Demonstration
__ Props	__ Short steps	__ Mirror	__ Physical assistance
__ Poly spots	__ Walk to the beat	__ Floor texture	__ Shaping
__ Footprints	__ Different movements	__ Limit noise	__ Verbal cues
__ Slow tempo	__ Slow tempo	__ Bigger area	__ Brailling
machine	__ Mirror partners	__ Use poly spots	__ Feedback
__ Slow	__ Respect classmates	__ Clear boundaries	__ Music
movements		__ Lights to the beat	__ Explanation
__ Lummi sticks		__ Decrease distractions	__ Use cues
__ Carpet squares			__ Command style
__ Music			__ Task cards
__ Scarves			__ Universal signs
__ Slow music			__ Hand signals
__ Visual aids			__ Corrective feedback
__ Large stereo			__ Write out lesson plan
__ Lights			
__ Music with bass			
__ Slow down music			
__ Task cards			

Example 1: Electric Slide

Task	Dancing: electric slide
Task description	Student will perform an entire line dance with 8 other students on team
Scale components	(a) ability to keep to the beat, (b) independence
Rubric level & color	**Rubric descriptors**
1-white	Student can perform the moves to the line dance Electric Slide, with no music, in one direction, with demonstration and verbal cues
2-yellow	Student can perform the moves to the line dance Electric Slide, with music, in one direction, with demonstration and verbal cues
3-orange	Student can perform the moves to the line dance Electric Slide, with music, in two directions, with demonstration and verbal cues

(continued)

(continued)

Rubric level & color	Rubric descriptors
4-green	Student can perform the moves to the line dance Electric Slide, with music, in all four directions, with demonstration and verbal cues
5-blue	Student can perform the moves to the line dance Electric Slide, with music, in all four directions, with only verbal cues, for the entire song
6-brown	Student can perform the moves to the line dance Electric Slide, with music, in all four directions, independently, for the entire song
7-black	Student can lead line dance Electric Slide, with music, in all four directions, for the entire song
Specific adaptations	

Individual Performance Report

Name: _____ Date: _____

Current performance: _____

_____

Product scores: _____

Adaptations: _____

Future goals: _____

Short-term objectives: _____

■ FISHING

Potential Modifications and Adaptations

Equipment	Rules	Environment	Instruction
__ Bamboo pole	__ From sitting	__ Calm water	__ Physical assistance
__ Velcro glove	__ No cast	__ No ledge to water	__ Demonstration
__ Short pole	__ Multiple tries for cast	__ Stocked pond	__ Assist with fish
__ Pole holder in belt	__ From boat with fixed chair	__ Few distractions	__ Peer tutor
__ Auto cast on pole	__ No time limit	__ Music or talking	__ Assist with baiting
__ Net to get fish			
__ Holder for pole			

Example 1: Casting

Task	Fishing: casting
Task description	Student will cast the fishing line with bait
Scale components	(a) skills, (b) independence, (c) distance of the cast
Rubric level & color	**Rubric descriptors**
1-white	Student can bait own hook with verbal prompting and some physical assistance
2-yellow	Student can bait own hook independently, and can bring rod back and cast forward without allowing reel to release
3-orange	Student can release the reel and get the line out by bringing rod across the body, most of the time
4-green	Student can release the reel, cast the line from behind the shoulder, and follow through out front, with line and bait casting at least 10 feet, some of the time
5-blue	Student can release the reel, cast the line from behind the shoulder, and follow through out front, with line and bait casting at least 10 feet, most of the time
6-brown	Student can release the reel, cast the line from behind the shoulder, and follow through out front, with line and bait casting at least 10 feet, 8 out of 10 times
7-black	Student can release the reel, cast the line from behind the shoulder, and follow through out front, with line and bait casting at least 15 feet, 8 out of 10 times
Specific adaptations	

Individual Performance Report

Name: _____ Date: _____

Current performance: _____

_____

Product scores: _____

Adaptations: _____

Future goals: _____

Short-term objectives: _____

■ MARTIAL ARTS

Potential Modifications and Adaptations

Equipment	Rules	Environment	Instruction
__ Mats	__ Mental imagery	__ Friendly	__ Shadowing
__ Loose clothing	__ No contact	__ Large space	__ Command
__ Visual aids	__ Personal space	__ Comfortable	__ Visual aids
__ Whistle	__ No kick below belt	__ Music	__ Demonstration
__ Books	__ Arm movements	__ Bright lights	__ Problem solving
__ Padding	while sitting	__ Flat, smooth surface	__ Emphasis on defense
__ Crutches	__ Lummi longer arm	__ Mirrors on walls	__ Self-defense
__ Lummi sticks	__ Modify moves	__ Acceptance	__ Peer tutor
__ Bright scarves	__ Right-left orientation	__ Posters	__ Direct
__ Smaller dummy	__ Move at own pace	__ Smaller boundaries	__ Brailling
__ Head gear	__ Two-step cushion	__ Locate in front of class	__ Feedback
__ Mouth guard	__ Alternate strikes	__ Bright colors	__ Task analyze
__ Gloves	__ No outside talking	__ Low noise	__ Short
__ Use tubes	__ Use freeze	__ Indoors or outdoors	__ Guided discovery
instead of sticks	__ Switch partners	__ Gymnasium	__ Hand signs
__ Use body only	__ Bow before technique	__ Decrease distractions	__ Physical assistance
__ Boards	__ Talk through steps		__ Breathing
__ Task cards	__ Side by side with tutor		__ Verbal cues
__ Punching bags	__ No face techniques		__ Visualization
__ Props			

Example 1: Martial Arts

Task	Martial arts: general
Task description	Student will go through a series of martial arts moves on command
Scale components	(a) number of moves, (b) form, (c) level of independence

Rubric level & color	Rubric descriptors
1-white	Student will execute one martial arts move correctly with demonstration and verbal assistance
2-yellow	Student will execute two martial arts moves correctly with demonstration and verbal assistance
3-orange	Student will execute three martial arts moves correctly with verbal assistance
4-green	Student will execute four martial arts moves correctly with verbal assistance
5-blue	Student will execute five martial arts moves correctly with verbal assistance
6-brown	Student will independently execute at least six martial arts moves correctly

Rubric level & color	Rubric descriptors
7-black	Student will execute an entire martial arts routine independently
	*Optional—student may lead others through the routine
Specific adaptations	

Individual Performance Report

Name: _____ Date: _____

Current performance: _____

_____

Product scores: _____

Adaptations: _____

Future goals: _____

Short-term objectives: _____

■ ROCK CLIMBING

Potential Modifications and Adaptations

Equipment	Rules	Environment	Instruction
__ Helmets	__ Safety	__ Indoors or outdoors	__ Project adventure
__ Ropes	__ Trust	__ Go for time	__ Demonstration
__ Beaners	__ Communication	__ Challenges	__ Peer tutors
__ Harness	__ Proper commands	__ Target at top to climb to	__ Verbal cues
__ Hiking boots	__ Climb across, not up	__ Use rocks	__ Visual aids
__ Wall or	__ Unlimited time	__ Bright lighting	__ Guided discovery
mountain	__ Adjustable surface	__ Spotters	__ Physical assistance
__ Picks	__ 1 person at a time	__ Wheelchair accessible	__ Direct or command style
__ Belay	__ Normal/unchallenged	__ Texture of rocks	__ Feedback
__ Cargo net	(rocks close together	__ More hand holds	__ Problem solving
__ Ladder	and simply placed)	__ Sloped walls	__ Safety
__ Stall bars	__ Belayer takes	__ Boundaries for height	__ Task analysis
__ Tandem belt	most of weight	__ Lower climbs	__ Inclusive
__ Smaller harness	__ Climb side by side	__ Safe climbs	__ Indirect
__ Smaller ropes	__ Double-check equipment	__ Good atmosphere	__ One-to-one
__ Smaller beaner	__ Always listen to cues	__ Sun not in eyes	__ Progress with height
__ Gloves	__ Only go comfortably	__ Decrease distractions	__ Small groups

(continued)

(continued)

Equipment	Rules	Environment	Instruction
__ Boots __ Safety lines __ High ropes course __ Low ropes course __ Whistle __ Task cards __ Red flags	__ Positively encourage __ State safety cues __ Always have buddy __ Wear proper clothing __ Go at own pace		__ Proper technique __ Harness in *c* position __ Review safety __ Lesson on board

Example 1: Basic Rock Climbing

Task	Rock climbing: basic (30-foot wall)
Task description	Student will climb a 30-foot rock wall with harness and helmet
Scale components	(a) preparation, (b) attempts at climbing, (c) descent
Rubric level & color	**Rubric descriptors**
1-white	Student can put on harness and helmet with assistance
2-yellow	Student can put on harness and helmet and understands the safety terminology to begin climbing
3-orange	Student attempts to pull body up with both hands up to 10 feet and climbs down
4-green	Student attempts to pull body up with both hands and feet up to 10 feet and climbs down
5-blue	Student uses both hands and feet, climbs 10-20 feet, and attempts the backward fall
6-brown	Student uses both hands and feet, climbs 10-20 feet, and properly executes the backward fall
7-black	Student uses both hands and feet, climbs 20-30 feet, and properly executes the backward fall
Specific adaptations	

Individual Performance Report

Name: _____ Date: _____

Current performance: _____

_____

Product scores: _____

Adaptations: _____

Future goals: _____

Short-term objectives: _____

■ IN-LINE SKATING AND SKATING ■

Potential Modifications and Adaptations

Equipment	Rules	Environment	Instruction
__ Velcro skates __ Brakes (front and back) __ Wrist and knee pads __ Helmet __ Trash can on wheels for support __ Shopping cart for support __ Walker on wheels __ Tether __ Bar held by peer __ Hula hoop held by peer	__ Skate slow __ Skate forward __ Skate backward __ Skate in a circle __ Skate with partner __ Obstacle course __ Skate for distance __ Skate for time __ Skate and dance __ Roller hockey __ Skate for transportation	__ Smooth surface __ Soft surface __ Inclined surface __ Limited space __ Larger space __ Challenge using obstacles __ Limited people in the way __ Supportive	__ Explanation __ Demonstration __ Physical assistance __ Problem solving __ Guided discovery __ Peer tutor __ Small group __ One-to-one __ Intervener explanation

Example 1: In-Line Skating and Skating

Task	In-line skating and skating
Task description	Student will in-line skate or skate in different directions, maintaining control
Scale components	(a) skill ability, (b) balance and control, (c) task complexity
Rubric level & color	**Rubric descriptors**
1-white	Student can skate forward, close to railing or wall, without falling, for 5 minutes
2-yellow	Student can brake, using the brake at will, 4 out of 5 times
3-orange	Student can skate forward on one foot, right, then left, then right, for 20 feet without losing balance, 4 out of 5 times
4-green	Student can skate in a circle 10 to 20 feet in diameter, clockwise and counterclockwise
5-blue	Student can skate backward for 20 feet without losing balance

(continued)

(continued)

Rubric level & color	Rubric descriptors
6-brown	Student can skate backward in a 10- to 20-foot circle once
7-black	Student can skate forward and change to backward while moving, in a straight line and in a circle, and can stop on command without losing balance, 4 out of 5 times
Specific adaptations	

Individual Performance Report

Name: _____ Date: _____

Current performance: _____

_____

Product scores: _____

Adaptations: _____

Future goals: _____

Short-term objectives: _____

A Disabilities in Kid Terms

This section contains definitions of many disabilities in terms easily understood by children. Each definition includes a description of the disability, some common characteristics kids may see in that child, and what they can do to make sure that child feels included in his or her educational setting.

It is important to note that instructors should emphasize similarities as well as differences. Instructors can easily think of similarities, but the following example demonstrates the presentation of similarities for each child.

The instructor might tell students, "You can make sure your friend is included in games and activities in your neighborhood or on the playground by adapting the equipment, the playing area, or the rules. He is just like you in many ways. He likes to play with his friends, eat ice cream, go to games, and be included in a group. You can help him feel good about himself by understanding who he is and what he needs. He will do the same for you if you give him a chance."

Arthrogryposis

- Children with arthrogryposis have a difficult time bending their arms and legs.
- They were born with very stiff joints. Their knees, wrists, elbows, ankles, and shoulders are very stiff in everything they do.
- They have a hard time walking, moving, eating, dressing, and playing.
- Some kids may walk with crutches, a walker, or a wheelchair.
- They may be able to push their own chairs, they may need help pushing the chair, or they may use an electric wheelchair.
- Most of the time these kids are able to think and talk just like anyone else.
- Sometimes you may need to be patient when they talk so that you can understand them.

Inclusion Ideas

- You can help these kids by pushing their chairs if they need you to, waiting for them if they walk a little slowly, or helping them put their coats on if they need you to.
- You may need to help them get things they can't get themselves, write down what they are thinking if they can't, or assist them in playing volleyball by helping their hands hit the ball.

- Other kids may look at them funny or tease them because of the way they look, but it is important to let others know that they are just like everyone else in more ways than not.

Asthma

- Children with asthma have a hard time breathing in certain situations. The difficulty breathing may occur after a stressful activity like running, if they are scared, or if they are overly tired.
- It may also happen if the person is allergic to pollen, grass, perfume, smoke, or animals.
- Either way, the problem will start with shortness of breath, and, if not taken care of, progress to wheezing, coughing, and perhaps even lack of air.
- Most people with asthma carry some type of inhaler, or breathing device, to help them when the problem starts so that it does not progress to a dangerous situation.
- This may be a very scary situation for the person who is having the attack.
- They will not only have to temporarily leave the current activity, but they will also feel embarrassed because they are different and attention was focused on them.

Inclusion Ideas

- You can help these kids by helping them remember to bring their inhaler or prescribed medication.
- You can also help by calming them if they do have an attack.
- Let them know that everything will be OK and it is not a big deal if they have to miss some of the class or game.
- You can put yourself in their situation and understand that it is hard to breathe and frustrating to have to sit out at any given moment.
- You can make sure the playing area is not too big if your friends have a hard time covering large areas.
- You could also make sure they get rest periods when they need them so that breathing does not get too difficult.
- It would also help if you and your friends had a signal for when they feel as though they are in too much trouble with their breathing and may need you to call the nurse, the teacher, or 911.

Attention Deficit Hyperactivity Disorder (ADHD)

- Children with attention deficit hyperactivity disorder have a hard time paying attention in school, at home, and in social and play situations. This is just the way they were born, and they may take medication to help them pay attention better.
- They are distracted very easily and sometimes make mistakes because they are rushing through an assignment or chore.
- They are often restless, fidgety, or hyperactive, and they may even run away from you in the middle of a game.
- Sometimes they have a hard time organizing schoolwork, their desks, or their lockers. They may interrupt a conversation or talk out of turn. They may seem lazy, unreliable, or uncaring.

Inclusion Ideas

- You can help these classmates to be organized and pay attention to what they need to do.
- If they become distracted in the middle of a game, group assignment, or conversation, then remind them of what they were doing and help them finish if possible.
- If they choose not to finish what they were doing at that time, remind them at another time, and help them remember what they had to do.
- If they run away from a game at recess, know that they will come back and welcome them when they do.
- You can understand that they may have a hard time paying attention to one thing for a long time, and perhaps help them structure their days so that they do not have to remain in one place for too long.
- Do not look at what they did not have time to do; look at what they did, and let them know they are doing a good job.
- Know that they are still your friends even if it appears that they are ignoring you, or if they run away from you.

Autism

- Children with autism have a difficult time relating to people.
- They may be more interested in playing with an object or watching their hand than in talking to a person.
- They may play in a corner all by themselves or run around for no apparent reason.
- They may have very limited communication or no communication, or what they do say may not make very much sense.
- They may be very good at some things and not be able to do other things at all.
- They may react to touch, noise, or lights very differently. Sometimes a low noise will seem very loud to them, so much that they will cover their ears.
- They may cry from a soft touch or cover their eyes from a dim light.
- Other kids may appear deaf when there is a loud noise, may seek out deep pressure or feelings, or may look for very bright lights to stimulate themselves.
- Each person with autism is very different, and you need to understand what your classmates want and need to be able to cope with their environment.

Inclusion Ideas

- You can help these classmates by talking clearly and only asking them one or two things at a time.
- You could help them when they don't know what to do, redirect them when they are doing the wrong activity, and help other people understand what they are good at and what they need help with.
- You can learn what makes them mad, frustrated, and happy, and you can help convey these feelings to the other classmates and teacher.

Blind or Visually Impaired

- Children who are blind or visually impaired have difficulty seeing.
- They have this disability because of a birth accident, an accident after birth, or a sickness.
- Some kids can see a little bit and walk around by themselves; some kids can see a little bit but need some help getting around; and some kids cannot see anything and need help in getting around.
- With practice and a cane or a seeing-eye dog, kids may be able to walk around school and their neighborhood by themselves.
- These kids will eat by themselves and use the clock system. You can tell them their milk is at 12:00, which means their milk is at the very top of their plate, and their fork is at 9:00, which means their fork is just to the left of their plate.
- They can dress themselves, and they know which clothes are which color by brailling the color on the tag of the shirt.
- They find out what is happening in their environment, who is around them, and where they are going by having people tell them.
- Do not be afraid to use the words "see" or "look" in a sentence. They will use these words and you can, too.

Inclusion Ideas

- You can guide your classmates by allowing them to grab your elbow and walk one step behind you. This will allow them to let go if they want to.
- You can assist them in getting their food in the lunch line, and you can tell them where their food is on their plates.
- You can describe their environment to them, such as who is in the room, what the weather is like, and what equipment is around the gym.
- You can answer their questions and make sure they are included in conversations.
- Do not ever leave a room without telling them you are leaving. They may want to talk to you and not know you are gone, and this is embarrassing.
- You can make sure they are included in games and activities in your neighborhood or on the playground by adapting the equipment, the playing area, or the rules.

Cerebral Palsy

- Children with cerebral palsy have a condition from birth that affects their arms and legs.
- They have this condition because their brains cannot tell their bodies what they want them to do.
- Their muscles contract and their body moves without control. This affects different kids in different ways.
- Sometimes they have difficulty walking, or they may look awkward when they walk.
- Children with cerebral palsy may walk with crutches, a walker, or a wheelchair.

- They may be able to push their own chairs; they may need help pushing the chair; or they may use an electric wheelchair.
- They may have difficulty with feeding themselves, getting dressed, or talking; and some kids with cerebral palsy communicate through a communication board or a voice synthesizer instead of with their voices.

Inclusion Ideas

- You can help your classmates who have cerebral palsy by pushing their chairs if they need a push or walking with them around school if they are a little slower so that they don't have to walk alone.
- You can go up the ramp or the elevator if they need to go a different way so that they do not have to go by themselves.
- You can be patient when they communicate with you and help others understand their wants and needs.

Congenital Heart Condition

- Children with a heart condition have a hard time breathing or functioning in certain situations.
- The difficulty breathing may occur after a stressful activity like running, if they are scared, if they physically stress themselves, or if they are overly tired.
- The problem will start with shortness of breath and, if not taken care of, progress to weakness and fatigue, or the person may even faint.
- Most people with a congenital heart disorder participate in activity at a slower rate or for short periods.
- This may be a very scary situation for the person who is having the attack. The person will not only have to temporarily leave the current activity, but he will also feel embarrassed because he is different and attention was focused on him.

Inclusion Ideas

- You can help these kids by helping them remember to work at a slower pace and take rest periods.
- You can also help by calming them if they do have an attack.
- Let them know that everything will be OK and it is not a big deal if they have to miss some of the class or game.
- You can put yourself in their situation and understand that it is hard to breathe and frustrating to have to sit out at any given moment.
- You could also make sure they get rest periods when they need them so that effort and breathing do not get too difficult.
- You could sit out with them when they are resting so that they do not have to sit out alone.
- It would also help if you and your friends had a signal when they feel as though they are in too much trouble with breathing and may need you to call the nurse, the teacher, or 911.

Deafness/Hard of Hearing

- Children who are deaf or hard of hearing cannot hear like you or I can.
- They hear much less than we do, and in some cases they cannot hear at all. This may be due to a fever their mother had during pregnancy, or their parents may be deaf and their children became deaf also. They may have been premature at birth, had a sickness after birth, or become deaf from an accident.
- Some kids wear hearing aids or have different hearing devices to help them hear better.
- Some kids can talk clearly, you can understand them, and they can read your lips.
- Some kids communicate using hand gestures and sign language.
- They may not be able to talk with their voices, and they may not be able to understand everything you say.
- Some kids will prefer to talk mostly to other deaf kids, and other kids will talk to and make friends with anyone, hearing or deaf.

Inclusion Ideas

- Because your classmates cannot hear, you can help them in many ways.
- If they use their voices and read lips, you can help by making sure you are looking at each other when you talk.
- You can tap them on the shoulder to get their attention if the teacher is talking, if there is a fire drill, or if someone wants to talk to them.
- You can make sure they understand the instructions when you are in class, and you can answer any questions they have.
- If your friends are totally deaf and use signs, you can learn some signs to aid in communication and, if you don't know the signs, you can look at them when you are talking and the interpreter will interpret what you say.
- Many kids who are deaf feel lonely and left out, so it is important to try to include them in all activities, both in school and out.
- It is also important that you do not make them feel bad if they do not understand something, but that you try to increase their understanding the best that you can.
- If you want to help students who are deaf or hard of hearing, always remember that you can make sure they are included in games and activities in your neighborhood or on the playground. Do this by communicating the rules, talking to them, and helping other kids understand them. They are just like you in many ways.

Dwarfism

- Children who have dwarfism are short in stature and may have shorter legs and arms than you have.
- For some kids this happens at birth because of the way their bones are formed.
- Other kids are this way just because they did not grow as fast or as much as you.

- They may have a high voice and may have a hard time moving their arms and legs like you can.
- They may walk a little slower than you, and may have trouble moving their bodies the same way you do.

Inclusion Ideas

- You can help these kids by walking with them if they are at the end of the line so that they are not alone.
- You can help them reach something that is out of reach or assist them in doing an activity that may be difficult for them in class or on the playground.
- Other kids may give them funny looks or tease them because of the way they look, but it is important that you let others know that your friends are just like them in more ways than not.
- You can make sure they are included in games and activities in your neighborhood or on the playground by adapting the equipment, the playing area, or the rules.

Emotional Disability/Serious Emotional Disturbance/Behavior Disability

- These children may exhibit physical or verbal attacks toward the teacher or other classmates.
- These attacks may include swearing, pushing, shoving, or destruction of property
- Sometimes the teacher or teacher's aide may have to physically restrain the students or take them out of the room.
- This behavior often affects the students' performance in class, and they may be out of the classroom frequently because of their behavior. This is not anyone's fault—it just happens because of outside factors.
- These students do not try to have excessive misbehavior; it is part of who they are and may remain this way for a while until teachers, parents, and administrators can figure out how to help decrease the behaviors.

Inclusion Ideas

- You can help these kids by giving them positive feedback when they are on good behavior.
- You could talk to them about everyday things and get to know who they are.
- You can be their partners when others may not want to and try to accept them after they come back from a time-out.
- Other kids may give them funny looks or tease them because of the way they act, but it is important that you let others know that your friends are just like them in more ways than not.

Learning Disability

- Children with learning disabilities have a difficult time in learning situations, with reading, or with comprehension. They are not stupid; their brains just have a hard time receiving information, processing information, or expressing or giving back information. This happens when they are born, and they look just like everyone else.

- These kids might also have problems with writing letters and numbers.
- These kids may have a hard time running the same way you do or playing a game in some situations. For example, they may run more slowly, or they have a hard time catching a ball or doing things with their upper bodies.
- Many kids with learning disabilities also have attention deficit hyperactivity disorder (ADHD). If they also have ADHD, please see the description on this to know the characteristics and how you can help them.

Inclusion Ideas

- You can help your classmates with learning disabilities by showing them the right way to catch a ball or run, assisting them in expressing their thoughts, and checking their writing if they need it.
- You can praise them when they accomplish their goals and encourage them when they are struggling.
- Because some activities or skills are more difficult for these classmates, you will need to be very patient and supportive.
- You can make sure that they are included in games and activities in your neighborhood or on the playground by adapting the equipment, the playing area, or the rules.

Mental Retardation

- Children with mental retardation may not be able to think the same way you do. This is because they had an accident before, during, or after they were born, involving their heads or the chemicals in their bodies.
- They will sometimes be able to understand parts of what you say, but not everything. They may also react to what they are asked in an unusual way because of the lack of understanding.
- These classmates may also have trouble communicating with you, taking care of themselves (such as feeding themselves), or putting on their coats.
- They may walk away when you are talking to them, or they may laugh for no reason. They may have trouble going out into the community on their own to do things such as taking a bus or going shopping.
- Sometimes during the day they may not know what they want to do, they may not be aware of danger in the environment, and they may need help to do classwork or recreational activities such as walking, riding a bike, or bowling.

Inclusion Ideas

- You can help these classmates by talking clearly and only asking them one or two things at a time.
- You could help them when they don't know what to do, redirect them when they are doing the wrong activity, and help other people understand what they are good at and how they can be helped.
- You can make sure they are included in groups, games, and activities by giving them clear instructions and demonstrations throughout the activity and praising them when they do something right.
- These kids have the same feelings you have. They are hurt when other kids don't want to play with them; they like eating ice cream, watching cartoons, and being part of the game.

Obesity

- Children who are obese may be this way for many reasons.
- They may be on medication, they may have a glandular problem, they may have inherited much of their body composition, or they may not have learned how to balance diet and exercise.
- Whatever the reason for the obesity, it makes movement difficult.
- They have a difficult time running, moving their bodies, and perhaps being involved in activities for a long period.
- They may be afraid or embarrassed to participate in certain activities such as gymnastics, dancing, or swimming.
- It is important to keep in mind that they can be involved in any activity with some minor modifications.
- They may need more rest time, they may need to cover less area in a game, or they may need to be involved in the activity in a different way.
- They also may need to substitute for activities that make their bodies hurt, such as walking instead of running, hopping, or jumping, or log rolls instead of forward rolls.
- Swimming is an excellent activity for children who are obese. Be sure to make them feel welcome and encourage them to swim to the best of their ability.
- They do need to be involved in activities, so it is important to allow them to modify any activity but continue to be involved to the maximum extent possible.

Inclusion Ideas

- You can help these kids by helping them remember to work at a slower pace and take rest periods.
- You can help them by giving them some positive feedback when they actively participate in a game.
- When they do something that you know is hard for them, be sure to give them a high five or a thumbs up, or just say, "Great job!"
- You can put yourself in their situation and understand that it is hard to move and frustrating not to be able to do everything all the other kids are doing.
- You can make sure the playing area is not too big if your friends have a hard time covering large areas.
- You could also make sure they get rest periods when they need them so that effort, movement, and breathing do not get too difficult.
- It would also help if you and your friends had a signal when they feel as though they are in too much trouble with breathing and may need you to call the nurse, the teacher, or 911.

Osteogenisis Imperfecta (Brittle Bones)

- These kids are born with very fragile bones that often break even when they are not doing anything. This is just the way their bones formed, and this will be their condition until they are teenagers.

- This can be very frustrating, because they always have to be careful when doing everything, and they spend a lot of time in the hospital or at home.
- They may walk with a waddling gait, with crutches or a walker, or they may use a wheelchair.
- They may push their own wheelchairs, need to be pushed, or use an electric wheelchair.
- They may also be overweight because they do not have the opportunity to exercise, run, and play.
- They are just as smart as all the other kids in your class, and they usually talk very clearly.
- It may be hard for them to reach things far away or to move very fast.
- They may need to play very modified games and cannot participate in activities that will place them in danger of breaking more bones.

Inclusion Ideas

- You can help them by pushing them if they need a push, slowing down if they are slow walkers, walking with them in class, or going up the ramp or elevator with them.
- If something is out of reach for them, you can help them get it by pushing it closer or getting it for them.
- You can help others understand how similar they are to you, and share your hopes and dreams for the future.

Spinal Cord Injury/Spina Bifida

- A spinal cord injury occurs at birth or from an accident or disease after birth.
- The part of the spine affected is either partially or totally severed, and the children have total or partial paralysis from that point down.
- The children have no feeling in or control of their legs, abdominal area, or, in some cases, arms.
- Spina bifida happens when a person is born and part of the spine does not close all the way.
- Their spinal cord is often not covered by skin or tissue.
- This is always corrected by surgery, but the children are most often left paralyzed, either totally or partially, from that area down.
- These kids will walk with an awkward gait, use crutches, walkers, or a wheelchair.
- They may push their own wheelchairs, need to be pushed, or use an electric wheelchair.
- They may urinate through a tube into a bag, and they may also have braces on their legs.
- They are just as smart as all the other kids in your class, and usually talk very clearly.
- They will need to use ramps and elevators to go up steps and to other floors, and they will need a bigger rest room stall than kids without wheelchairs need.
- Other than these few differences, these kids are just like you.

Inclusion Ideas

- You can help these classmates by pushing them if they need a push, slowing down if they are slow walkers, walking with them in class, or going up the ramp or elevator with them.

- If something is out of reach for them, you can help them get it by pushing it closer or getting it for them.

- You can help others understand how similar they are to you, and share your hopes and dreams for the future.

Traumatic Brain Injury

- Children with traumatic brain injury have had a bad accident or a blow to the head.

- This causes them to have short-term memory loss, sometimes their speech is slurred, and they may say whatever is on their minds.

- Because they don't remember what may or may not hurt others' feelings, they may say something that does not make sense or is mean.

- They do not do these things intentionally; it just happens because they do not know what is appropriate.

- They may look unbalanced when they walk, or they may use a cane, crutches, or a wheelchair.

- They may push their own wheelchairs, need to be pushed, or use an electric wheelchair.

- They may have a hard time doing simple, everyday tasks such as brushing their teeth, putting their coats on, or eating. This is because they have difficulty in controlling their muscles. Because of this, they may become frustrated with whatever they are doing.

- It is important for you to realize that they are not mad at you but frustrated with the situation, because they could do these simple things before but cannot perform them now.

Inclusion Ideas

- You can help these classmates by being patient when they try to talk and by listening and responding. You can also help other classmates listen and understand.

- You can push them if they need a push or walk with them if they walk slowly so that they don't have to walk alone.

- You can offer them your hand if it looks as though they will lose their balance.

- You can assist them in their daily activities until they can do them independently.

- You can show them how to do the things they forget. You can remind them of the things they forget and applaud the things they remember.

- Because some activities or skills are more difficult for this classmate, you will need to be very patient and supportive.

Note: It is just as important to emphasize the similarities between children as the differences. Please do not overlook this important point.

B Peer Tutor Training Program

As seen in chapter 5, peer tutoring programs are most effective when the peer tutor is trained. This appendix contains a general peer tutor training handout as well as the peer tutor written test. These should be used as part of a comprehensive peer tutoring program as described in chapter 5.

■ Peer Tutor Training Handout

Verbal Cue/Sign Cue

A verbal cue is a signal or sign to tell someone what to do.
Examples:
"John, run around the cones."
"Jane, it is your turn for pull-ups."
"Let's stand on the black circle."
"Sara, show me the crab walk."

Modeling

Modeling is a way of demonstrating how to do the activity. After you give a verbal cue, if the student does not do the activity or does the activity incorrectly, you should repeat the cue and demonstrate what it is you want him or her to do.
Examples:
"Mary, hop like this."
"Continue to perform sit-ups like this."
"Watch me participate in the relay race."
"When we get to station 3, do jumping jacks like this."

Physical Assistance

Physical assistance is used to help the student if he or she is unable to do the activity after you have given a verbal cue and modeled the activity. You should only physically assist the student by directing his or her body parts with your hands.

Examples:

Stand behind the student and physically assist with a sit-up.

Stand sideways in front of a student holding hands, bend your knees, and jump over the rope.

Tap the student on the shoulder when it is his or her turn to run or participate in fitness activities.

Positive General Feedback

Giving positive general feedback is making a supportive statement about the student's motor skill response.

Examples:

"Good skipping."

"Nice crab walk."

"Great!"

"Wow!"

Positive Specific Feedback

In positive specific feedback, the supportive statement includes exact information about what was good about the motor skill response.

Examples:

"Nice reaching up with your jumping jacks."

"Great high knees with your skip."

"I like the way you use your arms in your run."

"That's the way to keep your feet moving in that station!"

Skills

Cardiovascular Endurance

Running, skipping, galloping, hopping, walking, sliding

Muscle Strength and Endurance

Sit-ups, crab walk, pull-ups, push-ups

Flexibility

Sidebends, toe touches, trunk twists, hurdler's stretch, butterfly, sprinter's stretch

Examples of Scenarios

Scenario 1

Tutor: Cue ("Mary, jump over the rope.")

Student: Acceptable response

Tutor: Positive specific reinforcement ("Good job jumping over the rope so many times!")

Scenario 2

Tutor: Cue ("John, do five push-ups.")
Student: Unacceptable response
Tutor: Positive general feedback ("Good try!")
Tutor: Repeat cue and model ("John, do the push-ups like this.")
Student: Acceptable response
Tutor: Positive specific reinforcement ("Nice job! I like the way you bent your elbows all the way.")

Scenario 3

Tutor: Cue ("Sue, do the crab walk.")
Student: Unacceptable response
Tutor: Repeat cue and model ("Sue, do the crab walk like this.")
Student: Unacceptable response
Tutor: Questions the student ("Can I help you?")
Tutor: Provides physical assistance (Tutor helps student lift her hips up for a correct crab walk.)
Student: Acceptable response
Tutor: Positive specific reinforcement ("That's the way to lift your hips! Now try to do it yourself.")

Peer Tutor Quiz

Name: _____ Date: _____

Choose the correct answer from the list below for questions 1 through 5.

modeling
physical assistance
positive general feedback
positive specific feedback
verbal cue

1. A sign or signal to tell someone what to do is a _____.
2. If the student does not understand how to do the skill or is doing it incorrectly, you should use _____.
3. You should give _____ to the student only if the verbal cue and modeling does not work.
4. A statement that is supportive and gives exact information about what was good about a skill is called _____.
5. A statement that is supportive but does not give exact information about what was good about a skill is called _____.

Circle the correct answer for questions 6 through 10.

6. What is an example of a positive specific feedback statement?
   a. "Good job."
   b. "Good sliding sideways! I like the way you use your arms."

c. "Good try."

d. "Slide like this."

7. The student you are working with is unable to gallop. What is a verbal cue that you may give to help the student gallop?

a. "Slide your back foot to your front foot, then step with your front foot again."

b. "Gallop."

c. "Try again."

d. "You will get it this time."

8. After getting a verbal cue to jump with knees bent, the student is unable to do the skill correctly. What do you say?

a. "Almost! Try again."

b. "That was pretty good."

c. "Watch me! Bend your knees and jump."

d. "Good jump!"

9. After you give a verbal cue and model for the student, he or she is still unable to perform a hurdler's stretch correctly. What do you say?

a. "Is it OK if I help you?' (If the student agrees, sit beside him and put a hand on his outstretched leg.)

b. "Do you want me to take your turn for you?"

c. "Do you want to do something else?"

d. "Try again; I know you will get it."

10. "Good job throwing!" is an example of a

a. positive specific statement

b. corrective feedback statement

c. verbal cue

d. positive general feedback statement

C *Disability Awareness Activities*

Appendix C is a compilation of ideas for disability awareness activities for children. This list consists only of selected ideas and should assist the instructor in creating additional disability awareness activities at each level. These activities should be informative, fun, and memorable for the participants. Remember the rules of thumb for disability awareness activities from chapter 5.

▨ Disability Awareness Activities for Children

Level I: Exposure

Videos about individuals with disabilities

Newspaper or magazine articles about individuals with disabilities

Speakers with disabilities

Level II: Experience

Name of activity: Tunnel Vision Toss and Catch

Grade level: K-6

Disabilities: Retinitis pigmentosa or any visual impairment that results in tunnel vision

Materials needed: Safety goggles, masking tape, balls, paper, pens, bats

Time allotted: 30-40 minutes

Space needed: Gymnasium or large classroom

Description of activity: First discuss what tunnel vision is and why people have it. Next, have students wear goggles with peripheral vision blocked out. Divide the group into pairs. (You can have both students or one at a time simulate activity.) They need to toss and catch, kick, or bat a ball while simulating tunnel vision. If you have limited space, you could also have students write sentences on paper while simulating activity.

Safety considerations: Place students in stations or in static position to avoid collisions. Have students complete skills in same direction.

Variations: Vary the size of the holes (for example, 1/4-inch size, hole-punch size, pin hole, or others). Add another disability, such as wheelchair use or CP.

Questions the teacher can ask:

1. Can you see the sides?
2. Is it easy to see the target?
3. What would it be like to see like that all the time?
4. Is it easier to throw or catch the ball?
5. Which skills were harder?
6. How could you help a peer who has tunnel vision?
7. What other skills may be hard?

Innovators: Rodney Allen and Tim Eustice, Brockport, NY

Name of activity: Tag Games

Grade level: K-5

Disabilities: Autism

Materials needed: Wool sweaters, burlap bags, tape with loud sounds (everyday sounds), bright lights, strobe lights, tape, heavy jacket, other items

Time allotted: 30-40 minutes

Space needed: Gymnasium

Description of activity: Describe the disability of autism, the common characteristics, and what you may expect to see with that student. Students play various tag games wearing a wool sweater, burlap bag, or heavy coat. Music or noise is played extra loud, and bright light shines at children. You could also wrap tape around the children's wrists to simulate a watch or around the ankles to simulate socks.

Safety considerations: Use football flags or one hand to avoid excess contact. Use other normal tag game safety considerations.

Variations: Use different types of irritating material or latex material. Put tape or Velcro on children's arms so that it will catch on their clothes as they run.

Questions the teacher can ask:

1. How did the wool sweater make your skin feel?
2. Did the bright lights bother you?
3. Did the loud noises affect your concentration?
4. How did it feel to have your arms catch on your clothes?
5. Were you frustrated? Why?
6. What could you do to make the child with autism feel more comfortable in the classroom?

Name of activity: All Thumbs

Grade level: K-5

Disabilities: Muscular dystrophy, cerebral palsy, learning disability, juvenile rheumatoid arthritis

Materials needed: Gloves, mittens, Velcro, tape (enough for half the class)

Time allotted: 20-25 minutes

Space needed: Classroom or small gymnasium

Description of activity: Describe a disability in which children have fine motor difficulties (for example, muscular dystrophy, cerebral palsy, learning disability, or juvenile rheumatoid arthritis). This simulation will help them understand how those kids feel every day. All the kids try to tie their shoes, button their shirts, zip their pants, and braid shoelaces or hair with gloves, mittens, or other materials obstructing their hands.

Safety considerations: Common sense

Variations: Have kids try to type on the computer, open a door with a key, brush their hair, fasten buttons, open their lunch bags and their milk, or do other activities (anything fine motor).

Questions the teacher can ask:

1. What was hard about this exercise?
2. What was easy?
3. How did you feel?
4. How could you help a child with a fine motor problem?
5. What would you do if you had to go through your entire life with this disability?

Name of activity: Marshmallow Madness

Grade level: K-6

Disabilities: Cerebral palsy, Down syndrome, speech disorder

Materials needed: Bags of marshmallows (6 for each child), 3 × 5 cards containing short sentences

Time allotted: 20-30 minutes

Space needed: Classroom or small gymnasium

Description of activity: Teacher describes when and why some children have speech problems. Go over characteristics and common problems. Then each child gets a partner. One partner at a time puts 4 to 6 marshmallows in his or her mouth and tries to say a phrase or sentence that's on a card given by the teacher. The other student tries to understand what their partner is saying. Each partner has 2 to 3 tries, then the partners switch.

Safety considerations: Make sure they don't eat too many marshmallows. Don't continue if they are laughing too hard.

Variations: Allow them to make up phrases or sentences. Switch partners. Don't allow them to look at the student simulating activity.

Questions the teacher can ask:

1. What did you feel like when you were trying to talk and it was hard?
2. What did you feel like when you were trying to listen and it was hard to understand?
3. Were you clear on the phrase or sentence?
4. What would it feel like to talk like this every day?
5. What could you do to help a student with this problem?
6. Could you think of other effective ways of communicating?

Innovator: Dr. Georgia Frey, Indiana University.

Name of activity: Show Me the Sign

Grade level: K-12

Disabilities: Hard of hearing or deaf

Materials needed: Sign book, or teacher who knows sign

Time allotted: 10-15 minutes

Space needed: Classroom or small gymnasium

Description of activity: Teacher first describes the "culture" of deaf or hard of hearing people. He or she then talks about etiology and common characteristics. The teacher signs for 1 to 5 sentences and tries to see if any of the kids understand. This is very similar to a situation where a deaf child is sitting in a classroom, the teacher is talking, and there is no interpreter or clear communication.

Safety considerations: None

Variations: Turn on a TV with no volume and try to guess what is happening. Tell some of the kids, but not all, what was being signed, and the others will know what it is like to feel left out of the conversation. Tell a joke in sign and let some of the kids know. When they laugh, it will be frustrating for the others, just as it is for deaf kids.

Questions the teacher can ask:

1. How did you feel when you did not know what I was saying?
2. What would you do if you were in this situation?
3. What would you do if you were in this situation all the time?
4. How can you make a child who is deaf feel better in your classroom?
5. What would it feel like if all the kids in your school spoke sign and you were the only person who could speak and hear?

Community Awareness Activities

Accessible Transportation

Disability: Individuals who use wheelchairs

Description: Go to your local bus stop in a wheelchair and wait for a bus that is wheelchair-accessible.

Questions:

1. How many buses are accessible to people in wheelchairs and how many are not?
2. What is the average time a person in a wheelchair has to wait for a bus?
3. What is the average time a person who is not in a wheelchair has to wait for a bus?
4. Did the bus driver know how to use the wheelchair lift? Did he or she treat you the same as if you did not use a wheelchair?
5. Would the person in a wheelchair have to pay the same price for the ride as a person not in a wheelchair would pay?
6. Would you think this is a fair system if you used a wheelchair for your primary means of getting around?
7. What are some recommendations for the local bus company?
8. If this were a perfect world, what else would you ask for?
9. Other

Reaction to the project:

_____

_____

_____

Telecommunication Devices for the Deaf (TDDs or TTY)

Disability: Deafness

Directions: According to current legislation, all hotels are supposed to own a telecommunication device for the deaf (TDD), available 24 hours each day, for people who are deaf or who need to speak with someone who is deaf. You and a friend are to go to three or four local hotels and ask to use the TDD. Ask the clerks to teach you how.

Questions:

1. Do they have a TDD?
2. If so, is it available for you to use immediately?
3. Does the clerk know how to use one?
4. Do you feel you could call a person who is deaf?
5. If they did not have one, what was their excuse?
6. Do you think you could teach a peer how to use a TDD?
7. If you were deaf, do you feel you would have been treated well in each hotel?
8. What would you suggest for each hotel?
9. Other

Reaction to the project:

_____

_____

_____

Room for Individuals With Disabilities

Disability: Any

Description: Go to two to three local hotels and ask to see their room for people with disabilities. Then ask to see a room for guests without disabilities. Go in each room and see what is similar and what is different.

Questions:

1. What was different on the front door?
2. What was different in the bedroom (bed, bureau, mirrors)?
3. What was different about the bathroom (toilet, shower, bathtub, towel rack, sink, mirror, closet)?
4. Was closed captioning available on the television?
5. What about the doorways? Were they wider or narrower than in the room for people without disabilities?
6. How many rooms were available for people with disabilities?
7. Do the rooms for people with disabilities cost the same as the rooms for people without disabilities?
8. Ask the clerks if they would have the time to assist a person with a disability into his or her room if this was necessary. If so, have they ever helped a person with a disability?
9. What about the room may be difficult for a person in a wheelchair? What may be easier?
10. Other

Reaction to the project:

_____

_____

_____

Local YMCA or Health Club

Disability: Any

Description: Go to a local YMCA or health club and ask the following questions:

1. Do you have special programs for people with disabilities? If so, what are they? Are the people who run these programs qualified?
2. If you do not have special programs, can people with disabilities such as a visual impairment, cerebral palsy (in a wheelchair), deafness, or amputations join your activities (swimming, basketball, judo, weight training, gymnastics, dance, or aerobics)?
3. If so, what special accommodations do you make? Are these accommodations successful? Why or why not?
4. If not, where do these people go if they have an interest in physical activity yet can not be included in the local program?
5. Do you feel this YMCA or health club is or is not meeting the needs of people with disabilities? Why or why not?

6. What can you do to improve your current program? Would this be difficult to implement? Why or why not?

7. Is it the responsibility of the individual with a disability to make his or her own accommodations to be included in the local health club? Why or why not?

8. Other

Reaction to the project:

_____

_____

_____

Cars or Vans for Individuals With Disabilities

Disability: Spinal cord injury, dwarfism, spina bifida

Description: Go to a local automobile or van dealer and ask to see a car or van that is adapted to be accessible for people with spinal cord injuries, dwarfism, or spina bifida. If they do not have one, ask them where you can look at one. When you find one, answer the following questions:

Questions:

1. Who was the van adapted for?
2. What is different on the steering wheel?
3. What is different at the gas pedals?
4. Is the seat adapted? If so, how?
5. What is different about the back?
6. How is this van similar to a van that's not equipped for transporting people with disabilities?
7. Would this van cost more than the unadapted vans? If so, why? If not, why?
8. If the van costs more than the unadapted van, who pays for the adaptations?
9. Would you like this type of vehicle? Why or why not?
10. What did you learn from this project?
11. Other

Reaction to the project:

_____

_____

_____

Classroom Projects

Class bulletin board

Disability: Any

Description: Class must collect information about individuals with disabilities and create an informative bulletin board to share with your school. Be sure to collect information about different disabilities and both males and females.

Questions:

1. What different types of disabilities are represented here?
2. How many males and how many females are featured?
3. What were the major topics that were addressed about the individuals?
4. Was there anything that really impressed you that you did not know before?
5. Was there anything you already knew?
6. Was there anything missing that you thought your class would find in the newspapers or magazines?
7. How did other schoolmates react to the bulletin board? What was the most frequently stated comment?
8. What surprised you the most about their reactions?
9. Other

Reaction to the project:

_____

_____

_____

Speaker With a Disability

Disability: Any

Description: Invite a speaker with a disability to come in and talk about his or her life and how he or she overcame adversity to become who they are.

Questions:

1. What was the speaker's disability?
2. Was the speaker born with the disability, or acquired it later on in life?
3. How did or does the disability affect the speaker's life now?
4. Is the speaker's home adapted?
5. Did his or her family have to adapt to the disability? If so, how?
6. What does the speaker do now?
7. How are everyday things such as transportation, accessibility, or communication adapted for this individual?
8. What does he or she do for recreation or free time? Are there barriers to involvement in this activity? If so, what are they and how does he or she overcome those barriers?
9. What advice would this person give to other children with the same disability?
10. Other

Reaction to the project:

_____

_____

_____

Level III: Ownership

Class Disability Awareness Night (Ownership Experience for High School Students)

Disability: Any

Description: High school students organize a disability awareness night for the local middle school or elementary school. The students could send a preliminary questionnaire to the children who will participate; students could ask what they do and do not know about individuals with disabilities. The students would be responsible for setting up and implementing a variety of disability awareness activities for the younger community. They must teach the children about the particular disability, allow them to experience that disability, and conduct an activity to increase understanding and awareness about that disability. Student could teach basic sign language. On the same night, they could also bring in speakers who have disabilities. The questionnaires could be redistributed to assess whether the participants learned what was intended.

Questions:

1. What was the general response from the results of the preliminary questionnaire?
2. What were the common questions or comments on Disability Awareness Night?
3. Were there any misconceptions or myths about people with disabilities?
4. What effect did the experience have on the participants? Was this what you expected?
5. Did you learn any more than you already knew from this experience?
6. What would you do differently if you were to do it again?
7. Other

Reaction to the project:

_____

_____

_____

Cross-Aged Peer Tutoring (Ownership Experience for High School Students)

Disability: Any

Description: Students go through a 1- to 2-hour training session on teaching, feedback, and evaluation, which is held by the physical education teacher. Students then go to designated physical education classes for younger students with disabilities (adapted physical education). They serve as teachers and evaluators. This activity must be conducted for a specific period, such as a unit, quarter, or semester. It may work best if the adapted physical education class is at the same time as the high school students' study hall.

Questions:

1. What disability did the student or students you worked with have?
2. How did you assist in the physical education class?

3. What teaching and feedback techniques worked best with the students?
4. What was difficult about this experience?
5. What was easy about this experience?
6. What would be difficult if you had the same disability?
7. What would you do differently if you were to do the same experience again?
8. Other

Reaction to the project:

_____

_____

_____

Wheelchair Road Race (Ownership Experience for High School Students)

Disability: This race would benefit any person with a spinal cord injury or a person with limited use of the legs (cerebral palsy, spinal cord injury, spina bifida, multiple sclerosis, muscular dystrophy, and others)

Description: Students find local races and help organize a wheelchair race in conjunction with the race. The students are responsible for advertising, rewards, and recognition after the race. They must try to involve men and women in the race. It may be a good idea to interview the potential participants about their previous experience to determine if the race needs both open and amateur divisions. Students may need to go through the race course in a wheelchair or with someone in a wheelchair to make sure the course is safe. If not, they may need to alter the course. Be sure to advertise before the race and recognize participants and winners after the race in local papers, radio stations, and television stations.

Questions:

1. What did you learn about people who use wheelchairs?
2. What was the hardest part of this project?
3. What was the easiest part of this project?
4. Did you find the race course accessible? Why or why not?
5. Were the race organizers flexible with the parameters of the race?
6. Were the police helpful? Why or why not?
7. Other

Reaction to the project:

_____

_____

_____

Benefit Walkathon (Ownership Experience for High School Students)

Disability: Whatever disability the students want to highlight, such as cystic fibrosis, diabetes, cancer, or multiple sclerosis

Description: Students choose a particular disability and organize a walkathon to benefit that disability. Students must first contact a local chapter of that disability's organization, such as the local multiple sclerosis society, cystic fibrosis society, or diabetes chapter, and ask if the organization has a walkathon to raise money. If they already have a walk organized, the students can help with the existing walk. If they have no walkathon, the organization can work with the students in setting up one. The students must decide how far they want to walk (5 kilometers, 10 kilometers, 5 miles). Students must then help advertise and promote the walk. They have to distribute sponsor sheets and encourage participants to obtain a certain amount of money. They must organize the walk route with the community and local police. They must get local businesses to donate water, juice, food, and prizes such as gift certificates for people who collected the most money. They may also get local businesses to donate money. After the walk students will be responsible for collecting all the money from the participants and donating it to the local chapter of the chosen disability organization.

Questions:

1. What did you learn about the people you raised money for?
2. What was the hardest part of this project?
3. What was the easiest part of this project?
4. Did you find the walking course accessible? Why or why not?
5. Were the people from the local organization helpful in setting up the walk?
6. Were the police helpful? Why or why not?
7. Other

Reaction to the project:

_____

_____

_____

Fair or Festival Accessibility (Ownership Experience for High School Students)

Disability: Any

Description: Go to the local planning committee for your community fair or festival and ask the following questions:

1. Is the festival area accessible for wheelchairs?
2. Are the restrooms accessible for wheelchairs?
3. If there is music or a performance, is the area accessible for wheelchairs?
4. Will there be interpreters for deaf participants?
5. If there is a live performance, will interpreters be provided?
6. If there is a person who is blind, will a guide be provided for the duration of the fair?
7. Is there a number to call to inform the committee that a person with a disability will participate in the fair?
8. Is the committee willing to make necessary accommodations for individuals with disabilities?
9. How much will they charge people with disabilities?

Questions:

1. Is the fair accessible to people in wheelchairs?
2. Is the fair accessible to deaf people?
3. Is the fair accessible to people who are blind?
4. Was the committee open to students' suggestions and help?
5. If the committee already accommodates people with disabilities, did you learn anything new?
6. Did you make any suggestions?
7. How can you help this committee in the future?
8. Other

Reaction to the project:

_____

_____

_____
_____

Taken in part from Wilson, S. and Lieberman, L. 2000. Disability awareness in physical education. *Strategies* 13(6):12, 29-33.

D Aquatics Checklist

This appendix contains an aquatics skills checklist that is hierarchical and based on level of independence. It was created by Dr. Cathy Houston-Wilson. It should be used as an evaluation of initial swimming skills as well as for documenting progress on swimming skills.

SUNY Brockport Motor Fitness Clinic Aquatic Skills Checklist

By Cathy Houston-Wilson, PhD

Student: _____ Age: _____ Date: _____

Instructor: _____

	Independent	Needs Assistance	Total Assistance
Pool preparation			
Proper behavior en route to the pool			
Takes clothes off			
Hangs clothes in locker			
Puts bathing suit on			
Takes shower			
Awaits directions before entering pool			
Pool entry			
Sits at edge of pool, feet in water			
Puts water on body			
Lowers self into pool			
Climbs down stairs and enters pool			
Adjustment to water			
Splashes water around with no fear			
Holds gutter and kicks legs			
Kicks on front while being towed			
Kicks on back while being towed			
Moves arms and legs in swimming motion while being towed			
Blows bubbles			
Treads water for 30 seconds			
Puts whole face in water for 5 seconds			
Holds breath while submerged for 10 seconds			
Bobs up and down 5 times			

	Independent	Needs Assistance	Total Assistance
Continuous rhythmic breathing while holding side of pool and turning head to side 10 times			
Continuous rhythmic breathing from prone position while kicking with kickboard for 20 feet			

Floating skills

	Independent	Needs Assistance	Total Assistance
Floats on front while holding kickboard with arms fully extended and face submerged			
Front float			
Back float			

Basic propulsion

	Independent	Needs Assistance	Total Assistance
Flutter kicks with kickboard while on front for 15 feet			
Glides on front with push-off, holding kickboard with arms extended, and flutter kicks for 15 feet			
Glides on front with push-off and flutter kicks with no kickboard for 15 feet			
Glides on front with push-off and flutter kicks with face submerged and no kickboard for 15 feet			
Glides on back with push-off, holding kickboard with arms extended, and flutter kicks for 15 feet			
Glides on back with push-off and flutter kicks with no kickboard for 15 feet			
Rolls over, front to back, while gliding			
Rolls over, back to front, while gliding			

Swimming strokes

	Independent	Needs Assistance	Total Assistance
Does freestyle stroke, arms only, face out of water, for 10 strokes			
Does freestyle stroke, arms only, face submerged, for 10 strokes			
Does freestyle stroke, arms and legs, face submerged, for 10 strokes			

(continued)

(continued)

	Independent	Needs Assistance	Total Assistance
Swimming strokes			
Does freestyle stroke, arms and legs, with rhythmic breathing, for 10 strokes			
Swims under water for 10 feet			
Does side stroke on either side for 10 feet			
Does breast stroke for 10 feet			
Does back crawl stroke, arms only, for 10 strokes			
Does back crawl stroke, arms and legs, for 10 strokes			
Diving skills			
Dives from a sitting position			
Dives from squat or crouched position			
Dives from standing with knees slightly bent			
Dives from standing with spring and arm action			
Performs standing dive from end of low board			
Water safety and deep water skills			
Bobs 15 times			
Treads water for 30 seconds			
Survival floats			
Jumps feet first into water, surfaces, and swims back to side of pool			
Begins freestyle stroke after jumping or diving into pool			
Changes directions while swimming			
Changes position while floating and swimming (rolls from front to back)			
Changes from horizontal to vertical position while treading water			
Dives off side and swims under water for 15 feet			

For more information on adapted aquatics see Lepore, M., Gayle, W.G., and Stevens, S. (1998). *Adapted Aquatics Programming*. Champaign, IL: Human Kinetics.

Organizations in Adapted Physical Education and Disability Sport

These are lists of organizations in adapted physical education and disability sport. Each of these should be used as a resource for adaptation ideas, to assist the child in becoming involved in sport skills, to inform parents, to assist coaches who have a child with a disability on their team, and to increase coaches' and physical educators' awareness. The first list is in alphabetical order according to disability, whereas the second is alphabetized by sport.

Disability Organizations

Amputee Information Network
URL: **www.amp-info.net**

Australian Sports Commission
URL: **www.ausport.gov.au**

Disabled Sports USA
URL: **www.dsusa.org**

U.S. Disabled Athletes Fund
BlazeSports
URL: **www.blazesports.com**

Dwarf Athletic Association of America
URL: **www.daaa.org**

International Paralympic Committee
Adenauerallee 212-214
53113 Bonn
Germany
+49 228-2097-200
Fax: +49 228-2097-209
E-mail: **info@paralympic.org**
URL: **www.paralympic.org**

Skating Association for the Blind and Handicapped
URL: **www.sabahinc.org**

Special Olympics
URL: **www.specialolympics.org**

The United States Olympic Committee
Disabled Sports Services Dept.
URL: **www.usoc.org**

U.S.A. Deaf Sports Federation (USADSF)
3607 Washington Boulevard Suite 4
Ogden, UT 84403-1737
801-393-8710
Fax: 801-393-2263
URL: **www.usadsf.org**

United States Association for Blind Athletes
URL: **www.usaba.org**

U.S. Cerebral Palsy Athletic Association
URL: **www.uscpaa.org**

U.S. Les Autres Sports Association
Dave Stephenson, Executive Director
National Office
1475 West Gray Suite 165
Houston, TX 77019-4926
National Program Office
200 Harrison Avenue
Newport, RI 02840
401-848-2460

International Sports Organization for the Disabled
Idrottens Hus
Storforssplan 44
12387, Farsta
Sweden
Wheelchair Sports, USA
URL: **www.wsusa.org**

Asthma

Asthma and Allergy Foundation of America (AAFA)
1233 20th St. NW Suite 402
Washington, DC 20036
202-466-7643
800-7-ASTHMA
Fax: 202-466-8940
URL: **www.aafa.org**

American Lung Association (ALA)
1740 Broadway
New York, NY 10019
212-315-8700
URL: **www.lungusa.org**

Attention Deficit Disorder

Children and Adults With Attention-Deficit/Hyperactivity Disorder (CHADD)
8181 Professional Place Suite 201
Landover, MD 20785
800-233-4050
301-306-7070
Fax: 301-306-7090
URL: **www.chadd.org/other.htm**

National Attention Deficit Disorder Association (ADDA)
1788 Second St. Suite 200
Highland Park, IL 60035
847-432-ADDA
Fax: 847-432-5874
URL: **www.add.org**
ADD on About.com
URL: **www.add.about.com**

Autism

URL: **www.autism-resources.com**
URL: **www.autism.com/acap**
For more information call 503-978-3989

The Doug Flutie, Jr. Foundation for Autism
PO Box 767

233 Cochituate Road
Framingham, MA 01701
866-3AUTISM
508-270-8855
Fax: 508-270-8855
E-mail: **dougiesteam@yahoo.com**
URL: **www.dougflutiejrfoundation.org**

Autism Society of America
7910 Woodmount Avenue Suite 300
Bethesda, MD 20814
800-3-AUTISM
URL: **www.autism-society.org**

Blindness

Blindness Resource Center
URL: **www.nyise.org/blind.htm**
URL: **www.acb.org**

U.S. Association for Blind Athletes
Charlie Huebner, Executive Director
33 North Institute Street
Colorado Springs, CO 80903
719-630-0422
Fax: 719-630-0616
E-mail: **usaba@usa.net**
URL: **www.usaba.org**

International Blind Sports Association
Hybratenveien No. 7C
Oslo 10, Norway
Enrique Sanz Jimenez, IBSA President
C/o Quevedo 1
28014 Madrid, Spain
34-1-589-4537

Canadian Blind Sport Association
1600 James Naismith Drive
Gloucester, ON K1B 5N4, Canada
613-748-5609

Ski for Light
1455 West Lake Street
Minneapolis, MN 55408
612-827-3232
URL: **www.sfl.org**

American Foundation for the Blind
11 Penn Plaza Suite 300
New York, NY 10001
800-232-5463
Fax: 212-502-7777
URL: **www.afb.org**

Association for the Education and Rehabilitation of the Blind and Visually Impaired
PO Box 22397
4600 Duke Street Suite 430
Alexandria, VA 22304
703-823-9690
Fax: 703-823-9695
URL: **www.aerbvi.org**

Cardiac Conditions

URL: **www.bev.net/health/cardiac**

Cerebral Palsy
Cerebral Palsy Information Center
URL: **www.cerebralpalsy.com/links.html**

United States Cerebral Palsy Athletic Association
URL: **www.uscpaa.org**

United Cerebral Palsy Association
1660 L Street NW Suite 700
Washington, DC 20036
800-872-5827
URL: **www.ucpa.org**

National Disability Sports Alliance
25 West Independence Way
Kingston, RI 02881
401-792-7130
401-792-7132
E-mail: **info@ndsaonline.org**
URL: **www.uscpaa.org**

Jeffrey Jones, President, USCPAA
RIC Center for Health and Fitness
710 North Lake Shore Drive Third Floor
Chicago, IL 60611
312-908-4292
Fax: 312-908-1051
E-mail: **Ric-sports@nwu.edu**

United Cerebral Palsy Association of Miami
1411 NW Avenue
Miami, FL 33125
305-325-1080
URL: **www.ucpsouthflorida.org**

Miami Cerebral Palsy Residential Services
2200 NW 107th Avenue
Miami, FL 33172
305-599-0899

United Cerebral Palsy of Broward County
3117 SW 13th Court

Fort Lauderdale, FL 33312
954-584-7178

United Cerebral Palsy Association of Palm Beach and Mid Coast Counties
3595 2nd Avenue N
Lake Worth, FL 33461
561-357-7779

Cerebral Palsy-International Sports and Recreation Association (CP-ISRA)
Miss Elizabeth Dendy, President
9 Kingswood Road
London, W4 5EU
United Kingdom
44-181-994-4262
Fax: 44-181-994-4262
URL: **www.cpisra.org**

Trudie Rombouts
Secretariat CP-ISRA
6666 ZG HETEREN
The Netherlands
31-26-47-22-593
Fax: 31-26-47-23-914

Canadian Cerebral Palsy Sports Association
1010 Ploytek St Unit 2 2nd Floor
Ottawa, ON K1J 9H9 Canada
613-748-1340
URL: **www.ccpsa.ca**

American Academy for Cerebral Palsy and Developmental Medicine
6300 N. River Road Suite 727
Rosemont, IL 60018
847-698-1635
URL: **www.aacpdm.org**

Brain Injury Association
1776 Massachusetts Avenue NW Suite 100
Washington, DC 20036-0190
202-296-6443

National Easter Seal Society, Inc.
230 West Monroe Street Suite 1800
Chicago, IL 60606
800-221-6827
URL: **www.easter-seals.org**

Convulsive Disorder

URL: **www.meddean.luc.edu/lumen/meded/pedneuro/epilepsy.htm**

Cystic Fibrosis

Cystic Fibrosis Foundation
6931 Arlington Road
Bethesda, MD 20814
800-Fight CF
301-951-4422
Fax: 301-951-6378
URL: **www.cff.org**
E-mail: **info@ccff.org**

Deafness and Hearing Impairments

National Association of the Deaf
URL: **www.nad.org**

U.S.A. Deaf Sports Federation (USADSF)
3607 Washington Boulevard Suite 4
Ogden, UT 84403-1737
801-393-8710
Fax: 801-393-2263
URL: **www.usadsf.org**

National Information Center on Deafness
Gallaudet University
800 Florida Avenue NE
Washington, DC 20002-3625
202-651-5000

Canadian Deaf Sports Association
4545 ave. Pierre-Du Coubertin
CP 1000 Succ. M
Montreal, Quebec H1V 3R2 Canada
800-855-0511
URL: **www.assc-cdsa.com**

Deaf-Blindness

Deafness Information Center
URL: **www.nidcd.nih.gov**

Helen Keller National Center for Deaf-Blind
Youths and Adults
111 Middle Neck Road
Sands Point, NY 11050
516-944-8900
TTY: 516-944-8637
URL: **www.helenkeller.org/national**

National Information Clearinghouse on Children who are Deaf-Blind
800-438-9376
TTY: 800-754-7013
URL: **www.tr.wou.edu/dblink**

Diabetes

URL: **www.childrenwithdiabetes.com**

URL: **www.diabetes.org**
American Diabetes Association
1701 North Beauregard St.
Alexandria, VA 22311
800-DIABETES
800-342-2383
URL: **www.diabetes.org**

Down Syndrome

National Association for Down Syndrome
PO Box 4542
Oak Brook, IL 60522
630-325-9112
URL: **www.nads.org**

National Down Syndrome Society
666 Broadway
New York, NY 10012
800-221-4602
212-460-9330 (local NY)
Fax: 212-979-2873
URL: **www.ndss.org**

Dwarfism

Dwarf Athletic Association of America
URL: **www.daaa.org**

Little People of America
National Headquarters
Box 745
Lubbock, TX 79408
1-888-LPA-2001
URL: **www.lpaonline.org**
E-mail: **LPADataBase@juno.com**

Juvenile Rheumatoid Arthritis

URL: **http://jraworld.arthritisinsight.com**

Learning Disabilities

National Center for Learning Disabilities (NCLD)
381 Park Ave. South Suite 1401
New York, NY 10016
212-545-7510
Fax: 212-545-9665
Toll free: 1-888-575-7373
URL: **www.ncld.org**

LD Association of America
4156 Library Road
Pittsburgh, PA 15234-1349
412-341-1515

Fax: 412-344-0224
URL: **www.ldanatl.org**

The Council for Exceptional Children
1110 North Glebe Road Suite 300
Arlington, VA 22201
703-620-3660
TTY: 703-264-9446
URL: **www.cec.sped.org**

Council for Learning Disabilities
PO Box 40303
Overland Park, KS 66204
913-492-8755
URL: **www.acusd.edu/~ammer/proforg%
20folder/cld.html**

Mental Retardation

American Association on Mental Retardation
444 North Capitol St. NW Suite 846
Washington, DC 20001-1512
800-424-3688
202-387-1968
Fax: 202-387-2193
URL: **www.aamr.org**

Special Olympics International
Eunice Kennedy Shriver, Founder-Director
Timothy Shriver, CEO
Dr. Tom Songster, VP for Sports Policy and
Research
1325 G Street, NW Suite 500
Washington, DC 20005-3104
202-628-3630

Eunice Kennedy Shriver Center
200 Trapelo Road
Waltham, MA 02452-6319
781-642-0001
TTY: 800-764-0200
URL: **www.shriver.org**

International Sports Federation for Persons
With Mental Handicap (INAS-FMH)
Bernard Atha, Executive Director
13-27 Brunswick Place
London N1 6DX
United Kingdom
44-171-250-1100
Fax: 44-171-250-0110

Multiple Sclerosis

URL: **www.nmss.org**

Muscular Dystrophy/Neuromuscular Diseases

Muscular Dystrophy Association-USA
National Headquarters
3300 East Sunrise Drive
Tucson, AZ 85715
800-572-1717
URL: **www.mdausa.org/index.html**

Obesity

URL: **www.naaso.org**

Osteogenesis Imperfecta

URL: **www.oif.org**

Scoliosis

URL: **www.scoliosis-world.com**

Spina Bifida

URL: **www.asbah.org**

Spina Bifida Association of America
4590 MacArthur Blvd. NW Suite 250
Washington, DC 20007-4226
800-621-3141
202-944-3285
Fax: 202-944-3295
URL: **www.sbaa.org**

Wheelchair Sports, USA
3595 East Fountain Boulevard Suite L-1
Colorado Springs, CO 80910
719-574-1150
Fax: 719-574-9840
URL: **www.wsusa.org**

International Stoke Mandeville Wheelchair
Sports Federation
Stoke Mandeville Sports Stadium
Olympic Village, Guttman Road
Aylesbury, Bucks HP 21 9PP
United Kingdom
+44-(0)-01296-436179
Fax: +44-(0)-01296-436484
URL: **www.wsw.org.uk**

Canadian Wheelchair Sports Association
2460 Lancaster Road Suite 200
Ottawa, ON K1B 4S5 Canada
613-523-0004
Fax: 613-523-0149
E-mail: **info@cwsa.ca**
URL: **www.cwsa.ca**

Spinal Cord Injuries

Spinal Cord Injury Information Network
URL: **www.spinalcord.uab.edu**

National Spinal Cord Injury Association
6701 Democracy Blvd. Suite 300-9
Bethesda, Maryland 20817
301-588-6959
Fax: 301-588-9414
URL: **www.spinalcord.org**

Stroke

URL: **www.stroke.org**

Traumatic Brain Injury

URL: **www.biausa.org**

Brain Injury Society
427 Coney Island Ave.
Brooklyn, NY 11218
718-645-4401
URL: **www.bisociety.org**

Sport Organizations

Aerobics

Disabled Sports USA
Kirk Bauer, Executive Director
451 Hungerford Drive Suite 100
Rockville, MD 20850
301-217-0960
Fax: 301-217-0968
E-mail: **dsusa@dsusa.org**
URL: **www.dsusa.org**

Air Guns

NRA Disabled Shooting Sports
11250 Waples Mill Road
Fairfax, VA 22030
703-267-1495

Archery

Wheelchair Archery, USA
C/o Wheelchair Sports, USA
3595 E. Fountain Blvd. Suite L-1
Colorado Springs, CO 80910
719-574-1150
Fax: 719-574-9840

Basketball

National Wheelchair Basketball Association
Charlotte Institute of Rehabilitation
1100 Blythe Blvd.

Charlotte, NC 28203
704-355-1064
URL: **www.nwba.org**

Billiards

National Wheelchair Poolplayers Association
30872 Puritan
Livonia, MI 48154
702-437-6792
URL: **http://nwpainc.com/**

Boating

U.S. Rowing Association
201 South Capitol Ave. Suite 400
Indianapolis, IN 46225
800-314-4ROW
317-237-5656
Fax: 317-237-5646
E-mail: **members@usrowing.org**
URL: **www.usrowing.org**

Bowling

American Wheelchair Bowling Association
2912 Country Woods Lane
Palm Harbor, FL 34683-6417
Phone/Fax: 727-734-0023
URL: **www.awba.org**

Camping

Office of Special Programs and Populations
National Park Service
U.S. Department of the Interior
800 N. Capitol, NW
Washington, DC 20002
202-673-7647

Canoeing

American Canoe Association
Kayaking/Disabled Paddlers Committee
7432 Alban Station Blvd. Suite B-232
Springfield, VA 22150-2311
703-451-0141
Fax: 703-451-2245
URL: **www.acanet.org**

Fencing

U.S. Fencing Association
1 Olympic Plaza
Colorado Springs, CO 80909
719-578-4511
URL: **www.usfencing.org**

Flying

Challenge Air for Kids and Friends
Love Field, North Concourse
8008 Cedar Springs Road N106-LB24
Dallas, TX 75235
214-351-3353
URL: **www.challengeair.com**

Freedom's Wings International
1832 Lake Avenue
Scotch Plains, NJ 07076
908-232-6354
URL: **www.freedomswings.org**

International Wheelchair Aviators
Big Bear Airport
PO Box 1126
500 W Meadow Lane
Big Bear City, CA 92315
909-585-9663
URL: **www.wheelchairaviators.org**

Football

Parks and Recreation Department
Adapted Recreation Programs
Cabrillo Bathhouse
1118 E Cabrillo Boulevard
Santa Barbara, CA 93103
805-564-5421

Golf

Association of Disabled American Golfers
PO Box 280649
Lakewood, CO 80228-0649
303-922-5228
303-969-0447
URL: **www.golfcolorado.com/adag**

National Amputee Golf Association
11 Walnut Hill Road
Amherst, NH 03031-1713
800-633-6242
Fax: 603-672-2987
URL: **www.nagagolf.org**

Hockey

American Sled Hockey Association
Rich DeGlopper
21 Summerwood Court
Buffalo, NY 14223
716-876-7390
URL: **www.sledhockey.org**

Horseback Riding

North American Riding for the Handicapped
Association
PO Box 33150
Denver, CO 80233
800-369-7433
Fax: 303-252-4610
URL: **www.narha.org**

Hunting

NRA Disabled Shooting Services
11250 Waples Mill Road
Fairfax, VA 22030
703-267-1495

Motorcycling

Wheelchair Motorcycle Association
101 Torrey Street
Brockton, MA 02301
508-583-8614

Racquetball

U.S. Racquetball Association
1685 West Uintah
Colorado Springs, CO 80904
719-635-5396
URL: **www.usra.org**

Road Racing

U.S. Handcycling Federation
Ian Lawless
115 Du Four St.
Santa Cruz, CA 95060
831-457-7747
E-mail: **info@ushf.org**
URL: **www.ushf.org**

Wheelchair Athletics of the USA/WSUSA
3595 E. Fountain Blvd. Suite L-1
Colorado Springs, CO 80910
719-574-1150

Rowing

U.S. Rowing Association
201 South Capitol Ave. Suite 400
Indianapolis, IN 46225
800-314-4ROW
317-237-5656
Fax: 317-237-5646
E-mail: **members@usrowing.org**
URL: **www.usrowing.org**

Rugby

U.S. Quad Rugby Association
Jim Bishop
5861 White Cypress Drive
Lake Worth, FL 33467-6230
561-964-1712
Fax: 561-642-4444
E-mail: **jbishop@quadruby.com**
URL: **www.quadrugby.com**

Sailing

Access to Sailing
6475 East Pacific Coast Hwy.
Long Beach, CA 90802
562-499-6925
Fax: 562-437-7655
URL: **www.access2sailing.org**

National Ocean Access Project
451 Hungerford Dr. Suite 100
Rockville, MD 20850
301-217-0960

Scuba Diving

Handicapped Scuba Association
1104 El Prado
San Clemente, CA 92672
949-498-4540
Fax: 949-498-6128
E-mail: **hsa@hsascuba.com**
URL: **www.hsascuba.com**

Shooting

NRA Disabled Shooting Services
11250 Waples Mill Road
Fairfax, VA 22030
703-267-1495

National Skeet Shooting Association
5931 Roft Road
San Antonio, TX 78253
210-688-3371
Fax: 210-688-3014
E-mail: **nssa@nssa-nsca.com**
URL: **nssa-nsca.com/nssa**

Amateur Trapshooting Association
601 W. National Road
Vandalia, OH 45372
937-898-4638
Fax: 937-898-5472
URL: **www.shootata.com/ATAHome.cfm**

Snow Skiing

Wheelchair Athletics of the USA/WSUSA
3595 E. Fountain Blvd. Suite L-1
Colorado Springs, CO 80910
719-574-1150

Disabled Sports USA
Kirk Bauer, Executive Director
451 Hungerford Drive Suite 100
Rockville, MD 20850
301-217-0960
Fax: 301-217-0968
E-mail: **dsusa@dsusa.org**
URL: **www.dsusa.org**

U.S. Disabled Ski Team
PO Box 100
Park City, UT 84060
801-649-9090

Softball/Baseball

National Wheelchair Softball Association
1616 Todd Court
Hastings, MN 55033
612-437-1792
URL: **www.wheelchairsoftball.com**

Challenger Baseball
Little League Headquarters
PO Box 3485
Williamsport, PA 17701

National Beep Baseball Association
C/o Jeanette Bigger
231 West 1st St.
Topeka, KS 66606-1304
913-234-2156
URL: **www.nbba.org**

Swimming

U.S. Wheelchair Swimming, Inc.
Liz DeFrancesco
105 Jenne St.
Santa Cruz, CA 95060
E-mail: **bizde@got.net**

Aquatics Council (Adapted Aquatics)
Dr. Monica Lepore, Chairperson
West Chester University
Department of Kinesiology
West Chester, PA 19382
610-436-2516

Council for National Cooperation in Aquatics
C/o Louise Priest
901 W. New York Street
Indianapolis, IN 46202
317-638-4238

Table Tennis

American Wheelchair Table Tennis Association
Jennifer Johnson
23 Parker St.
Port Chester, NY 10573
914-937-3932
E-mail: **johnsonjennifer@yahoo.com**

Tennis

National Foundation of Wheelchair Tennis
940 Calle Amanecer Suite B
San Clemente, CA 92672
714-361-3663
URL: **www.htwt.org**

Track and Field

Wheelchair Athletics of the USA/WSUSA
3595 E. Fountain Blvd. Suite L-1
Colorado Springs, CO 80910
719-574-1150

Water Skiing

American Water Ski Association
1251 Holycow Road
Polk City, FL 33868
800-533-2972
Fax: 863-325-8259
URL: **http://usawaterski.org**

Weightlifting

U.S. Wheelchair Weightlifting Federation (WSUSA)
39 Michael Place
Levittown, PA 19057
215-945-1964

Wilderness

Breckenridge Outdoor Education Center
PO Box 697
Breckenridge, CO 80424
970-453-6422
Fax: 970-453-4676
URL: **www.boec.org**

Cooperative Wilderness Handicapped Outdoor Group
PO Box 8128
Idaho State University
Pocatello, ID 83209
208-236-3912
URL: **www.isu.edu/departments/cwhog/index.html**

Pacific Crest Outward Bound School
0110 SW Bancroft
Portland, OR 97201
800-547-3312
URL: **www.pcobs.org**

Voyager Outward Bound School
101 Chapman Street
Ely, MN 55731
218-365-7790
URL: **www.vobs.com**

Wilderness Inquiry
808 14th Avenue SE Box 84
Minneapolis, MN 55414-1516
800-728-0719
612-676-9400
URL: **www.wildernessinquiry.org**

Wilderness on Wheels
3131 S Vaughn Way Suite 224
Aurora, CO 80014
303-751-3959
URL: **www.wildernessonwheels.org**

General Resources in Adapted Physical Education and Sport

Committee on Sports for Disabled
Mark Shepherd, COSD Chair
United States Olympic Committee (USOC)
1750 East Boulder Street
Colorado Springs, CO 80909-5760
719-578-4818

Disabled Sports USA
Kirk Bauer, Executive Director
451 Hungerford Drive Suite 100
Rockville, MD 20850
301-217-0960
Fax: 301-217-0968
E-mail: **dsusa@dsusa.org**
URL: **www.dsusa.org**

National Sports Center for the Disabled
PO Box 1290
Winter Park, CO 80482
970-726-1540
303-316-1540
Fax: 970-726-4112
URL: **www.nscd.org**

National Sports Network
A Sports Program for People With Disabilities
PO Box 47799
St. Petersburg, FL 33743-7799
800-699-4494
Fax: 727-345-7130

Palaestra: Forum of Sport, Physical Education, and Recreation for Those With Disabilities (Magazine)
PO Box 508
Macomb, IL 61455
309-833-1902
E-mail: **challpub@macomb.com**
URL: **www.palaestra.com**

Sports 'N Spokes (Magazine)
PVA Publications
2111 East Highland Street Suite 180
Phoenix, AZ 85016-4780
URL: **www.sportsnspokes.com**

U.S. Organization for Disabled Athletes (USODA)
143 California Avenue
Uniondale, NY 11553
800-25-USODA
516-485-3701

Equipment Companies

This list includes the names of equipment companies, what they make, the number to call to order a catalog or ask questions, and their Web site if they're on the Internet. This information will assist the general physical education teacher as well as inform parents about equipment availability.

Access to Recreation: Adaptive recreation equipment for the physically challenged.
800-634-4351 to order catalog
805-498-8186 fax
www.accesstr.com

Community Play Things: Safe and adapted playground equipment for young children.
800-777-4244 customer service
800-336-5948 fax
www.communityplaythings.com

Project Adventure Equipment Catalog: A source book for ropes courses and adventure programs.
800-796-9917
www.pa.org/equipment.asp

RehabTool LLC: High-tech assistive, adaptive, and accessibility aids for children and adults with disabilities and special needs.
281-531-6106
281-531-6406 fax
info@rehabtool.com
www.rehabtool.com

S&S Worldwide Games: Sports equipment for every occasion.
800-243-9232 to order catalog
800-566-6678 fax
www.snswwide.com

Sportime/Abilitations: Sports, recreation, and games equipment with a variety of textures, shapes, and colors, for all individuals, including those with sensory impairments and physical disabilities.

800-850-8602 to order catalog

800-845-1535 fax

E-mail: **catalog.request@sportime.com**

Things From Bell: A variety of sports, recreation, and game equipment in many colors, shapes, and textures.

800-543-1458

800-566-6678 fax

Toledo: Physical education supply company with inexpensive sports and playground equipment.

800-225-7749 to order catalog

800-489-6256 fax

www.tpesonline.com

Vital Signs: Instrumentation for rehabilitation, sports medicine, and physical fitness.

608-735-4718 to order catalog

608-735-4859 fax

Wolverine Sports: Sports, gymnastics, and coaching equipment.

800-521-2832 to order catalog

800-654-4321 fax

www.wolverinesports.com

G Additional Resources

Here are a few suggested resources, in addition to the references used in each chapter, to assist the general physical educator with adapted physical education.

Books

American Alliance for Health, Physical Education, Recreation and Dance. 1989. *The best of practical pointers.* Reston, VA: AAHPERD.

American Alliance for Health, Physical Education, Recreation and Dance. 1991. *Sports instruction for individuals with disabilities: The best of practical pointers.* Reston, VA: AAHPERD.

DePauw, K.P. and Gavron, S.J. 1995. *Disability and sport.* Champaign, IL: Human Kinetics.

Dunn, J. 1997. *Special physical education: Adapted, individualized, developmental.* 7th ed. Madison, WI: Brown and Benchmark.

Grosse, S.J. and Thompson, D. 1993. *Play and recreation for individuals with disabilities: Practical pointers.* Reston, VA: AAHPERD.

Kasser, S.L. 1995. *Inclusive games.* Champaign, IL: Human Kinetics.

Lieberman, L.J. and Cowart, J.F. 1996. *Games for people with sensory impairments.* Champaign, IL: Human Kinetics.

McCall, R.M. and Craft, D.H. 2000. *Moving with a purpose: Developing programs for preschoolers of all abilities.* Champaign, IL: Human Kinetics.

Sherrill, C. 1998. *Adapted physical activity, recreation, and sport: Crossdisciplinary and lifespan.* 5th ed. Boston, MA: WCB McGraw-Hill.

Winnick, J. 2000. *Adapted physical education and sport.* Champaign, IL: Human Kinetics.

Adapted Physical Education Web Sites

ADAPT-TALK: A listserv for the purpose of dialogue about adapted physical education. Supported by Sportime.
www.lyris.sportime.com/adapt-talk-index.html

The National Center on Physical Activity and Disability: An organization that provides a tremendous amount of information on physical activity programming for individuals with disablities.
http://ncpad.cc.uic.edu/home.htm

The National Consortium on Physical Education and Recreation for Individuals With Disabilities: An advocacy group to promote adapted physical education and recreation.
http://ncperid.usf.edu/index.html

Adapted Physical Education National Standards (APENS): The Web site for information about the national certification exam for adapted physical education.
www.twu.edu/o/apens

Project INSPIRE: Information about inclusion, disabilities, and adapted physical education. Supported by Texas Woman's University.
www7.twu.edu/~f_huettig

Disability Sports Web Page: Information pertaining to adapted physical education, adapted sport, and adapted technology. Supported by Michigan State University.
http://ed-web3.educ.msu.edu/kin866

Physical Activity For All: Information about inclusion, adapted physical education, and disabilities. Supported by University of South Florida.
http://pe.usf.edu/pafa

Sign Language: Sign language taught in a simple and understandable way. Includes sport signs.
www.handspeak.com

Camp Abilities: A developmental sports camp for children who are blind.
www.brockport.edu/campabilities

Disability Sport Information: A web site that provides up-to-date disability sport information with profiles of disabled athletes.
www.wemedia.com

Publications

Palaestra: A forum of sport, physical education & recreation for those with disabilities.
www.palaestra.com

Sports 'N Spokes: A publication covering the latest in competitive wheelchair sports and recreational opportunities.
www.sportsnspokes.com/sns/default.htm

Active Living Magazine: The cross-disability "how-to, where-to, and what-to" magazine for people who want to attain or maintain a healthy, active lifestyle.
www.cripworld.com/themall/activeliving.shtml

Adapted Physical Activity Quarterly: The official journal of the International Federation of Adapted Physical Activity; the latest scholarly inquiry related to physical activity for special populations.
www.humankinetics.com/products/journals

State Directors of Special Education

States

Alabama

Special Education Services
State Department of Education
PO Box 302101
Montgomery, AL 36130-2101
334-242-8114
TTY: 334-242-8406
Fax: 334-242-9192
URL: **www.alsde.edu/html/sections/section
_detail.asp?section=65&menu=
sections&footer=sections**
E-mail: **mabreyw@alsde.edu**

Alaska

Teaching And Learning Support
Alaska Department of Education and Early
Development
801 West 10th Street Suite 200
Juneau, AK 99801-1894
907-465-8693
TTY: 907-465-2970
Fax: 907-465-2806
URL: **www.eed.state.ak.us/tls/sped/home.
html**

Arizona

Exceptional Student Services
Department of Education
1535 West Jefferson Street Bin 24

Phoenix, AZ 85007
602-542-3184
800-352-4558
TTY: 602-542-1410
Fax: 602-542-5404
URL: **www.ade.state.az.us/ess**
E-mail: **jgasawa@ade.az.gov**

Arkansas

Special Education
Department of Education Building
Room 105-C
4 State Capitol Mall
Little Rock, AR 72201-1071
501-682-4221
Fax: 501-682-5159
E-mail: **dsydoriak@arkedu.k12.ar.us**

California

Special Education Division
State Department of Education
515 L Street Suite 270
Sacramento, CA 95814
916-445-4602
Fax: 916-327-3706
E-mail: **aparker@cde.ca.gov**

Colorado

Special Education Services
Department of Education
201 East Colfax Avenue

Denver, CO 80203
303-866-6694
TTY: 303-860-7060
Fax: 303-866-6811
URL: **www.cde.state.co.us/cdesped/index.htm**
E-mail: **sped@cde.state.co.us**

Connecticut

Bureau of Special Education and Pupil Services
State Department of Education
25 Industrial Park Road
Middletown, CT 06457
860-807-2025
Fax: 860-807-2047
URL: **www.state.ct.us/sde**
E-mail: **george.dowaliby@po.state.ct.us**

Delaware

Exceptional Children and Early Childhood Education
Department of Education
PO Box 1402
Dover, DE 19903-1402
302-739-5471
Fax: 302-739-2388
URL: **www.doe.state.de.us/exceptional_child/ececehome.htm**
E-mail: **mbrooks@state.de.us**

District of Columbia

State Office of Special Education
825 North Capitol Street NE 6th Floor
Washington, DC 20002
202-442-4800
Fax: 202-442-5517
URL: **www.k12.dc.us/dcps/home.html**
E-mail: **specialeducation@k12.dc.us**

Florida

Clearinghouse Information Center
Department of Education
Bureau of Instructional Support and Community Services
325 West Gaines Street
Tallahassee, FL 32399-0400
850-488-1879
Fax: 850-487-2679
URL: **www.firn.edu/doe/commhome**
E-mail: **CICBISCS@mail.doe.state.fl.us**

Georgia

Division for Exceptional Students
Department of Education
1870 Twin Towers East
Atlanta, GA 30334
404-656-3963
Fax: 404-651-6457
URL: **www.doe.k12.ga.us/sla/exceptional/exceptional.asp**
E-mail: **pbragg@doe.k12.ga.us**

Hawaii

Special Education Section
State Department of Education
637 18th Avenue
Room C102
Honolulu, HI 96816
808-733-4990
800-297-2070
Fax: 808-733-4841
URL: **// doe.k12.hi.us/specialeducation/index.htm**

Idaho

Special Education Department
Department of Education
PO Box 83720
Boise, ID 83720-0027
208-332-6910
800-432-4601
TTY: 800-377-3524
Fax: 208-334-4664
URL: **www.sde.state.id.us/SpecialEd**
E-mail: **rbrychen@sde.state.id.us**

Illinois

Office of Special Education
Illinois State Board of Education
Mail Code E-228
100 North First Street
Springfield, IL 62777-0001
217-782-4826
866-262-6663
TTY: 217-782-1900
Fax: 217-782-0372
URL: **www.isbe.state.il.us/spec-ed**
E-mail: **griffel@isbe.net** or **jshook@smtp.isbe.state.il.us**

Indiana

Division of Special Education
Department of Education
State House, Room 229
Indianapolis, IN 46204-2798
317-232-0570
877-851-4106
TTY: 317-232-0570
Fax: 317-232-0589
URL: **web.indstate.edu/soe/iseas/dse.html**
E-mail: **marrab@speced.doe.state.in.us**

Iowa

Bureau of Children, Family, and Community
Services
Department of Education
Grimes State Office Building
Des Moines, IA 50319-0146
515-281-5294
Fax: 515-242-5988
URL: **www.state.ia.us/educate/programs/
ecese/cfcs/index.html**
E-mail: **brenda.oas@ed.state.ia.us**

Kansas

Student Support Services
State Department of Education
120 Southeast 10th Avenue
Topeka, KS 66612-1182
785-291-3097
800-203-9462
TTY: 785-296-6338
Fax: 785-296-6715
URL: **ww2.nekesc.org/ksde/services.html**
E-mail: **apochowski@ksde.org**

Kentucky

Division of Exceptional Children Services
State Department of Education
500 Mero Street Eighth Floor
Frankfort, KY 40601
502-564-4970
TTY: 502-564-4770
Fax: 502-564-6721
URL: **www.kde.state.ky.us**
E-mail: **marmstro@kde.state.ky.us**

Louisiana

Division of Special Populations
PO Box 94064

Baton Rouge, LA 70804-9064
225-342-3633
TTY: 225-219-4588
Fax: 225-342-5880
URL: **www.doe.state.la.us**
E-mail: **vberidon@mail.doe.state.la.us**

Maine

Office of Special Services
State Department of Education
23 State House Station
Augusta, ME 04333-0023
207-624-6650
TTY: 207-624-6800
Fax: 207-624-6651
URL: **www.state.me.us/education/specserv.
htm**
E-mail: **dstockford@doe.k12.me.us**

Maryland

Division of Special Education/Early Intervention Services
Department of Education
200 West Baltimore Street Fourth Floor
Baltimore, MD 21201
410-767-0238
TTY: 800-735-2258
Fax: 410-333-8165
URL: **www.msde.state.md.us**
E-mail: **cbaglin@msde.state.md.us** or
nFeather@msde.state.md.us

Massachusetts

Massachusetts Director of Special Education
State Department of Education
350 Main Street
Malden, MA 02148-5023
781-388-3388
Fax: 781-388-3396
URL: **www.doe.mass.edu/sped**
E-mail: **MMittnacht@doe.mass.edu**

Michigan

Office of Special Education and Early Intervention Services
Department of Education
608 West Allegan
Lansing, MI 48933
517-373-9433
TTY: 517-373-9434

Fax: 517-373-7504
URL: **www.mde.state.mi.us/off/sped**
E-mail: **RowellF@state.mi.us**

Minnesota

Division of Special Education
Department of Children, Families, and Learning
1500 Highway 36 West
Roseville, MN 55113-4266
651-582-8289
Fax: 651-582-8729
URL: **http://children.state.mn.us**
E-mail: **norena.hale@state.mn.us**

Mississippi

Office of Special Education
Mississippi Department of Education
PO Box 771
359 North West Street Suite 338
Jackson, MS 39205-0771
601-359-3498
Fax: 601-359-2198
URL: **www.mde.k12.ms.us**
E-mail: **thoover@mde.k12.state.ms.us** or
dennis@mde.k12.ms.us

Missouri

Division of Special Education
Department of Elementary and Secondary
Education
PO Box 480
Jefferson City, MO 65102
573-751-5739
Fax: 573-526-4404
URL: **www.dese.state.mo.us/divspeced**
E-mail: **mfriedeb@mail.dese.state.mo.us**

Montana

Division of Special Education
Office of Public Instruction
PO Box 202501
Helena, MT 59620-2501
406-444-4429
Fax: 406-444-3924
URL: **www.metnet.state.mt.us**

Nebraska

Special Populations Office
Department of Education
301 Centennial Mall South

PO Box 94987
Lincoln, NE 68509-4987
402-471-2471
888-806-6287 (NE Residents only)
TTY: 402-471-2471
Fax: 402-471-5022
URL: **www.nde.state.ne.us/SPED/sped.html**

Nevada

Educational Equity Team
State Department of Education
700 East Fifth Street Suite 113
Carson City, NV 89701
775-687-9171
TTY: 800-326-6888
Fax: 775-687-9123
URL: **www.nde.state.nv.us**

New Hampshire

Special Education Services
Department of Education
101 Pleasant Street
Concord, NH 03301-3860
603-271-3741
TTY: 800-735-2964
Fax: 603-271-1953
URL: **www.ed.state.nh.us/SpecialEd/**
special1.htm

New Jersey

Office of Special Education Programs
Department of Education
PO Box 500
Trenton, NJ 08625-0500
609-633-6833
TTY: 609-984-8432
Fax: 609-984-8422
URL: **www.state.nj.us/education**
E-mail: **bgantwer@doe.state.nj.us**

New Mexico

New Mexico State Department of Special
Education
300 Don Gaspar Avenue
Santa Fe, NM 87501
505-827-6541
Fax: 505-827-6791
URL: **http://sde.state.nm.us/divisions/**
learningservices/specialeducation/
index.html
E-mail: **bpasternack@sde.state.nm.us**

New York

Office of Vocational and Educational Services
for Individuals with Disabilities
One Commerce Plaza, Room 1624
Albany, NY 12234
518-486-7584
800-222-5627
TTY: 518-474-5652
Fax: 518-473-5387
URL: http://web.nysed.gov/vesid
E-mail: vesidspe@mail.nysed.gov

North Carolina

Exceptional Children Division
North Carolina Department of Public Instruction
301 North Wilmington Street
Raleigh, NC 27601-2825
919-807-3969
Fax: 919-807-3243
URL: www.ncpublicschools.org/ec
E-mail: lharris@dpi.state.nc.us

North Dakota

Office of Special Education
Department of Public Instruction
600 East Boulevard Avenue 10th Floor
Bismarck, ND 58505-0440
701-328-2277
TTY: 701-328-4920
Fax: 701-328-4149
URL: www.dpi.state.nd.us/speced/index.
shtm
E-mail: landerso@mail.dpi.state.nd.us

Ohio

Office for Exceptional Children
State Department of Education
25 South Front Street Second Floor
Columbus, OH 43215
614-466-2650
Fax: 614-728-1097
E-mail: john.herner@ode.state.oh.us/
exceptional_children

Oklahoma

Special Education Services
State Department of Education
2500 North Lincoln Boulevard Room 411
Oklahoma City, OK 73105-4599
405-521-3351
TTY: 405-521-4875
Fax: 405-522-3503
URL: http://sde.state.ok.us
E-mail: darla_griffin@mail.sde.state.ok.us
or   john_corpolongo@mail.sde.state.
ok.us

Oregon

Office of Special Education
Department of Education
255 Capitol Street NE
Salem, OR 97310-0203
503-378-3600
TTY: 503-378-2892
Fax: 503-378-7968
URL: www.ode.state.or.us/sped/index.
htm
E-mail: steve.johnson@state.or.us

Pennsylvania

Bureau of Special Education
Pennsylvania Department of Education
333 Market Street Seventh Floor
Harrisburg, PA 17126-0333
717-783-6913
TTY: 717-787-7367
Fax: 717-783-6139
URL: www.pde.psu.edu
E-mail: fwarkomski@state.pa.us

Rhode Island

Office of Special Needs
State Department of Education
Shepard Building Fourth Floor
255 Westminster Street
Providence, RI 02903
401-222-4600, Ext. 1-2504
TTY: 800-745-5555
Fax: 401-222-6030
URL: www.ridoe.net/special_needs
E-mail: tdipaola@rideoe.net

South Carolina

Office of Exceptional Children
Department of Education
Rutledge Building 1429 Senate Room 808
Columbia, SC 29201
803-734-8806
Fax: 803-734-4824

South Dakota

Division of Education and Resources
Office of Special Education
700 Governors Drive
Pierre, SD 57501-2291
605-773-3678
TTY: 605-773-6302
Fax: 605-773-3782
URL: **www.state.sd.us/deca/special/special.htm**
E-mail: **michelle.powers@state.sd.us**

Tennessee

Division of Special Education
Department of Education
Fifth Floor Andrew Johnson Tower
710 James Robertson Parkway
Nashville, TN 37243-0380
615-741-2851
TTY: 615-741-2237
Fax: 615-532-9412
URL: **www.state.tn.us/education/msped.htm**
E-mail: **jfisher@mail.state.tn.us**

Texas

Division of Special Education
Texas Education Agency
1701 North Congress Avenue
Austin, TX 78701
512-463-9414
800-252-9668
TTY: 512-475-3540
Fax: 512-463-9560
URL: **www.tea.state.tx.us/special.ed**
E-mail: **sped@tea.tetn.net**

Utah

Services for At-Risk Students
Utah State Office of Education
250 East 500 South
Salt Lake City, UT 84111-3204
801-538-7711
Fax: 801-538-7991
URL: **www.usoe.k12.ut.us/sars**
E-mail: **mtaylor@usoe.k12.ut.us**

Vermont

Family and Educational Support Team (Vermont)

State Office Building
120 State Street
Montpelier, VT 05620-2501
802-828-5118
Fax: 802-828-3140
E-mail: **mmartin@doe.state.vt.us** or **dkane@doe.state.vt.us**

Virginia

Office of Special Education
Department of Education
PO Box 2120
Richmond, VA 23218-2120
804-225-2402
800-292-3920
TTY: 800-422-1098
Fax: 804-371-8796
E-mail: **dougcox@mail.va.k12.edu**

Washington

Special Education Section
Old Capitol Building
PO Box 47200
Olympia, WA 98504
360-725-6075
TTY: 360-586-0126
Fax: 360-586-0247
URL: **www.k12.wa.us/specialed**
E-mail: **speced@ospi.webnet.edu**

West Virginia

Office of Special Education
Department of Education
Building 6 Room 304
1900 Kanawha Boulevard East
Charleston, WV 25305
304-558-2696
800-642-8541 (WV residents only)
TTY: 800-642-8541
Fax: 304-558-3741
URL: **http://wvde.state.wv.us**
E-mail: **dbodkins@access.k12.wv.us/ose**

Wisconsin

Division for Learning Support: Equity and Advocacy
Department of Public Instruction
125 South Webster Street
PO Box 7841
Madison, WI 53707-7841

608-266-1649
800-441-4563
TTY: 608-267-2427
Fax: 608-267-3746
URL: **www.dpi.state.wi.us/dpi/dlsea/index.html**
E-mail: **michael.thompson@dpi.state.wi.us**

Wyoming

Special Education Unit
State Department of Education
Second Floor Hathaway Building
2300 Capitol Avenue
Cheyenne, WY 82002-0050
307-777-7417
Fax: 307-777-6234
URL: www.k12.wy.us/speced
E-mail: **rwalk@educ.state.wy.us**

Territories

American Samoa

Special Education Division
Department of Education
PO Box 2202
Pago Pago, AS 96799
684-633-1323
Fax: 684-633-7707

Commonwealth of the Northern Mariana Islands

No Entry

Federated States of Micronesia

Office of Special Education
Special Education
Federated States of Micronesia National Government
Kolonia, Pohnpei, FM 96941
691-320-2609
Fax: 691-320-5500

E-mail: **mkeller@mail.fm**

Guam

Division of Special Education
Department of Education
PO Box DE
Agana, GU 96910
671-475-0549
TTY: 671-475-0550
Fax: 671-475-0562
E-mail: **guamsped@ite.net**

Puerto Rico

Department of Special Education
Department of Education
PO Box 190759
San Juan, PR 00919-0759
787-753-7981
Fax: 787-753-7691

Republic of Palau

Special Education Coordinator
PO Box 189
Palau, PW 96940
680-488-2568
Fax: 680-488-5808
E-mail: **spedcor@palaunet.com**

Republic of the Marshall Islands

No Entry

Virgin Islands

Division of Special Education
44-46 Kongens Gade
St. Thomas, VI 00802
340-776-5802
Fax: 340-774-0817
E-mail: **bwoneal@usviosep.org**

Data generated from EROD database Aug 16, 2001. Please report any discrepancies to **mheeg@aspensys.com**.

References

Andrews, S.E. 1998. Using inclusion literature to promote positive attitudes toward disabilities. *Journal of Adolescent & Adult Literacy* 41(6):420-426.

Auxter, D., Pyfer, J., and Huettig, C. 1997. *Principles and methods of adapted physical education.* 8th ed. St. Louis: Mosby.

Auxter, D., Pyfer, J., and Huettig, C. 2001. *Principles and methods of adapted physical education.* 9th ed. St. Louis: Mosby.

Barfield, J.P., Hannigan-Downs, S.B., and Lieberman, L.J. 1998. Implementing a peer tutor program: Strategies for practitioners. *The Physical Educator* 55(4):211-221.

Blinde, E.M., and McCallister, S.G. 1998. Listening to the voices of students with physical disabilities. *Journal of Physical Education, Recreation and Dance* 69:64-68.

Block, M.E. 1998. Don't forget the social aspects of inclusion. *Strategies* 12(2):30-34.

Block, M.E. 2000. *A teacher's guide to including students with disabilities in general physical education.* 2nd ed. Baltimore, MD: Paul H. Brookes.

Block, M.E., and Horton, M.L. 1996. Including safety in physical education: Do not exclude students with disabilities. *The Physical Educator* 53(2):58-72.

Block, M.E., Lieberman, L.J., and Conner-Kuntz, F. 1998. Authentic assessment in adapted physical education. *Journal of Physical Education, Recreation and Dance* 69(3):48-56.

Briggs, D. 1975. Across the ages. *Times Educational Supplement* 15:9.

Bruininks, R.H. 1978. *Bruininks-Oseretsky Test of Motor Proficiency: Examiner's Manual.* Circle Pines, MN: American Guidance Service.

Burton, A.W., and Miller, D.E. 1998. *Movement skill assessment.* Champaign, IL: Human Kinetics.

Conatser, P., Block, M., and Lepore, M. 2000. Aquatic instructors' attitudes toward teaching students with disabilities. *Adapted Physical Activity Quarterly* 17(2):197-207.

Cooper Institute for Aerobic Research. 1994. *FITNESSGRAM.* Reston, VA: AAHPERD.

Davis, W., and Burton, A. 1991. Ecological task analysis: Translating movement theory behavior into practice. *Adapted Physical Activity Quarterly* 8(2):154-177.

Delquadri, J., Greenwood, C.R., Whorton, D., Carta, J.J., and Hall, R.V. 1986. Classwide peer tutoring. *Exceptional Children* 52(6):535-542.

DePaepe, J.L. 1985. The influence of three least restrictive environments on the content, motor-ALT, and performance of moderately mentally retarded students. *Journal of Teaching in Physical Education* 5:34-41.

Dunn, J.M. 1997. *Special physical education*. Madison, WI: Brown and Benchmark.

Dunn, J.M., Morehouse, J.W., and Fredericks, H.D. 1986. *Physical education for the severely handicapped: A systematic approach to data based gymnasium*. Austin, TX: Pro-Ed.

Education for All Handicapped Children Act of 1975 (Public Law 94-142).

Franck, M., Graham, G., Lawson, H., Lougherty, T., Ritson, R., Sanborn, M., and Seefelt, V. 1992. *Outcomes of quality physical education programs*. Reston, VA: National Association of Sport and Physical Education.

Frankenberg, W.K., and Dodds, J.B. 1991. *The Denver II Developmental Screening Test*. Denver, CO: University of Colorado Medical Center.

French, R., Henderson, H., Kinnison, L., and Sherrill, C. 1998. Revisiting Section 504, Physical Education and Sport. *Journal of Physical Education, Recreation and Dance* 69(7):57-63.

Fronske, H. 1997. *Teaching cues for sports skills*. Needham Heights, MA: Allyn and Bacon.

Greenwood, C.R., Carta, J.J., and Hall, R.V. 1988. The use of peer tutoring strategies in classroom management and education instruction. *School Psychology Review* 17(4):258-275.

Henderson, H.L., French, R., and Kinnison, L. 2001. Reporting grades for students with disabilities in general physical education. *Journal of Physical Education, Recreation and Dance* 72(6):50-55.

Housner, L.D., ed. 2000. *Integrated physical education: A guide for the elementary classroom teacher*. Morgantown, WV: Fitness Information Technology.

Houston-Wilson, C., Dunn, J.M., van der Mars, H., and McCubbin, J.A. 1997. The effect of peer tutors on motor performance in integrated physical education classes. *Adapted Physical Activity Quarterly* 14(4):298-313.

Houston-Wilson, C., and Lieberman, L.J. 1999. Becoming involved in the Individualized Education Program: A guide for regular physical educators. *Journal of Physical Education, Recreation and Dance* 70(3):60-64.

Houston-Wilson, C., Lieberman, L.J., Horton, M., and Kasser, S. 1997. Peer tutoring: A plan for instructing students of all abilities. *Journal of Physical Education, Recreation and Dance* 68(6):39-44.

Individuals With Disabilities Education Act Amendments of 1997. U.S. Public Laws 105-17. *Federal Register*, 4 June, 1997.

Johnson, R.T., and Johnson, D.W. 1983. Effects of cooperative, competitive, and individualistic learning experiences on social development. *Exceptional Children* 49(4):323-329.

Kelly, L.E. 1995. *Adapted physical education national standards*. Champaign, IL: Human Kinetics.

Kiphard, E. 1983. Adapted physical education in Germany. In *Adapted physical activity from theory to application*, Eason, R., Smith, T., and Caron, F., eds., p. 25-32. Champaign, IL: Human Kinetics.

LaMaster, K., Gall, K., Kinchin, G., and Siedentop, D. 1998. Inclusion practices of effective elementary specialists. *Adapted Physical Activity Quarterly* 15(1):64-81.

Lepore, M., Gayle, G.W., and Stevens, S. 1998. *Adapted aquatics programming*. Champaign, IL: Human Kinetics.

Lieberman, L.J. 1999. Physical fitness and adapted physical education for children who are deaf-blind. In *Deaf-blind training manual*. Logan, UT: SKI-HI Institute Press.

Lieberman, L.J., and Cowart, J.F. 1996. *Games for people with sensory impairments.* Champaign, IL: Human Kinetics.

Lieberman, L.J., and Cruz, L. 2001. Blanket medical excuses from physical education: Possible solutions. *Teaching Elementary Physical Education* 12(4):27-30.

Lieberman, L.J., Dunn, J.M., van der Mars, H., and McCubbin, J.A. 2000. Peer tutors' effects on activity levels of deaf students in inclusive elementary physical education. *Adapted Physical Activity Quarterly* 17(1):20-39.

Lieberman, L.J., Houston-Wilson, C., and Aiello, R. 2001. *Developing and implementing a peer tutor program.* Presentation at the American Alliance for Health, Physical Education, Recreation and Dance National Conference, Cincinnati, Ohio.

Lieberman, L.J., Houston-Wilson, C., Brock, S., Aldrich, K., and Kolb, L. 2000. *Setting up a peer tutor training program for your inclusive program.* Presentation at the New York State Association for Health, Physical Education, Recreation, and Dance Conference, Hudson Valley, NY.

Lieberman, L.J., and McHugh, B.E. 2001. Health related fitness of children with visual impairments and blindness. *Journal of Visual Impairment and Blindness* 95(5):272-287.

Lieberman, L.J., Newcomer, J., McCubbin, J.A., and Dalrymple, N. 1997. The effects of cross-aged peer tutors on the academic learning time in physical education of students with disabilities in inclusive elementary physical education classes. *Brazilian International Journal of Adapted Physical Education* 4(1):15-32.

Long, E., Irmer, L., Burkett, L., Glasenapp, G., and Odenkirk, B. 1980. PEOPLE. *Journal of Physical Education and Recreation* 51:28-29.

Loovis, M.E., and Loovis, C.L. 1997. A disability awareness unit in physical education and attitudes of elementary school students. *Perceptual Motor Skills* 84:768-770.

Mach, M. 2000. Using assistants for physical education. *Strategies* 14(2):8.

Melograno, V.J. 1994. Portfolio assessment: Documenting authentic student learning. *Journal of Physical Education, Recreation and Dance* 65(8):50-61.

Melograno, V.J. 1998. *Professional and student portfolios for physical education.* Champaign, IL: Human Kinetics.

Mills v. Board of Education of the District of Columbia, 348 F. Supp. 966 (1972).

National Association for Sport and Physical Education. 1995. *Moving to the future: National standards for physical education.* St. Louis: Mosby.

Nirje, B. 1969. The normalization principle. In *Normalization, social integration, and community services,* Flynn, R.J. and Nitsch, K.E., eds., p. 31-49. Baltimore, MD: University Park Press.

Peabody Developmental Motor Scales. 1974. *IMRID Behavioral Monograph No. 25.* Nashville, TN: George Peabody College.

Pender, R.H., and Patterson, P.E. 1982. A comparison of selected motor fitness items between congenitally deaf and hearing children. *Journal for Special Educators* 18:71-75.

Pennsylvania Association for Retarded Children v. Commonwealth of Pennsylvania, U.S. District Court, 343 F. Supp. 279 (1972).

Powers, L.E., Wilson, R., Matuszewski, J., Phillips, A., Rein, C., Schumacher, D., and Gensert, J. 1996. Facilitating adolescent self-determination: What does it take? In *Self-determination across the lifespan: Independence and choice for people with disabilities,* Sands, D.J. and Wehmeyer, M., eds., p. 257-284. Baltimore, MD: Paul H. Brookes.

Rehabilitation Act of 1973. Public Laws 93-112. U.S. Congress, 1973.

Rehabilitation Act Amendments of 1992. U.S. Public Laws 102-569, Section 102 (p) (32), 1992.

Rink, J.E. 1998. *Teaching physical education for learning.* Boston, MA: McGraw Hill.

Shephard, R.J. 1990. *Fitness in special populations.* Champaign, IL: Human Kinetics.

Sherrill, C. 1997. *Adaptation theory: Epistemological perspectives.* Presentation at the International Symposium on Adapted Physical Activity, Quebec City, Quebec, Canada.

Sherrill, C. 1998. *Adapted physical activity, recreation and sport: Crossdisciplinary and lifespan.* 5th ed. Boston, MA: WCB McGraw-Hill.

Short, F.X. 2000. Individualized education programs. In *Adapted physical education and sport.* 3rd ed. Winnick, J.P., ed., p. 47-60. Champaign, IL: Human Kinetics.

Sinibaldi, R. 2001. Peers: Partners and equals, exceptional and regular students. *Strategies* 14(4):9-13.

Smith, T.K. 1997. Authentic assessment: Using a portfolio card in physical education. *Journal of Physical Education, Recreation and Dance* 68(4):48-52.

Stein, J.U. 1994. Total inclusion or least restrictive environment? *Journal of Physical Education, Recreation and Dance* 65(9):21-25.

Tripp, A., French, R., and Sherrill, C. 1995. Contact theory and attitudes of children in physical education programs toward peers with disabilities. *Adapted Physical Activity Quarterly* 12(4):323-332.

Ulrich, D.A. 2000. *The Test of Gross Motor Development.* Austin, TX: Pro-Ed.

Webster, G.E. 1987. Influence of peer tutors upon academic learning time-physical education of mentally handicapped students. *Journal of Teaching in Physical Education* 7:393-403.

Wehmeyer, M.L., Agran, M., and Hughes, C. 1998. *Teaching self-determination to students with disabilities: Basic skills for basic transition.* Baltimore, MD: Paul H. Brookes.

Werder, J.K., and Bruininks, R.H. 1988. *Body skills: A motor development curriculum for children.* Circle Pines, MN: American Guidance Service.

Wessel, J.A., and Kelly, L. 1986. *Achievement-based curriculum development in physical education.* Philadelphia: Lea & Febiger.

Wessel, J.A., and Zittel, L.L. 1995. *Smart start: Preschool movement curriculum designed for children of all abilities.* Austin, TX: Pro-Ed.

Wessel, J.A., and Zittel, L.L. 1998. *I CAN Primary Skills K-3.* Austin, TX: Pro-Ed.

Wiggins, G. 1997. Practice what we preach in designing authentic assessment. *Educational Leadership* 54(4):18-25.

Wilson, S. and Lieberman, L. 2000. Disability awareness in physical education. *Strategies* 13(6):12, 29-33

Winnick, J.P., ed. 2000. *Adapted physical education and sport.* 3rd ed. Champaign, IL: Human Kinetics.

Winnick, J.P., and Short, F.X. 1985. *Physical fitness testing for the disabled: Project UNIQUE.* Champaign, IL: Human Kinetics.

Winnick, J.P., and Short, F.X. 1999. *The Brockport Physical Fitness Test.* Champaign, IL: Human Kinetics.

Wolfensberger, W. 1972. *Normalization.* Toronto: National Institute on Mental Retardation.

Yell, M.L. 1998. The legal basis of inclusion. *Educational Leadership* 56(2):70-73.

Yun, J., Shapiro, D., and Kennedy, J. 2000. Reaching IEP goals in the general physical education class. *Journal of Physical Education, Recreation and Dance* 71(8):33-37.

Zittel, L.L. 1994. Gross motor assessment of preschool children with special needs: Instrument selection consideration. *Adapted Physical Activity Quarterly* 11(3):245-260.

Index

Note: An italic *t* after the page number indicates a table.

About the Authors

Lauren Lieberman, PhD, is an associate professor in the department of physical education and sport at the State University of New York (SUNY) at Brockport. She teaches graduate and undergraduate courses in adapted physical education and coordinates five practicum programs, including Camp Abilities, a developmental sports camp for children who are blind. She conducts research in inclusion and physical activity for people with sensory impairments. She coauthored the books *Games for People With Sensory Impairments* (Human Kinetics) and *Case Studies in Adapted Physical Education*.

In 1995, Lieberman earned her PhD from Oregon State University in human performance with a minor in movement studies and disabilities. While there, she taught classes in adapted physical education and coordinated a play-based program for infants and toddlers. Her research at Oregon State focused on inclusion of deaf children in physical education.

Cathy Houston-Wilson, PhD, is an associate professor in the department of physical education and sport at the State University of New York at Brockport, where she coordinates the physical education teacher education concentration. She earned her PhD in adapted physical education from Oregon State University in 1993.

Houston-Wilson has taught general and adapted physical education, and she developed the early childhood inclusive motor program at SUNY Brockport. Currently, she advises school districts on appropriate inclusion of students with disabilities into general physical education.